Lawson's Leaves of Love

Daily Meditations

William A. Lawson

Printed in United States of America

For information address:
Biblical Dogs Publishing, Division of Biblical Dogs, Inc.
305 N. McNeil
Memphis, TN 38112-5109
phone   240-447-3620
email   BiblicalDogs@aol.com

Library of Congress Cataloging-in-Publication Data

Lawson, William A., 1928–
  Lawson's Leaves of Love: Daily Meditations / by
William A. Lawson
p. cm.
Includes bibliographical references and index.
LCCNumber: 2004093904
ISBN 0970372280

  1. Meditations. 2. Young adults—Prayer-books and
devotions—English   I. Title.

BV4850.L39 2004   248.8'4
                         QB133-2053

cover concept by: Technimedia, Inc.—Neal Brooks & Donald Flenoy
book design by: www.madhof.com

ACKNOWLEDGMENTS

This book of meditations is a gift to me, given by the congregation of Wheeler Avenue Baptist Church in Houston, on the occasion of my 75th birthday and my 57th year in the ministry of Jesus Christ. They honored me by selecting from 25 years of weekly meditations in our Sunday bulletins 366 to go in this volume. Our Associate Pastor, Rev. Marcus D. Cosby, came up with the idea (knowing that I have never desired material gifts for special occasions), recruited a Deacon and Deaconess, Dr. Harold and Mrs. Laura Mullins, to spearhead the project. The Mullins' selected four brilliant ladies to pore through hundreds of old bulletins: Professors of English Dr. Patricia Williams, Dr. Betty Taylor-Thompson, and Mrs. Joyce McEwing, and the former medical examiner Dr. Joye Carter. These pages are the result of the meticulous labor of those six people.

FOREWORD

It happens to us all. We are dragging behind us the burdens of the day, complaining about how unfair life is to us. We may even slide into blaming God for the unfairness. But the day is gray and gloomy.

Then, sometimes gradually, sometimes suddenly, a sunbeam brightens and warms the day, and our burdens fall into perspective. We are far more blessed than somebody else we know; and our God knows and cares about us. (When those burdens fall into perspective, we may even understand that God intends some pain that we might build stronger spiritual muscle.)

Those sunbeams injecting our gloom with unexpected peace and timely understanding are often sent into our lives by chance remarks, an article we happen to pick up, an insight suddenly emerging from a personal experience, a passage of scripture we have read dozens of times that yells cheer at us just when we need it.

The meditations in this book were intended when they were written for our church bulletin over several decades to provide gentle reminders that our Shepherd loves us, that He is not blind nor deaf to our predicaments, and that our faith in Him ought to be as consistent and unfailing as His love for us. Some of them will pass through your consciousness without touching sides or bottom.

But we pray that one or two of them will be that unexpected but welcomed sunbeam that tells you that despite present challenges, you are being watched over and quietly guided—that it's going to be O.K.

Welcome to God's 'leaves of love.'

All biblical scriptures are taken from
the King James Version
of the Holy Bible.

The date at the end of the daily note reflects the
original date that Rev. William A. Lawson delivered
his sermon & presented the "Sunday Note."
His wisdom has a timeless quality.

January 1

How Will This Year Be?
How Did You Define Last Year?

On this first day of the year, we can look at this new year as a bundle of opportunities to do things better, or as more set-backs, disappointments, and calamities. If we saw last year through the eyes of a complainer, this year will be a lousy year. If we recognized the hand of GOD in both advances and adversities last year, and could praise Him for having sustained us through it, this year will be another year He will give us reason to thank Him.

Trivia books give information that nobody really needs to know. One such trivia item relates the following: Kimberly-Clark Company produced a very absorbent, cotton-like substance during World War I (1914–1918) to be used as a filter for gas masks used by U.S. GI's. When the war was over, the company was stuck with massive surpluses of the soft stuff called Cellucotton. Kimberly-Clark could have gone bankrupt. But somebody was optimistic and creative enough to think the company could find some use for the super-soft stuff—and it did. It produced handkerchief-like tissues used by actors and actresses on Broadway to remove makeup. Those tissues, developed to squeeze profit out of an oversupply of Cellucotton, became what we now classify "Kleenex." No home could be without it, and most other facial tissues are called by that same brand name.

We cannot face any year alone. Last year was too depressing, and the year before was equally bad. If we just look at the pile of surplus headaches left over from last year, we may be tempted to swallow a bucket of Valiums. But we can face this year with joy and hope and thanksgiving if we ask GOD to tell us what to do with the problems. Our grief may help us to be more compassionate. Our blunders will certainly help us be more watchful. Problems can bowl us over—until we give them to the LORD. Then we discover in truth what we already know from scripture.

Happy New Year!

But my GOD shall supply all your need according to His riches in glory by Christ Jesus. Philippians 4:19

January 7, 1990

January 2

Define Yourself

His name is a household word in virtually every nation and language on earth. He was once considered somewhere between a nuisance and a monster among conservative Anglos, but now even the most ultra-right Southerners rank him as somewhere between a great leader and a saint. He has been painted with scandal, and blamed for urban violence, but his integrity has lifted him above it all.

These are labels others ascribed to Dr. Martin Luther King. But he defined himself as a preacher of the gospel of Jesus Christ, an advocate of the exhortations of the Old Testament prophets, a drum major for justice. He never called himself a civil rights leader, never ran for elected office nor accepted an appointed position. He was a servant of the LORD, by his own definition.

2

If people call you incompetent or stupid, ignore them. If people call you the greatest thing since sliced bread, thank them politely—and ignore them. Do not let other people determine who you are. GOD has brought you into the world, and GOD has some role for you to play, and GOD is providing for you the equipment with which to play that role. You don't have to live up to an image imposed upon you by the people. Ask GOD each morning what He wants you to be about that day; and ask GOD at the end of each day how well you satisfied His assignments for you.

People will lift you to stardom, trample you as scum, or overlook you as inconsequential. Ignore all of their labels—and seek to be a servant of the LORD: His is the only evaluation that counts!

For I say, through the grace given unto me, to every man that is among you, not to think of himself more highly than he ought to think: but to think soberly, according as GOD hath dealt to every man the measure of faith. Romans 12:3

January 17, 1999

January 3

"Happy(?)" New Year

The common salutation during this first week of January is "Happy New Year." As people of GOD, we take this greeting with some advisement. We believe you deserve more than a "happy" year.

"Happiness" is an unstable state. The word comes from an old English root, "hap," meaning "chance" or "luck." Our words "happenstance" and "haphazard" are related to that root. Small wonder, then, that whether you are happy or unhappy often depends on external circumstance, or "luck." Sudden wealth should make you happy—but with the wrong circumstances, it can bring you grief.

How can you be "blessed" if people are scandalizing your name? Well, if your joy depends on external circumstances, you cannot. But if you have a joy that comes from your relationship with the Almighty, then you can laugh even when you are hurting.

We will not wish anyone a "happy" New Year, because not all happenstances in the new year will be pleasant. But we can wish everyone a blessed New Year, because with Jesus, whatever the situation outside, the inside will be joy. Jesus ends His beatitudes with a contradiction.

3

Blessed are ye, when men shall revile you, and persecute you, and shall say all manner of evil against you falsely for My sake. Matthew 5:11

January 5, 1997

January 4

What Kind of Year Will the New Year Be?

That depends upon one's attitude.

Letters from jail are common to some people. The letters tell how inmates are unjustly detained, how they were framed or set up by the police or by relatives and friends, how bad prison conditions are—from bad food to abuse by guards and fellow inmates, and how those on the outside ought to work for the prisoners' release (and maybe for the punishment of the bad people who framed these innocent souls).

So it seems odd to read in a letter from jail these words:

Here is a last piece of advice: All that is true;

all that is dignified;

what is right, what is pure;

whatever is endearing;

all the fine, good things in others;

whatever is lofty and whatever is praiseworthy;

there let your thoughts dwell

4

(Philippians 4:8, Modern Translation).

These are from a letter sent from the jail at Philippi by the Apostle Paul. Despite the filth, the rats and roaches, the shackles and chains—and the fact that he was unjustly incarcerated—he recommends that we think positive thoughts rather than to complain!

We can moan and groan about last year and about a society that is going to pot. And we will find this year to be a miserable one. Or we can remember the blessings of GOD, the best qualities of the people we know, the great opportunities for praise, for love, and for service. And this new year will be the best year yet!

Not that I speak in respect of want: for I have learned, in whatsoever state I am, therewith to be content. Philippians 4:11

January 5, 1992

January 5

Before You Ask

Your personal relationship is in the garbage can? Don't shoot your mate, or sell the kids, or install a bomb in your parents' car, or pour poison in your friend's coffee. GOD knows how you groan inwardly. Tell Him (but be willing to do some bridge-building, some conceding, some forgiving, etc.); and don't hang an "incurable" sign on that relationship. Try to mellow down into a quiet trust.

A deep love—a really deep love, like the love a mother has for her child—has a characteristic you can always expect. The person who loves you anticipates your needs. Somehow he or she can sense when you need to have company, or when you need space by yourself; when you want to talk, or when you prefer silent solitude; when you are feeling great, or when you are in pain of soul (despite the happy face you bravely display). All of us have known times when Mama or That Special Person said or did just the right thing at precisely the time when we needed it said or done. A deep love feels your needs before you express them.

5

If Mama or That Special Person loves you like that, how much more does GOD love you like that?

Jesus taught us The Model Prayer (or "The LORD's Prayer," Matthew 6:9-13). He told us that the Father knows our need even before we come to Him in prayer (Matthew 6:8).

You need to be healed? By all means ask Him; the prayer of faith can heal the sick. But He knows already exactly how scared you are. Try to mellow down into a quiet trust.

You are financially pinned to the wall? Tell Him—but don't be frantic. He has the most accurate fix on your P & L there is. If you need to have money, He can provide it. If you need to lose something in order to gain something, He has already organized the process by which you can make it through the transition intact. Try to mellow down into a quiet trust.

Before you ask, He knows. So trust Him!

...pray to thy Father which is in secret; and thy Father which seeth in secret shall reward thee openly for your Father knoweth what things ye have need of, before ye ask him. Matthew 6:6, 8b

January 24, 1993

January 6

Not Later—Now

It is an irrevocable axiom. We have so little time to do so much. There are some opportunities that flash on the screen of our lives for an instant, and then are gone. In the final month of the 20th century, we dealt with fourteen families who lost loved ones. There was great variety in the deaths. They were young and elderly, well-known and obscure, from large clans and virtually alone. But a common thread ran through all of them, as it does through the millions of other deaths that occur annually throughout the world.

Their deaths ended any chance for brightening their days with good words or deeds.

While death brings pain, it also should bring wisdom. While we can, we must bring some sunshine to the lives of those we touch regularly. A bright greeting, a compliment, a hug, a cheap but thoughtful gift—these are among the "points of light" we ought to offer on a regular basis. It is nine days into the new century now. It is not too late to establish for ourselves a sunshine regimen. You don't have to be a party animal or a radiant personality to spread sunshine. But all of us can improve in the way we speak to those closest to us. We can do better in the way we think of an encouraging word for family members, for co-workers (especially those subordinate to us who think we do not appreciate them), for hassled waiters, waitresses, salespeople. We can learn how to talk to children so we do not intimidate or frighten or demean them. We can come up with ways to be warm to strangers and people remote from us.

While we have people with us, before we have to make up eloquent lies about them at their funerals, we can brighten the corner where we are. That is better than resolving to lose enough to get into your wedding dress or the tuxedo you wore in 1975.

Life is short. Time is precious. Let's be thoughtful while we still can.

Say not unto thy neighbor, Go, and come again, and tomorrow I will give; when thou hast it by thee. Proverbs 3:28

January 9, 2000

January 7

Too Much

It was the Queen's birthday in Hong Kong, at that time not a part of mainland China, but a Royal Colony of the United Kingdom. We had been invited to dinner at the home of a Baptist deacon who was a leading banker in the city. The guest list included the cream of Hong Kong society. The event was held in the Grand Ballroom of the Hotel Nikko Hong Kong (where a room is $1,950 a night). It was formal—I didn't have a tux, but did have a black bow tie. The meal was fourteen courses. We were in high cotton!

And then I learned a new thing about Chinese etiquette.

The waiters over-filled the soup bowls. And they splashed green tea over the rim of the cup. And they splattered rice and duck and caviar on the gleaming white tablecloth. Between courses, they took away the soiled cloth and the dirty dishes, replaced them with new linen and new china and crystal, and started slopping food again. This messy way of serving symbolized prosperity—you were complimenting the guest by saying that he was worthy of prodigal abundance. You did not carefully measure the servings, but poured and splashed and sloshed excessively, because the guest was worthy of excess hospitality.

GOD treats us like that.

David says "my cup runneth over." Jesus provided so much bread and fish that the disciples gathered twelve baskets of leftovers. When He directed His disciples, who had caught nothing, to let down their nets, the excess of fish almost broke the nets. Paul rejoices in a GOD Who is "able to do exceeding abundantly above all that we ask or think." And Jesus is not satisfied that we might have life; He wants us to "have it more abundantly."

GOD does not measure His grace and His mercy carefully—He sloshes it over us excessively, extravagantly, far more than we deserve. We sin against Him. We rebel against Him. We blaspheme His Name. And He pours out on us His very best, because He wants us to know that we are precious to Him, that we are worthy of excessive love.

I am come that they might have life, and that they might have it more abundantl. John 10:10b

July 16, 2000

January 8

Remember

Is there a number that represents too many times to remember what GOD has done for us? We may wash ourselves daily. We eat and drink several times a day. We do what is important often. Nothing is more important than being redeemed from our sins, being rescued from the worst death row in any prison anywhere. When we are broke, we have an open line to Heaven. When we are sick, or our loved one is, there is no waiting to reach GOD to ask for healing. When we are heartbroken because we have lost somebody very dear to us, we need not wait in line to ask for comfort. We do not have to prove to GOD that we have been sinless when we need to beg for a miracle. How did we get such a clear access to all the Power, all the Wisdom, all the Presence in the universe?

Our GOD had pity on us long before we knew ourselves and went to the cross for us. And what does He ask of us? That we yield our hearts to Him, accept Him as our personal Savior, and enlist in His army of witnesses to tell the entire world what He has done for us and for all of them. The tiny morsel of bread and the tiny cup of wine used in the ordinance of communion remind us to remember what He has provided for us every minute of every day of our lives. Remember!

This is My body which is given for you: this do in remembrance of Me. Luke 22:19

May 4, 2003

January 9

Nothing New under the Sun

The calendars change. Last year's new car is now an old model. Different top tunes or box office smashes hit the scene. Individuals have just begun their diet or their attitude improvement or their new habit of organizing their days. Everything is new.

Another murder has already been added to last year's, and the police are pursuing suspects in last year's robberies. Your arthritis carries over from last year to this year, and the holiday celebration that ended December 31 has to be paid for this year. Everything is old.

Both statements are true.

GOD has sustained us throughout years past. And the good news is your LORD is the same yesterday, today, and forever. And Satan has been scheming to overthrow our faith ever since we first split the silence at birth. (Fortunately, he will not be there forever.) So there is nothing new with GOD and the adversary. But that same GOD, Who never changes, is with us right this minute. We can tell Him about our arthritis or our bills or our soul-pain today—right now. His provision for you is as new as the morning (and as old as creation). It would be great if Satan had been swept out with the Christmas decorations. However, unfortunately, he is also right beside us, right now, maybe telling us to be mad at our neighbor or to design a brand new scheme to defraud a client. Yes (Sigh!), he also followed us into this new year. So we cannot afford to take off our armor.

9

We should thank GOD for the blessings of our lifetime, and for the ones we are receiving right now and we should depend on Him to help us grow in grace and kick Satan out of our lives—right now.

Cast thy burden upon the LORD, and He shall sustain thee: He shall never suffer the righteous to be moved. Psalm 55:22

January 6, 1991

January 10

Projection

"Hindsight " is the ability to reflect on the past. "Projection" is the attempt to plan for the future. Projection means literally "to stick out," like a pier into a body of water. And that is the nature of looking into a new year—forcing hopes and plans into the unknown and properly anticipating the hazards and opportunities in that frightening void we call the future.

Wise projection is always a careful laying out of plans based on hindsight with aim on interpretation of yesterday. We try to learn from mistakes we made yesterday. We capitalize on whatever worked yesterday and direct our efforts toward repeating the more effective things we did yesterday. We examine yesterday in detail before poking our talents and resources into the unknown.

But the most important study of yesterday is based on spiritual attitudes.

10

If we think all our victories were won because we are so sharp, we will swagger into the future without asking GOD's help. If we are aware that we cannot even take the next breath without Divine help, we will certainly not plunge into tomorrow without beseeching GOD for guidance. If we look back and focus on the sorrows and heartaches of the past, we may see the future as bleak and failure as guaranteed. If we count the blessings of yesterday, we will march confidently into tomorrow, knowing that the same GOD Who provided for us last year is faithful to provide for us this year, too. And our pessimism or optimism is self-fulfilling.

So as we make big plans for the new year, we expect some of them to be fulfilled and some of them to fall by the wayside. We will have some sunshine and some gloomy days—even a storm or two. But sensible projections take three simple steps:

1. Spend some time reflecting on the past. Remember your mistakes. Be thankful for your victories. Give GOD credit for victories and for survival through mistakes. And admit that there were more blessings than headaches.

2. Stand still before making a move, and talk it over with GOD. Open yourself to His direction. Ask for it. Beg for it. Do not move without it.

3. Put on a smile. Throw your shoulders back. Go out ready to meet Satan, circumstance, and tomorrow. GOD will be in front of you. Trust Him all the way.

The meek will He guide in judgment: and the meek will He teach His way. Psalm 25:9

September 6, 1992

11

January 11

A New Year's Dialogue with GOD

Well, LORD, this is the first Sunday in a new year. I want to make some changes in my life which You will certainly appreciate. For starters, I will join the Courtesy Corps, provided they do not ask me to be on duty more than once a month.

Know ye that ye are not your own? For ye are bought with a price.

Of course, I know that. But that is not all I plan to do this year—let me finish! You know when the preacher asks us to pray for somebody on the sick list? I will pray for two people every week (except when my calendar is over-full).

But in all things approving ourselves as the ministers of GOD in much patience, in afflictions, in necessities, in distresses.

Now, LORD, don't push it! I intend to make some sacrifices; but You are asking for the total sacrifice of body and mind! Suppose I throw in volunteering to help serve coffee (on third Sundays in odd-numbered months). Now you know that's a sacrifice, because I will miss brunch at the Warwick!

12

You know You make it difficult to make resolutions! So You are asking for body and mind, for denial of myself, for a total, almost suicidal surrender! O.K., O.K.—I get the message! First fruits of time? You got it. Talents? (Groan) You got it. Income? (Ugh) All right. Give it cheerfully? (Sigh) I'm smiling! I'm smiling!

For all the law is fulfilled in one word, even in this: Thou shalt love thy neighbor as thyself. Galatians 5:14

September 6, 1998

January 12

Why Should I Make Resolutions?

What difference will it make that a number is changed on the calendar, on your checks, on the dating of your letters and memos? The old problems, the old obstacles, the old frustrations are on the other side of that boundary waiting for you. You listen to the air-headed guests on the talk shows, chattering meaninglessly about resolutions they are making for the new year. They will screen scripts better, write better songs, be more responsive to their families and their fans—Bah, Humbug!

When you were younger (and more naïve), you used to make resolutions about how you would improve your behavior or your performance or your appearance. And you failed to live up to most of it. So why fool yourself that one year could be any better than another just because you made some promises you are bound to break?

Because you are not alone.

Life at its best is pressing toward what is good, better, best. You can never be satisfied with who and what and where you are. "But," you ask, "how can I keep civil toward that scoundrel? How can I stay on a weight-loss regimen? How can I remember to pray twice, three times a day?"

13

The answer is not with Anne Landers, nor with Chuck Swindoll. Check Paul again for the answer.

We then as workers together with Him, beseech you also that ye receive not the grace of GOD in vain. II Corinthians 6:1

December 31, 1995

January 13

Put Down That Gun

You are tired! You woke up tired. No, not tired as in after cleaning the garage or driving 1,200 miles—tired as in "What's the use? I have not accomplished much in my life; nobody really appreciates me; I am still struggling with this sickness; I cannot go on now that Mama/Daddy/my child has passed on. Life is not worth living any more."

Don't feel alone. While there is one who never stops smiling, there are 99 more of us who share these "down" times. Such times come after a death or other devastating event. Sometimes they don't need a catalyst—they just rise like a dark mist from a bed of daily complaints. It isn't even abnormal; but down times ought to be treated quickly before they lead to our quitting before we have to, or withdrawing from people who love us, or even thinking suicide is not such a dumb idea.

While there is no absolute insulation from down moments, there is a ready and effective antidote for them. It is a blend of reflection and praise.

14

You look at yourself and reflect that GOD woke you up this morning; and that even while you do not feel like doing somersaults, you are alive. You look around and reflect that there is somebody who considers you precious—a parent, a mate, a child, a grandchild, a pet. You look behind and reflect that while you have not discovered a cure for cancer, you have done some good that improved your world (helped to rear or teach a child? encouraged somebody who had given up? written a good speech, or letter, or poem?). You look above and realize that you have a Savior Who considered you so valuable that He died to redeem you.

Upon reflection, we have more reason to praise GOD than to curse the day of our birth. The more we reflect upon our blessings, and the more we praise GOD for life, for loved ones, for accomplishments, however small, for salvation through Christ Jesus, the more we think "Hallelujah!" And the less we think cyanide.

I will give thee thanks in the great congregation: I will praise thee among much people. Psalm 35:18

January 12, 2003

January 14

A Drum Major for Justice

That is how he said he wanted to be remembered. But his life was cut short, by an assassin's bullet in Memphis, Tennessee, when he was only 38 years old. On the 15th, the nation—and much of the world—commemorates the birth and the legacy of Dr. Martin Luther King, Jr.

For most of us, the term "justice" belongs to the world of law enforcement with its court system, its police and sheriff networks, and its prosecutors: district, state, and federal. But what Martin had in mind was nothing so secular and bureaucratic as that. He counted himself a preacher, a spokesman for GOD, one who exhorted us as GOD's creatures to:

But let judgment run down as waters, and righteousness as a mighty stream. (Amos 5:24)

The kind of justice Dr. King wanted to represent was a moral and spiritual justice that is not enforced by weapons and sentences and barred buildings. He wanted people to live together because they cared about and respected each other, not because strong laws forced them to. If I treat you right only under threat of penalty, I am not just; I am grudgingly practical. But if the love of GOD in me drives me from within to respect you and to do unto you as I would that you should do unto me, we have achieved true justice. And for that kind of justice, Martin wanted to be remembered as a "drum major."

15

January 18, 1998

January 15

Praise & Obedience

If Martin
Could leave his place
In the bosom of Abraham
And pay a visit
To the world today,
Surely he would rejoice
That bearing his name
Are streets and schools
And hospitals and public buildings;
That children recite his speeches
Who never knew the divided world
Of bus seats and drinking fountains.

Surely he would rejoice—
Or would he?

Maybe instead he would be sad
That some of us got good jobs
And were admitted to once-closed schools
And moved out of the hated ghetto
Into places where our children could have white playmates—
And forgot the masses who still hurt.
Maybe he would ask us
To keep the plaques
And the street names
And give him the assurance
That we did not forget the dream
That Jesus gave to him
And that he passed on to us
And to our children.

And why call me, LORD, LORD, and do not take things which I say? Luke 6:46

January 14, 1990

January 16

We Only Knew

The sweetest words flow in times of tragedy. Funeral eulogies select the best qualities and the finest achievements of the loved one, and no one mentions his or her faults or blunders. However we may have nodded in agreement while Dr. Martin Luther King was being criticized during his lifetime, we frown at the bad taste of anybody who criticizes him now. And during the height of campaign battle, all of us sling labels and throw rocks at politicians. But during a crisis people of all political persuasions and from every ethnic background come together repeatedly to pray for those victimized.

This is not hypocrisy. It is the nature of the corrupt human animal to criticize and complain. But virtually all of us know enough good about many people we vilify to say some good things about them. The shame is that it sometimes takes tragedy to make us remember those good things.

Jesus accepts us despite our faults and urges us to take up His commitment to touch all the nations of the world, to embrace them as kin, and to feed them as His sheep. How can He accept us, knowing what kind of rogues and scalawags we are?

17

He knows us. We are His sheep (John 10:14,15).

The better we know a person, the more we can understand the balance between the qualities we agree with and the qualities we don't agree with. If we are very close to someone, and we know how much he feels compassion for people, we are not surprised that he is a bit gullible and that he may be extravagant. If we understand someone's penchant for efficiency and his tendency to be a perfectionist, we are not insulted when he curtly cuts off a rambling conversation or rewrites a sloppy letter. Jesus wants us to love others as He loves us. And He loves us in an intimate, knowing, understanding way. If we love others that way, we don't have to wait until a funeral to say the best about the deceased. We know it right now.

These things I command you, that ye love one another. John 15:17

August 13, 1989

January 17

The Devil Made Me Do It

Children of elementary school age will not remember it. But virtually everybody else recalls the funny excuse given by a popular comedian for his breaking of the rules. But long before Flip Wilson tickled our funny-bones with that theme sentence, the Apostle Paul was complaining about a law prompting him to do wrong. Devil has been busy for a long, long time.

We are surrounded by, saturated with, immersed in a climate of rule-breaking. Popular athletes are accused of drug abuse, spouse abuse, even murder. A rising young actor is convicted of lewd behavior with a prostitute, and a high-priced prostitute is not convicted of prostitution, but of tax evasion. Author Shere Hite trumpets statistics of 70% of all married couples struggling with unfaithfulness. And do any college or graduate or professional students do honest preparation for tests and examinations any more? Dishonesty is no longer a vice—it has become a national pastime.

So since you can't beat them, why not join them?

Because your Boss is not popular practice and opinion; because you must try to pass on to the children you influence some sense of value and ethics; because while dishonesty may bring quick gains, evil ultimately destroys.

The majority may rule, but it is never right. Masses rush to destruction, says Jesus, but only a trickle climb the road to right thinking and doing, even when nobody is looking over their shoulder. Be part of that minority!

I find then a law, that, when I would do good, evil is present with me. Romans 7:21

August 6, 1995

January 18

Check Your Qualifications

We often emphasize visiting the sick and shut-in. All of us will endure going to the hospital or to a home when a relative or close friend or associate is sick. But it may not be the most desirable form of recreation to go to the bedsides of people who are not in your circle. So why not just mention their name in prayer when you see it on the prayer list, or at best send them a nice "Get Well" card, especially one that costs more than a dollar?

Because it goes on a divine resume.

Do you know who qualifies for Heaven? No, not the preacher or the deacon, or the Sunday School Superintendent with the thirty-year certificate. Jesus describes the qualifications of those who will be admitted to His "good side" in Heaven. And there is not a single mention of the soloist who tears up the church, or the usher with the proudest military strut! He puts down a litany of acts of mercy toward the hungry, the naked, the stranger, the sick, the incarcerated. As a matter of fact, He makes it crystal clear that if those acts of mercy are not on your resume, you will be rejected in spite of the years you spent as Secretary of the District Association!

So take seriously Jesus' definition of "the righteous" and ask yourself: Whose bedside do I visit beside my family and my friends? You are qualified as a church member—try to qualify as a Christian!

And the King shall answer and say unto them, Verily I say unto you, Inasmuch as ye have done it unto one of the least of these my brethren, ye have done it unto Me. Matthew 25:40

July 30, 1995

January 19

A Little Goes a Long Way

One of the most graphic metaphors of Jesus is from His sermon on the mount—referring to the salt of the earth. The LORD was referring to salt as a preservative for meat. We do not commonly see it used that way today. But it is a very important seasoning for us. You may not appreciate its importance until your doctor takes you off of salt, and you have to live with bland green beans, pasty potatoes, and meat that tastes like paper.

And the funny thing is, only a few grains make a huge difference between delicious and awful!

So when Jesus calls us "salt," He is saying at least two things to us:

1. We can make a major difference in our world.
2. We don't have to be rich or powerful or brilliant or famous.

Ever notice how after a miserable day, one hug from a child can lighten your heart? Or how a simple "Thank you" can make a sacrifice worthwhile?

20

Somebody needs a word from you. Perhaps they need to hear a simple compliment. Or maybe it would help if you just asked how they were doing, and sounded as though you really cared. Or, chances are, somebody needs to know that Jesus has made a difference in your life, and if you shared that with them, it would nudge them to try Him for their needs, too. Just a sprinkle could make a big difference!

Ye are the salt of the earth: but if the salt have lost his savour, wherewith shall it be salted? Matthew 5:13

May 21, 1995

January 20

Form & Dynamic

Physics is a tough subject. In the first place, it demands concentration, and teenage boys are not generally long on concentration. In the second place, it is not practical, like learning to hook a shot from half-court or memorizing "cool" lines with which to destroy girls' resistance. In high school, students memorize theory like the relationship of form to dynamic. What red-blooded boy cares about that boring stuff?

How could such boring stuff determine that a football was oval, a basketball was round, and a baseball was hard enough to be hit by a bat? How a thing is made determines how a thing can be used. "Form determines dynamic." Wow!

So what is the church for?

It has a dais with a lectern on it and a choir stand behind it, and hundreds of seats facing it. So it is designed for performing before an audience. Right? Wrong.

Jesus did not ordain any of that junk. He established a family, held together by a common experience of regeneration in Christ and sent out into the entire world with a commission. Its form is not audience, but witnesses; therefore, its dynamic is not performance, but mission—to persuade the world to return to GOD through Jesus Christ.

It may be boring stuff, but we do not throw footballs through netted hoops. If we know what we were made to do, all we need to do is to do it!

Thy hands have made me and fashioned me; give me understanding, that I may learn Thy commandments. Psalm 119:73

December 29, 1991

January 21

The Secret of Long Life

It is not a wonder cosmetic or a miracle drug. It is not some elusive fountain whose waters could miraculously increase one's life span. In fact, it is nothing so physical as to be consumable or injectable or even perceived with the five senses. It is obedience to a Divine order.

Strange, how unfailing are the dynamics of obedience or rebellion. The one blesses, the other guarantees disaster. Our nation glorifies youth and discards the aging. So did the European civilizations which preceded our own nation. So history has watched these youth-adoring civilizations rise, shine brightly for a few centuries, then die from the inside. But the civilizations of Africa and Asia, based on respect for family and for the elderly, have lasted for thousands of years. Honor elders and live; dishonor elders and die. Why can we not learn the lessons of scripture and of history?

Your parents and grandparents may not be highly educated, but respect their wisdom. Your life depends upon it!

Honour thy father and thy mother: that thy days may be long upon the land which the LORD thy GOD giveth thee. Exodus 20:12

January 29, 1995

January 22

He's Already There

Among the sermonic gems of Dr. Jeremiah Wright is his creative interpretation of the three Hebrew boys in the fiery furnace of Nebuchadnezzar. As only Jerry Wright can do it, he paints a picture of a conversation in Heaven. These three faithful young men are sentenced to be incinerated in the furnace. GOD needs a Heavenly protector to go down to be in the fire with them. Wright says the Archangel Michael volunteers. "LORD, I can be there in one minute!" The Father says, "That's too slow." The giant angel Gabriel pleads, "LORD, I can make it in ten seconds!" GOD says, "That's still a little slow." GOD the Son (who has not yet been named Jesus) volunteers. "How fast can you make it, Son?" asks the Father. The answer is like an echo from the bottom of a well: "I'm already there!" (Appropriate shouting and hand-clapping.)

That is a bit more than pulpit histrionics. It is a sober truth we can lean on. When the crisis hits you, you immediately reach for GOD's help. Your loved one has died. Your home is falling apart. Your child is in serious trouble. A terrible illness has struck very close to you. You have been backed into a financial corner, and there is no visible way out. And when the crisis strikes, you scream to GOD for mercy.

It takes a little time for the doctors or the banker or your closest friends to rally. And they may even have to shrug their shoulder and admit they cannot help at all. But the good news is that you don't have to wait on GOD. Before you prayed, before the crisis hit, before you were born, GOD was there with all the help you need.

23

He answered and said, Lo, I see four men loose, walking in the midst of the fire, and they have no hurt; and the form of the fourth is like the Son of GOD. Daniel 3:25

March 19, 1995

January 23

When the Shoe Is on the Other Foot

Ever notice how easy it is to get irritated when you are on top?

Moses fouled out with GOD in Kadesh, because after forty years of leadership, after having been used of GOD to work countless miracles for the children of Israel, Moses got cocky about his role as agent for the miracles. The people were complaining (they were surely brothers and sisters), and they got on Moses' last nerve. So in his arrogance, Moses claimed credit for a miracle, and GOD penalized him.

Our church has been used by GOD to help thousands of people. So, naturally, my own "Moses pride" swells up every now and then. I am driving my new car down Scott Street in a driving rain. Great radio, air conditioner on "normal," 73°, good suspension system floating over potholes, this is the elevator to Heaven! Then I see them—shabbily dressed man and woman and two children. Man recognizes me, waves frantically. It is pouring, and they are all wet. If I stop, they mess up my seats. For a Moses second, I consider pedal to the metal.

Then I remember a young preacher in Kansas, stranded on a snowy road with a flat tire, passed by a speeding Cadillac with a "clergy" tag, and then a couple of guys from a Leavenworth tavern stopping to help me change the tire. And deep in my gut I feel the reprimand: "Don't ever forget what it feels like to be out there instead of in here!"

LORD, I was not really going to pass them by! You know how religious I am! I just hadn't noticed them—but as soon as I did, I was going to stop for them! Honest, I was! Yes, I do remember Leavenworth.

24

And the LORD spake unto Moses and Aaron, Because ye believed me not, to sanctify me in the eyes of children of Israel, therefore ye shall not bring this congregation into the land which I have given them. Numbers 20:12

September 28, 1997

January 24

Put on a Happy Face

Let me have about me men that are fat;
Sleek-headed me and such as sleep o' nights:
Yon Cassius hath a lean and hungry look;
He thinks too much: such men are dangerous
Shakespeare's Julius Caesar, Act I

These are the words of Roman emperor Julius Caesar, unaware that he is about to be assassinated, not by the lanky Cassius, but by the more healthy-looking Brutus. But it is not surprising that he is less attracted to the gaunt, grim-looking Cassius. Some of those naturally thin do not like that play at all.

But even folks with their own "lean and hungry look" are drawn to people with cheerful countenances. In a group we often find ourselves subconsciously looking repeatedly toward whoever smiles or laughs. Our favorite people are probably people with a gentle sense of humor, who smile easily.

25

The world is full of hurt and pain. Most people are not eager to be dumped on by our own hurt and pain; they have enough of their own. But everybody can appreciate a joyous and positive attitude, the kind of spirit that spreads sunshine. We need not go around reciting Pollyanna "I'm-so-happy-I- could-die" platitudes. Just wearing a pleasant expression and saying something positive rather than sourly critical or pessimistically negative makes a difference.

It is not hard to do. What is in one's heart often shows on his face. Don't screw your face up into a smile when you hate the world. Count your blessings and say over and over again, "Thank you, LORD," and be glad to be alive. GOD is good!

Keep thy heart with all diligence; for out of it are the issues of life.
Proverbs 4:23

April 5, 1987

January 25

And Then I Saw A Man Who Had No Feet

You have those days. Everything goes wrong. You stub your toe getting out of bed. You slip in the shower. The dog has torn up your newspaper. Your boss starts yelling before you get all the way into the office. The light company is threatening to cut off your power, and you get a call from the school that your child is sick in the nurse's office. Maybe you shouldn't have gotten up today.

How many times have you felt like screaming at GOD, "Why me, LORD? Why me?"

While you are fixing your flat, you see a man, his wife, and a child pushing a grocery cart to no place in particular. A friend tells you his mother is lying comatose in a hospital five states away. An ambulance screams by, rushing without just cause the dead body of a teenager killed in a drive-by, and its wail is barely louder than the wail of the child's devastated mother. You remember the feeling of helplessness in the pit of your stomach as you stood by the bedside of a once-strapping man, now barely skin and bones as he wasted away before your eyes.

And you say to yourself as you gaze at the dent in your fender bequeathed by somebody's careless backing out, "I don't have it so bad at all!"

Of course, you have reasons to complain. And complaining is a privilege GOD allows you. So yell at the cat who tore up your garbage bag—but remember how good GOD is to you, and whisper, "I love you, LORD!"

26

I know both how to be abased, and I know how to abound: everywhere and in all things I am instructed both to be full and to be hungry, both to abound and to suffer need. Philippians 4:12

August 24, 1997

January 26

Positive Negativism

This is an oxymoron. Ox/y/mo/ron (ok'si mor'on), n., a figure of speech in which words of opposite meaning or suggestion are used together. But it is a fitting description of the Christian journey.

You should aspire to the best you can do or be. That's positive. But you should be constantly dissatisfied with your current level of performance, always wanting to do or be better. That's negative—but good negative.

The Apostle Paul tells us he had a heritage to boast about: the purest Jew, "circumcised the eighth day, of the stock of Israel, of the tribe of Benjamin, an Hebrew of the Hebrews; as touching the law, a Pharisee; concerning zeal, persecuting the church; touching the righteousness which is in the law, blameless" (Philippians 3:5,6). He was obviously proud of who he was. That's positive.

But he was not satisfied with who he was. The same proud Jew says he is not yet what he wants to be.

So you love Jesus, and you belong to church. That's positive. But you know you do not always act as Jesus would act under stress. So work on it. You come to a monthly auxiliary or Family Group meeting. That's good. But you have not made a sacrificial commitment of your time or talent for children or youth or seniors or the indigent. Push toward doing that. You tip GOD $50.00 every month. Bless your little heart! But you know that the first tenth of your income would be more like $300.00, before an offering. Deal with it. You can shout in church. Hallelujah! But you still cannot witness to your business partner. Be proud of one—get to work on the other. Be negatively positive!

Nevertheless, whereto we have already attained, let us walk by the same rule, let us mind the same thing. Philippians 3:16

September 13, 1998

January 27

Hindsight

It is the only land most of us have.

GOD has endowed us with memory, but not usually with clairvoyance. We can reflect on yesterday, but cannot generally predict tomorrow. If hindsight is 20-20, foreknowledge is legally blind. While there is a tiny number of Jeanne Dixons among us, most of us learn from looking back, not from being able to see ahead.

We can see patterns of GOD's purpose and our own failings, as we look back, but still do not know what is going to happen twenty-four hours (or twelve or two) from now.

That is why faith is such a critical attribute for the child of GOD.

Only He sees what is in our path as we plow ahead through opportunities and dangers. Only He knows the reasons for our victories and our losses and foresees when we will have reason to rejoice and when we will be beaten to our knees by calamity or depression. We cannot adequately equip ourselves against the hazards of the future; we have no way of knowing what they will be.

But the GOD Who woke each one of us up this morning and started us on our way knows precisely the maze of events, circumstances, and obstacles through which we must wind our way today and tomorrow and the day after. He "opens doors you cannot see," and "makes a way out of no way." Those phrases did not come from the brilliant sages of antiquity; they are from old saints who could not depend on human wisdom and learned to depend on Jesus.

As we face the unknown challenges (many of them the same kinds of challenges we wrestled with last year and the year before that), we do not need to stock up on tranquilizers and headache medicines. All we need is to commit to Jesus our tomorrows and then lie down to peaceful dreams.

As we look at yesterday, we know already Who is in charge; and we have seen Him consistently handing victories to us at exactly the right time. We may have to suffer; but we do not have to worry. And we do not need to foreknow; we have great hindsight.

Casting all your care upon him; for he careth for you. I Peter 5:7

28

August 30, 1992

January 28

Keep Starting Up

It is a common sight at weddings. The vows have been spoken, and the rings have been exchanged. Ladies are sniffling, men are thinking about the big game they are missing, the flower girls and ring bearer are unashamedly bored. It is time to light the Unity Candle, the gorgeous set of candles symbolizing the covenant of love between the radiant young woman and her nervous groom.

They float to the Unity set like clouds, smoothly extricate the two side candles from their sockets, and bring the tiny flames together over the wick of the thick candle which represents their union. While every eye, even the eyes of the men with visions of end-zones dancing through their heads, focuses on this bit of ceremony, the worst happens!

The big candle does not light.

Nervous coughing. Throats clearing. Quiet sighs. The couple keeps trying to get the wick to light. A faint flicker, and a wisp of smoke—it goes out. They know not to leave this business undone, so while perspiration beads the forehead of the groom, and the bride stubbornly keeps her stiff smile in place, they try again. It goes out. On the third (charmed) try, a healthy little flame appears, and the candle is lit, and the bride's fake smile becomes a real one. The guests dare not applaud, but they want to.

29

So what does that have to do with anything?

You made a promise to GOD and yourself. You were going to do something better in the new year. Now it is a few days into the year, and you have already broken your promise. Don't give up! You do not learn to walk without first learning to stumble and fall. If you have to apologize to GOD and yourself, go ahead—but re-commit, and then when your flame goes out again, hang in there for a third, and fourth, and fifth time. Improvement is not always a first-time achievement, but it is worth the stubborn effort.

And Samuel said, Hath the LORD as great delight in burnt offerings and sacrifices, as in obeying the voice of the LORD? Behold, to obey is better than sacrifice, and to harken than the fat of rams. I Samuel 15:22

January 7, 2001

January 29

Headlights & Reverse Lights

Every driver in America has learned how to spot them. Foreign drivers sometimes wonder how we know when a parking space in the mall lot is about to be available. They think Americans are naturally brilliant and do not know about the white backup lights that tell us a driver is coming out of a space.

But that is not the purpose of that white light. It was designed as a safety feature so that when we must back up at night we can see obstacles that may be behind us. But most of us use it most often to grab a scarce parking space.

There is a message in that backup light.

If you cannot be clairvoyant, then celebrate memory.

30

Most of us cannot see very far ahead of us. We do not know what tomorrow brings. Therefore, we cannot use our spiritual "headlights" to see what GOD has in store for us. But we can use our "reverse whites" to remember what He has done. In fact, most of us learn the will of GOD by looking back over what has happened already rather than by visions from Heaven about what will happen next.

In Acts 16, Paul and his companions are planning an evangelistic campaign. They lay out a planned route through what is now called Turkey and then envision an extension into the Far East—maybe as far away as India. But the Holy Spirit kept closing doors in their faces. Every time they attempted to travel to a church in Turkey, they were blocked by the Spirit and kept getting forced westward. When they were pushed all the way to the west coast of Turkey, Paul had his famous vision of the Macedonian man, begging him to come to preach in Europe. He realized, in hindsight, that GOD's will had been for them to go west, not east! What he could not see in his headlights, he saw illumined by his rear-view lights.

Don't worry about tomorrow. You will understand it better by and by

And the peace of GOD, which passeth all understanding, shall keep your hearts and minds through Christ Jesus. Philippians 4:7

July 26, 1992

January 30

By Force of Habit

Does anyone ever notice how easy it is to get into a bad habit and how hard it is to replace it with a good one? Interrupting other people's conversation too often, or saying "Uh" or "You know" too much, or picking one's nose, or scratching the right itch at the wrong time. But if we decide we are going to remember birthdays and anniversaries, or be on time, or drink eight glasses of water, or buckle up before we put the gear in drive, we have to work at it. It seems that human nature coasts to vices, but must climb to virtues.

If we realize that good habits, have to be forced, then we will schedule prayers twice or three times a day. We must put forth an effort to study GOD's Word daily, and we have to force our family/friends/co-workers out of our thought during those dedicated moments.

So why not think of some things to do for the Master and figure out ways to remind ourselves to do them until they become automatic. We will be glad when we realize that we are thinking more good thoughts about people than critical thoughts; that our mind goes to prayer without our having to look at the note stuck on our desk; that we wear a pleasant expression even when we are not conscious of it; that we include Jesus in casual conversation without contriving it; that we unconsciously think "Thank you, LORD," before we cry out, "Why me, LORD?"

31

Bad habits? They slip into our lives without any effort. Good habits? We have to roll up our spiritual sleeves and work at them!

Commit thy works unto the LORD; trust also in Him, and He shall bring it to pass. Psalm 37:5

September 17, 1989

January 31

Aren't You Glad You Use Dial?

If you are the middle passenger in the car pool or the last person who can possibly squeeze into the elevator, you are glad. But how often, after you have bathed and deodorized and put on your best face and your most flattering outfit, do you feel incomplete because you have not prayed? How often does it occur to you that although you have had your Scope and two dabs of your best cologne, you have not gotten rid of a foul disposition? It is much easier to clean or dress or cosmeticize the outside than it is to rightly direct or consecrate the inside.

On this last day in January, check out your resolutions, if you made any. If you did not, it is not too late to make some now. But do not make cosmetic resolutions. Weight loss or exercise or throwing out cigarettes are not "transforming" resolutions. A transforming, mind-renewing resolution is to make fervent, thankful prayer a habit several times a day; or to tell at least one person per day what Jesus Christ has done for you; or to set aside time for Bible study as being more important than catching the news or the sports or the weather; or to be understanding, forgiving, peace-making even when you feel you are being mistreated.

32

A better soap is fine. A more contemporary wardrobe would make you look better. A dynamite new hairdo is worth the cost and the trouble. But the most important change in your life must be basic, essential, internal, spiritual to really give you real joy and peace and power.

So use Dial (or Zest or Coast or Dove or Tone or whatever before you squeeze into the elevator). But make sure that the inside is as fresh and beautiful as the outside, and you will be much more than acceptable—you will be a blessing!

And be not conformed to this world: but be ye transformed by the renewing of your mind, that ye may prove what is that good, and acceptable, and perfect, will of GOD. Romans 12:2

January 31, 1993

February 1

The Shame of Pride

We are proud. Today is the first day in Black History Month. What was once a celebration for African-Americans becomes a celebration for an entire nation. Schools that are predominantly non-black, companies with mostly white employees, agencies and organizations without large black clientele or memberships will recognize February not only for Presidents' Day, Ash Wednesday, and Valentine's Day, but also a time to affirm the African-American community. We are proud.

But we ought to be ashamed a little, too.

The very celebration of Black History Month is a gentle indictment of our national priorities and emphases. If we had not excluded from our education the history and culture and contributions of African-Americans, we would need no "Black History Month," or "Black History Week" as it began. There is no "English History Month" or "German History Month" although all of us are immigrants from somewhere else.

33

So the best thing we can do is not to plan better and better Black History Months throughout the 21st century, but to emphasize the oneness of our personhood as children of a common Father, as sinners redeemed by a common Saviour, Whose death we commemorate.

Our LORD is a "whosoever will" LORD, who represents GOD's love for the entire world—not for the rich or the white or the powerful. And we do not have to aspire to be rich or "synthetic white" or powerful to be somebody. We can be proud we are black, but even more thankful we belong to the elect of GOD through Jesus Christ.

But ye are a chosen generation, a royal priesthood, an holy nation, a peculiar people; that ye should shew forth the praises of Him Who hath called you out of darkness into His marvelous light. I Peter 2:9

February 3, 1991

February 2

Be Who "You" Is

If you are black and struggling, we can all identify with that. But if you tell me your problems are because of racism and the absence of jobs, you have just pulled the string that starts my recorded speech.

"Anybody who really wants to make it can. Let me tell you a story about a man I met who established and ran a successful business before the Civil Rights Movement. He was a quadriplegic, paralyzed from the neck down. But when you saw him being wheeled into the bank on his reclined wheelchair, he was dressed to the nines from snappy Homburg to spats and mirror-shined shoes. Since he was totally disabled, he and his family took some small savings and set up a telephone answering system in his home, with controls he could handle with the six fingers he could use. When I met him, virtually every black physician and lawyer in Houston (there were not many then) used McDonald's Answering Service. So don't tell me about the obstacles to your finding something to support yourself!"

34

The month of February is not just about bragging on the Sojourner Truths and the Frederick Douglasses and the Martin Luther Kings. It is about the pride and possibilities of all of Africa's children. We can observe the heroes and heroines of the past to persuade ourselves that the same GOD Who led them is leading us, and we can depend on Him to make a way out of no way for us, too.

Let's turn in our excuses for determination, our whining for prayer, our apathy for effort. We are somebody—we are black!

In the day of my trouble I sought the LORD: my soul ran in the night and ceased not: my soul refused to be comforted. Psalm 77:2

February 4, 1996

February 3

Built for Punishment

Remember when you could drop a telephone and nothing would happen to it? Maybe with all the computerized features of modern telecommunications, a phone has to be much more delicate than the old Western Electric instruments with the circular dials. But sometimes, don't you wish we could have some of the strength of those things that were part of the Bell monopoly?

African-Americans ought to be very proud of their heritage, because we have endured slavery, Jim Crow, and are still producing strong adults in a climate of second-class citizenship. Does anybody think we have achieved first-class citizenship? Is it that we have been toughened by all the greens and fatback and generations of hard physical labor? Could it be that the snuff and moonshine have hardened rather than weakened us?

35

Or is the real reason for our strength that we are the results of a better manufacturing process? Our founding fathers have woven an eloquent rhetoric about differences in humans: "All men are created equal." But since it is clear that all men are not treated equally, is it possible that all men are not really created equally? Slavery exterminated some people, it did not exterminate Africans. Social ostracism engendered neurosis, even suicide, in some societies. It just drove us to our knees and made us cuddle closer to our GOD.

Maybe, we are not as delicate as some folk because the Maker Who put us together actually designed us for tribulation and made us out of tougher stuff. If so, we have to do much more than brag about our toughness. We have to use our muscle to lift our community. GOD built us that way!

He giveth power to the faint; and to them that have no might he increaseth strength. Isaiah 40:29

February 2, 1992

February 4

Why Me, LORD?

Troubles cluster. Hard times pile up. Tribulations accumulate. "When it rains..."

But you have not been a mass murderer, or an armed robber, or a wife beater, or a child abuser. You are a good person, and you love the LORD and try to live by His precepts. It is understandable when a person who has mistreated everybody who crosses his path gets his comeuppance through two or three calamities in quick succession. It makes sense when the corrupt leader or the constant manipulator gets sick or loses two loved ones within a few months of each other.

But what is GOD punishing you for?

There is no answer at our level for that question. It may be difficult to trust GOD when He does not explain adversities to us—but we have to trust Him.

He chose a good man to absorb hurt when He chose Job (Job, chapters 1 and 2). And even after GOD restored to Job all that he had lost, GOD never explained to Job why he suffered, of all the men who lived during his time.

But the best Man Who ever lived was GOD's own Son, Jesus. When Jesus cried, "My GOD, my GOD, why?" (Matthew 27:46), we are never told that GOD responded with an explanation.

Trials do not come because we are bad people, or because we deserve punishment. They come to us all, even those of you who have been fastidiously righteous. But the good news is that GOD is in charge of good days and bad days, and He is with us, even in the midst of the fire. So trust Him anyhow!

The law of His GOD is in his heart; none of his steps shall slide.
Psalm 37:31

January 23, 2000

February 5

Black & Precious

This month features Valentine's Day and Presidents' Day. It is also very special to some 40 million Americans of African ancestry. February is Black History Month.

On the surface, there seems to be little difference in the circumstances of Americans of different ancestry. Kids whose ancestors came from Europe or from Latin nations or from Asian cultures or from Africa all have to take tough academic tests; they all are subject to the laws of the land; and they all are represented among the successful and the rich and the famous. But that is on the surface.

The kids with African ancestors had to overcome more than mediocre upbringing. They are the only ones whose ancestors were enslaved by law, and whose bondage was supported by the Constitution of the United States. So while they are capable of being CEO of a major corporation, or of winning a Grammy, an Oscar, or a Super Bowl ring, they must never forget what their forebears went through to gain for them the privilege of first class citizenship.

37

In a curious combination of the grace of GOD and the spiritual toughness of African slaves, there was forged a unique character—the African-American. He/she prays and "cusses." He/she hangs loose and hangs tough. He/she accepts insults and stereotypes and still puts out excellence. He/she does super-dumb things and is incomparably brilliant. This nation has been made infinitely richer by the presence and the contribution of Aunt Hagar's children.

And all who know that GOD orchestrated our slavery, our suffering, and our strength must make sure that our children praise Him for it!

We will not hide them from their children, shewing to the generations to come the praises of the LORD and his strength, and His wonderful works that He hath done. Psalm 78:4

February 2, 2003

February 6

Who Are We?

This month must be celebrated. Our children are subject to miss the significance of this month as we gain new opportunities and place less emphasis on black history. It is less and less politically correct to talk about race. The more fashionable position is the patriotic one—we are all Americans.

Jesus urged us to remember. In an upper room somewhere in Jerusalem, the night before He was crucified. He "took bread, and gave thanks, and brake it, and gave unto them, saying, This is my body which is given for you: this do in remembrance of me" (Luke 22:19). We should look forward to our goals; we should have a positive outlook toward future successes. But we must never forget the sufferings that made those goals and successes possible. Behind us is beauty and ugliness. The glories of ancient empires, the pain of slavery and Jim Crow, the struggles for civil rights, and the emergence of new opportunities—all are part of our past. We need to remember both the beauty and the ugliness so that we understand the price GOD pays that we may have abundant life.

38

The Jew remembers the Law and the Prophets. The Oriental remembers the dynasties and the sages. The African still pays respect to the kings and chieftains, even when they wear Armani and drive Mercedes SUV's. So we, who have evolved from slaves called by masters' names from "colored" to "Negro" to "black" to "African-American" to "Mr. or Ms. Jackson," must take the time to teach our children the glories and the agonies of their background. They need to know that they are somebody. But they need to know that it cost Somebody's blood to give them that title.

Tell ye your children of it, and let your children tell their children, and their children another generation. Joel 1:3

February 3, 2002

February 7

So What's Good about It?

Are you a "griper"? Many of us are, although few of us would admit it. We are bundles of peeves. It's too warm if it is 73°, but downright chilly if it is 71°. A fly or a mosquito can totally destroy an otherwise great day. We are sure that because somebody looked our way, they were talking about us. If we don't get the job or the promotion, it's racism. If we do and somebody else complains, they are paranoid. The sad thing is, we are not that upset by the plight of children or by the very real pains of the poor or the sick. We just gripe about lukewarm coffee or slow service or a gift we didn't like.

The more you gripe, the more things are wrong, until you wake up to face a lousy day.

But there is an exercise that helps you trim your "gripe-line." It is called "thanks." If you thank the LORD, because His mercy endures forever (Check out Psalm 136—beautiful redundancy!), you will find yourself appreciating more and more little things. You can rejoice about the sunshine and celebrate the rain. You can praise Him for strength with which you can help others and for weakness that gives you compassion for others. You can glory in family and be downright thrilled with the noise of children. And before long you will find yourself thanking GOD for meager food (somebody somewhere has none) and for a paycheck too small (somebody who is jobless cannot even look forward to that).

39

You have really arrived when you can be reviled and persecuted and lied on, and can rejoice and be exceeding glad, knowing that you are now numbered with such greats as Martin King and the Christian martyrs and the Old Testament prophets, and with Jesus Christ Himself. When you can smile under those conditions, you have shed your "gripe complex" and have achieved the abundant life.

Rejoice in the LORD alway; and again I say, Rejoice. Philippians 4:4

May 16, 1999

February 8

GOD Don't Make No Junk

That ungrammatical clause is part of a proud self-affirmation that "GOD made me," with the obvious implication that therefore I am good stuff. This month is about proud self-affirmations. But it is not about boasting. You are black and beautiful; however, your beauty is not something you can take credit for. You are part of a community that has greatly improved America; but not because of your own genius or hard work. You are part of a Master Plan by which GOD uses us all as witnesses to His glory.

Once, at a seminar, the diversity consultant gave a parable about a giraffe and an elephant who were friends. The giraffe invited the elephant home, but his house was tall and narrow, with windows at the top, and the elephant could not get through the doors. The point was when you invite an elephant, you have to alter your home to accommodate an elephant; when you diversify a company, you have to make changes to accommodate minorities, females, the handicapped, the aged, etc.

GOD did not make you a dark-skinned white person; so you do not need to try to "Anglicize" yourself to be complete. You can say "Amen" or raise your hands or pat your feet and still be considered civilized. Your background should have taught you tribal neighborliness, concern for children, respect for elders, a work ethic, the centrality of GOD—do not abandon these principles because you live in a culture dominated by Anglo-Saxon values. Help remodel the giraffe's house so that all of us can feel at home here. It is GOD's will; and GOD don't make no junk.

I will praise Thee; for I am fearfully and wonderfully made; marvelous are Thy works; and that my soul knoweth right well. Psalm 139:14

February 1, 1998

February 9

Angels from the Bottom

She was a nobody.

She was the "espoused wife" of Joseph, according to Luke. Matthew paints her the color of shame, because "before they came together, she was found with child," and Joseph, not wanting to degrade her publicly, considered an annulment. (Matthew makes it clear that she was found with child "of the Holy Ghost.") We don't know who her family was. Some Biblical scholars say her daddy was Heli, named in Luke 3:23. While Matthew, a typical chauvinist Jew, listed Joseph's genealogy in the first sixteen verses of his first chapter, Luke, the brilliant Gentile physician, correctly listed Mary's lineage rather than Joseph's, since Joseph was not the real father of the Holy Baby.

But that is only a theory. She was a nobody, rejected by the innkeeper, a poor traveler far from home, with no significant connections in Bethlehem, forced to have her baby in a stall where animals were kept. How low can one go?

A nobody? Somehow, of all the young women in the world in the first century, GOD selected this poor young wife of a carpenter to be the mother of the most precious Baby ever born! Millions of the super-rich would have given all their fortunes to have their daughter so favored. And in a moment of spiritual ecstasy, this humble young nobody was moved to prophesy that "from henceforth all generations shall call me blessed" (Luke 1:48).

As in the case of Mary, however lowly we may be in men's eyes, if GOD favors us, He can exalt us beyond anything ever expected.

For promotion cometh neither from the east, nor from the west, nor from the south. But GOD is the judge: he putteth down one, and setteth up another. Psalm 75:6-7

41

March 9, 2003

February 10

"You Can Take the Boy Out of the Country...

...but you can't take the country out of the boy." There is more truth than humor in that dictum. If you were reared in a certain style or in a certain environment, there are always echoes of that background in your present behavior and attitudes. For persons fortunate to journey to Africa, their feelings are a bit more than the usual pre-trip excitement.

They are going home.

In the streets and homes of West Africa a strange sense of déjà vu overwhelms visitors. Sights and sounds and smells never experienced before seemed oddly familiar. Children playing in the streets of Accra or Lagos singing ditties in Yoruba or Hausa use tunes familiar to children even in St. Louis. And the plump lady who offers goat-meat and yams looks shockingly like Cousin Rose in Kansas City. Over 370 years of Americanization have not changed the strut-and-swagger walk of the teenage boy, whether in Monrovia or Monroe, Louisiana.

42

Our ancestors brought strong traits from Africa to America, and we have kept many of them. They also brought a strong value system, and it survived all the persecutions of the centuries. We are picking up many things from the technologically advanced, economically affluent, militarily strong West. We are learning greed, arrogance, cruelty, and addiction. But we must never forget reverence for GOD, respect for elders, and the self-discipline that drives bright children to become responsible adults. We have left home, but must not leave home training.

Train up a child in the way he should go: and when he is old he will not depart from it. Proverbs 22:6

February 9, 1992

February 11

The Cost of Honesty

Perhaps it was Benjamin Franklin in his oft-quoted "Poor Richard's Almanac." Maybe, it was some sage Roman senator or Greek playwright. But whoever said it, he (or she) has been quoted as gospel for a long time: "Honesty is the best policy."

As rare as truth is, as seldom as we find a person whose word is his or her bond, honesty is certainly a precious commodity (as diamonds or four-leaf clovers are precious). But it can also be expensive, unless we know how to use it in the right amount at the right time. If a child is always messy, it would be honest to tell him that, maybe even with a scowled face and a few examples to drive home the point. But honesty at that time could discourage the child and even guarantee that he or she would never develop order and neatness. The accusation could become a self-fulfilling prophecy. On the other hand, a word of praise for one of the few times he was not messy could begin a path toward not being messy.

43

What is even more significant is that brutal honesty may clear someone's conscience or get some things off his chest; but that same brutal honesty can cause people to avoid certain people. Some people enjoy being put down (and then get guest spots on popular talk shows), but more do not like being slapped. It may be harder to find things to compliment in people, but one word or note of affirmation may do more than fifty good, honest chewings-out.

So is honesty not the best policy? Maybe what we are calling "honesty" is not honesty at all, just shoot-from-the-hip blatant frankness. Christian honesty cares about the person to whom we speak and knows when to leave some "truths" unsaid. We do not have to lie to be kind. We can have the honesty of GOD as Jesus describes Him. That's the best policy.

...that we may lead a quiet and peaceable life in all godliness and honesty. I Timothy 2:2b

May 6, 1990

February 12

GOD Is a "He"

(Pause for angry female screams and hoots.)

February is a good month to celebrate males. In many communities, males are the endangered half of us. While GOD gives us an equal number of newborn males and females, we quickly begin wiping out our males. Violence, drugs, and prisons take them. They drop out of school, become illegitimate fathers, end up as drifters or as gays. By the time they are adults, we have lost massive numbers of them.

The old Hebrew concept of family celebrated males. So it is significant that when we think of GOD the Father, we conceive of a "Him." When we worship GOD the Son, we revere a "Him." Even when we tell our children the story of creation, we must tell them that GOD's first human was a male and that from that male came females and all children. Whether we like that order or not, it is the Biblical order. We may write off males as nuisances or as unredeemable, but GOD celebrates males, too.

44

If we are true to the Biblical order, we must revitalize family, which means trying to bring back home prodigal sons. (Of course, we must try to improve our daughters, but they are nowhere near as endangered as our sons; and Jesus teaches us that we leave the safe ones in the fold and go out to rescue the endangered ones. Luke's story of the shepherd in his chapter 15 relates that to us.)

Parents must demand the best of their boys. Men must consciously set good examples for the boys who watch them. They must volunteer to mentor at least one boy—their own boy, a male relative, a neighbor's boy, a male student.

GOD redeems the billions of people on earth one re-birth at a time. We rehabilitate an old house board by board, pipe by pipe, wire by wire, brick by brick, etc. You cannot suddenly correct all the problems of African-American males with a media blitz, but we can make a difference by touching the life of at least one boy. And GOD will help us (HE is a chauvinist!).

But if any provide not for his own, and specially for those of his own house, he hath denied the faith and is worse than an infidel. I Timothy 5:8

October 11, 1992

February 13

When the Eagle Flies

The eagle is the symbol of the Boy Scouts, a major character-building program for boys. It represents strength, endurance, and leadership. And this noble creature is the symbol of our nation, the most powerful one.

This creature also represents triumph over obstacles. As the eagle rises above the low landscape to soar in the upper air, to leave behind rubbish on the ground to seek out mountain peaks, so, says the prophet Isaiah, shall be those who "wait upon the LORD" (Isaiah 40:31). They shall "renew their strength," and overcome the weary and the slow.

The eagle is a fitting symbol for a nation which, despite her failings, is a leader among the nations of the world. And it is a significant symbol for boys who aim to be strong men, leaders in their fields. How much more a prophetic statement that it represents African-American boys, pledging faith in GOD and country, and developing the attitudes and attributes of the highest levels of black manhood. We can be justly proud of the Pack and Troop which bears the likeness of the majestic bird.

45

But Isaiah is not talking patriotism. He is a proud Jew, loyal to the principles of the Children of Israel—but he says we shall be strengthened and elevated not by our loyalty to nation, but by our faith in GOD. Likewise, we hope boys will rise with their eagles in scholarship, in leadership, in achievement—and with the Son of GOD as their Master, they can soar to the mountaintops.

But they that wait upon the LORD shall renew their strength; they shall mount up with wings as eagles; they shall run, and not be weary; and they shall walk, and not faint. Isaiah 40:31

February 14, 1999

February 14

The Anatomy of Love

A decade ago, Dionne Warwick warbled huskily,
"What the world needs now is love, sweet love;
That's the only thing that there's just too little of."
The song is outmoded, but the words relay a timeless reality. The violence, the cynicism, the almost unconscious abuse of other people make it seem that there is not only "too little of" it, but that there is no longer true love at all. We use the term with incredible looseness: We love pieces of merchandise and vehicles and sports and foods. The incessant coupling on the soap-opera screen is liberally smothered under "I love you's" and heavy breathing. What, really, is love?

The model for all things begins with the Creator. He made all matter, all energy, all personality. He designed love (the corrupt version we express is a far cry from the agape which originated with GOD). So if we want to know what love really is, we must ask Him. Jesus, of course, will answer for Him.

46

Jesus gives a bewildered Peter with a real definition of love. Love does not simply talk; love gives, nurtures, cherishes, feeds. Who do you claim to love? Now—who do you really love? Your actions answer for you.

He saith to him again the second time, Simon, son of Jonas lovest thou Me? He saith unto him, Yea, LORD, thou knowest that I love Thee. He saith unto him, Feed my sheep. John 21:16

September 22, 1996

February 15

Mirror-Images

A major disadvantage of being thin, it seems, is that the person has a "Cassius image." Shakespeare has Julius Caesar say that he wants around him men who are fat, who enjoy food and laughter, because "yon Cassius has a lean and hungry look. He thinks too much." So it surprises no one that little children sometimes shrink from Ichabod Crane gauntness.

But every once in a while a child is so loving and affectionate that even the old rawbones does not push him or her away.

Even when not "huggable," someone chooses to love us anyway, not because we are loveable, but because that person is loving. (There is a difference.)

Love is not determined by external circumstance, but by internal attitudes. We do not love on the basis of appearance or personality or even in response to good deeds. Real and lasting love is based on much deeper attitudes in both the lover and the beloved. We can feel nothing for a person of great beauty and love deeply a parent or a child who is plain or even homely.

47

The loving nature of a child reflects, mirror-like, what kind of environment he has. His parents, both doctors, might have given him a cold, rational, unfeeling environment. But apparently they have hugged him, affirmed him, loved each other in his presence, and conditioned him to love. So he could express love even for a Cassius.

The Bible reminds us that we reap what we sow, that bread cast on the waters shall return. If we send out loving vibrations, they come back. If we surround people with love, they transmit it to others. We ought to love much. Some Ichabod needs to be on the receiving end!

Cast thy bread upon the water: for thou shalt find it after many days.
Ecclesiastes 11:1

August 14, 1983

February 16

Divine Engineering

We puttered away at routine chores; we talked on phones and wrote out our calculations and cared for babies and buffed floors and pecked out information on computers. It was a perfectly normal morning. The sky was dark and angry, and the throaty roar of distant thunder provided gentle percussion for our routine. It was a perfectly normal morning.

A blinding flash of lightning, an ear-splitting explosion of thunder, and suddenly buffers and typewriters and computers and telephones went dead. A baby screamed in the darkened nursery. A quick glance outside revealed that the whole neighborhood was without power.

Except us.

An emergency telephone line became instantly available. Soft lights from a backup lighting system provided enough visibility for us to leave buildings if we needed to. We had built into our system some "in case" safeguards so that we had some light and some communications.

48

A certain automobile calls itself "the best engineered car in the world." That company does not know what real engineering is!

GOD has engineered His universe so that we can be saved by His "in case" system. He made us innocent and without sin. But in His own foreknowledge, He developed a plan of salvation for sinners before the foundation of the world. He did not design us to sin, but because He designed us with free will, He also engineered a backup system called Jesus on Calvary and through His Son provided for us to have communication with Heaven and enough light to get out of the mess we get ourselves into.

For with the heart man believeth unto righteousness; and with the mouth confession is made unto salvation. Romans 10:10

September 9, 1990

February 17

Getting Prepared

On the second Sunday in February, we observe Boy Scout Sunday. It is fitting that during Black History Month we encourage building the character for boys, for boys are our most valuable human resource. Black boys are our most endangered species. If we cannot produce good men, then women and children are in trouble. One cannot produce a strong society with only women and children. So we praise GOD for the gift of boys.

The motto of Boy Scouts is "Be Prepared." The emblem of Boy Scouts includes the most majestic of all birds, the eagle. That bird symbolizes the highest level of achievement to which a scout can aspire: the coveted Eagle badge. Few boys ever get it. But in order to get it, a long and demanding process of earning twenty-one merit badges has to be achieved. A boy must prove himself able to do everything from cook to survive in the wilderness. If he prepares well, he may wear the Eagle badge.

49

Whoever does so prepare can be sure of several things. He will complete school. He will not go to jail. He will not succumb to drug addiction. He will go on to prepare for gainful employment and for productive manhood.

We preach Jesus Christ as redeemer and every sinner as redeemable. We want to guarantee life in a realm without sin or crime or human conflict. Jesus offers it, if we make preparations now. We can accept Him as our Savior, or re-dedicate ourselves to Him, and we will go through the process that ends in His awarding each one of us as a "good and faithful servant," welcome to the "joys of your LORD." As we push our hoys to prepare for excellence in scouting, we must push ourselves to prepare for the rejoicing of angels as we receive our crowns!

Therefore be ye also ready: for in such an hour as ye think not the Son of Man cometh. Matthew 24:44

February 10, 1991

February 18

Who Opened That Door?

"Timmy!" shouted the frustrated mother of the four-year-old with the untied shoe and the shirt partially tucked in, "Get away from that door!" Then, somewhat apologetically to the store manager, "I'm sorry, sir; I'll keep him with me. Come on over here, boy!"

His lip quivered a bit, and a silent tear rolled down his smudged cheek. He had committed the crime of childish curiosity and had been reprimanded for it. But it is the nature of four-year-olds to marvel at the wonders of their world. They may find special fascination in the clatter of neatly-stacked cooking pots, or in the swirl of a Kleenex in the flushing toilet, or in the miracle of a fusillade of images when they press the "channel" button on the remote control device.

He had just discovered that if someone stood in a certain spot at the store's entrance, the huge glass doors opened without anybody touching them. How could anyone convict him for wanting to see why that happened?

50

The Apostle Paul describes GOD's provision of an opportunity for the Gospel to cross from Asia into Europe by declaring that "a door was opened unto the LORD" (II Corinthians 2:12).

Our elders drew from that testimony a phrase every African-American Christian knows well: "He opens doors we cannot see." That has happened for all of us. We were in the corner, against the wall. And GOD opened for us some door we did not know was there.

He always does that. He does not guarantee that we will know in advance how things are going to work out. Certainly, He provides no promises that they will work out as we prescribe them to work out. But He calls us to be faithful and promises He will not leave us comfortless, or alone, or without guidance. We do not need to know how He opens the door. We do not need to instruct Him in when to open the door. We do not even need to wake Him up to tell Him how urgent it is that He open the door now. All we need to do is to stand in the right place, at the right time, and wait prayerfully.

Ask, and it shall be given you; seek, and ye shall find; knock, and it shall be opened unto you. Matthew 7:7

March 21, 1993

February 19

What Language Does GOD Speak?

At the Tower of Babel (Genesis 11), GOD took away the universal language of His rebellious children and replaced it with many languages so they could no longer work together in their rebellion. On the Day of Pentecost (Acts 2), GOD gave back the universal language to His followers so they could be understood by all the people despite the diversity of languages. Luke describes that universal language as "other tongues" (Acts 2:4).

So what is this universal language of GOD? It seems to be "get up and do something."

When GOD made the first couple, He immediately ordered them to be administrators of creation. After man's sin had gotten unbearable, He told Noah to get up and build an ark. Then He shook Abram awake in Ur of the Chaldees and told him to get out of town. He told Moses to leave the quiet of the desert and go back to confront Pharaoh. And so with Joshua, Gideon, David, Solomon, Josiah, and all the prophets.

What do you think GOD is saying to His people right now? Surely not, "Relax and enjoy air- conditioned inspiration." When the Holy Spirit, who speaks in GOD's universal language, brings us a message from Him, it is what it has always been: "Get up and do something." Jesus tells us that the Father always works, and so does He (John 5:17). So if you are trying never to be where work- assignments are being handed out, you do not speak the language of GOD. It is not English, or French, or Hindustani, or Swahili. It is action to make GOD's will done!

Thy Kingdom come. Thy will be done in earth, as it is in Heaven!.
Matthew 6:10

August 25, 1991

February 20

Hold My Mule

At least ten thousand preachers have told the story about the farmer who was reprimanded by a dignified fellow church member because he was overly emotional in church; and who, while telling why he had to praise GOD, asked the shocked member to hold his mule while he shouted.

One lighted candle turns Calvary's mourning into Easter's joy. The resurrection of Jesus is the reason we worship on Sundays instead of Saturdays. And the joy we have in GOD's salvation is why Christians sing. Many other religions of the world do not; some are emulating the Christian church by adding music, even gospel music, although they have no Jesus to praise. We are "the singing faith." You can hardly imagine a Christian worship service without music. It is the way we tell GOD how much we love Him—it is not "performance," or display of our talent.

52

One of the earmarks of a true child of GOD is how he or she deals with the burdens of this life. Constant complaints, criticisms? Synthetic Christian. Praise so spontaneous that he or she lights up a gloomy place? The real McCoy. In fact, hold my mule...

And Jesus came and spake unto them, saying, All power is given unto me in heaven and in earth. Matthew 28:18

December 15, 1996

February 21

When You Are Up, Reach Down

The way of our world is to push upward, to make more money, to acquire more "stuff," to establish more power, to gain more prestige. Both. major presidential candidates are promising a better economy, because the more you can garner, the better your quality of life. Right?

Wrong. That is the gospel of Upward Mobility. GOD's way is not upward mobility, but embracing the underclasses.

He began with a slave nation, and its kings were counted as good or bad depending on how they treated the masses of Israel. Every prophet told Israel she must care for "widows and orphans." Jesus was the classic example of downward mobility, ministering to publicans, sinners, the sick, the poor.

On a Mission Sunday, we must try to act more like GOD, and extend ourselves and our resources to those further down on the ladder, whether in the ghettoes and barrios of Houston or among the struggling in the Third World. It is what Christ established the church for.

53

Ye have heard that it hath been said, Thou shalt love thy neighbor, and hate thine enemy. Matthew 5:43

September 29, 1996

February 22

Walk in My Shoes

If you are a child, you think of "growing up" as getting bigger and older and having more privileges. Once you become an adult, you know that even after you have attained full size and have begun to go downhill rather than uphill, you have not finished "growing up." Jesus urges us to be perfect. The word translated "perfect" in our King James Bibles is not "flawless," but "mature, finished, full- grown."

A major part of growing up is being able to feel other people's needs or joys or pains, not just your own. It is difficult for a teenager to be a good parent, because he or she may not yet have developed the ability to nurture an infant, who always needs and never gives back. He or she may still be in the needing stage him- or herself!

Have you matured enough to feel the needs of those around you? Do you care that your friends or family or associates may be carrying heavy burdens behind their carefully-displayed smiles? Are you willing to inconvenience yourself to comfort them, listen to them, pray with them?

54

We consider the needs of those who never have to complain about loud music or pointless gossip or fingernails on the chalkboard. They cannot hear such things. If one can hear the cough of a baby in the next room, the whimper of a puppy trying to get in, the gentle "I love you" of a small child, he should be thankful and be sensitive. Grow up!

Be ye therefore perfect, even as your Father which is in heaven is perfect. Matthew 5:48

September 15, 1996

February 23

The Strength of the Sea

She is small of build and of light weight. She is feather-gentle with the new-born she suckles at her breast. The most apt image of her is "flower," delicate and soft.

But Heaven help whoever becomes a threat to her baby. Whether the mother is a bird or a cat or a human, she becomes a killing machine when her beloved is in danger. There is a sudden and unexpectedly fierce power in even a small mother protecting the ones she loves.

Paul says he has learned to accept his infirmities, even to glory in them. An odd contradiction in terms!

In February, we celebrate blackness. But the long history of black peoples is one of oppression, exclusion, hardship, even enforced bondage. What do we have to celebrate? We could fantasize about the glorious kingdoms of antiquity and try to identify with the kings and emperors and pharaohs of great dynasties. But we know deep down inside that most of us were not kings or queens, nor part of their courts. Most of us were ordinary folk, whether in Africa or in the New World. But we can celebrate an unexpected strength that comes from hardship. We were built to stand against storms—under GOD, we are survivors.

GOD sustained us when we were oppressed by cruel tyrants in Africa, and He has sustained us under oppression by the powerful in the West. And under GOD, we are stronger than those who oppress us. That is what we celebrate: the strength of the weak!

Therefore I take pleasure in infirmities, in reproaches, in necessities, in persecutions, in distresses for Christ's sake: for when I am weak, then I am strong. II Corinthians 12:10

February 5, 1995

February 24

We Are the World

While we tell our children about "their history," events make it clear to them that we have left out some parts. They have heard of Philadelphia and Richard Allen, but where is Soweto and who is Desmond Tutu? They remember names like Nat Turner and Martin Luther King, but why all the headlines about Nelson Mandela?

If we could think as GOD thinks and see as GOD sees, we would not limit our interests to those closest to us. But we do not think GOD-thoughts nor see GOD-perspective.

GOD made a world, not a nation. He created a human race, not Caucasoid, Negroid, and Mongoloid branches. And the predicament of sin and the plan of salvation are universal, not local. We always see our family, our friends, our kind. GOD sees His children as "all flesh."

We cannot think as GOD thinks; we cannot see what GOD sees. But we can rise above our little clans and cliques to learn the way Jesus defines "neighbor." And we can teach our children that Black History tells the story of African-Americans and the peoples of sixty-odd nations in Africa, and African children in South America and the Caribbean and Asia and Europe. So if we try to learn for whom GOD wants us to pray and for whom GOD wants us to care, we must include the poor in Addis Ababa and Alexandria and Cite Soleil as well as the families in the Fourth Ward. And if we would teach real Black History, our children must learn about Alan Boesak. They may not be our American family, but they are our family.

For my thoughts are not your thoughts, neither are your ways, my ways, saith the LORD. For as the heavens are higher than the earth, so are my ways higher than your ways, and my thoughts than your thoughts. Isaiah 55:8-9

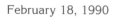

February 18, 1990

February 25

"You Can't Do That!"

Anyone ten or older must have heard the parable. It is the one about the bumble-bee not being able to fly because its body is too oddly-shaped with its bulbous trunk and its tiny wings. According to the laws of aerodynamics (which is Greek to most), the plump little insect should not be able to fly. But, says the parable, since the bumble-bee does not know the laws of aerodynamics, he flies away.

Often, we accept challenges that seem impossible. In tough economic climates, some financial undertakings are ill-advised. Our personal finances may in many cases be so bad we ought to be declared disaster areas. Major corporations may file bankruptcy or lay off employees by the thousands. To put it bluntly, sometimes things just seem impossible.

But we worship a Christ Who faced blind people, and they saw; Who touched lepers, and they were made clean; Who produced wine where there was none; and Who fed multitudes with a child's lunch. Our LORD, without equivocation, gives us hope when situations seem hopeless.

57

So when we try to save up our gift for GOD and Satan slaps us with a cracked engine block or a child's broken collar-bone or greetings from the IRS, we just groan a bit, drop to our knees, tell Satan to go to Hawaii, and tell GOD we are still on the case.

We acknowledge some things cannot be done, but we do not have sense enough to accept that as the last word. We have seen GOD do some other things that could not be done, so praise the LORD for ignorance!

With men it is impossible, but not with GOD: for with GOD all things are possible. Mark 10:27

February 13, 1983

February 26

He Always Opens Doors

February says two things simultaneously: one explicitly and one implicitly. Explicitly Black History Month says that African-Americans have made significant contributions to the life and development of this nation. We glory in the achievements of giants in science and education, literature and the arts, entertainment and industry, government and human rights. So February tells us that we are somebody.

The other thing BHM tells us is that Somebody has made it possible for an oppressed people to transcend their adversities and to do great things in spite of those adversities. The old folk had a saying for it: "He opens doors I cannot see; He makes a way out of no way." That is implicit rather than explicit, but behind the Douglasses and the Tubmans and the DuBoises and the Malcolms and the Kings is the clear and indisputable truth: GOD made it possible.

58

As we marvel at the greatness of a Colin Powell or a William Gray or a Marguerite Ross Barnett, we must remember that they had to struggle against the same obstacles that face each of us. There would have been no national renown or global reputation had not the LORD been with them. The reason we can point our children to them is that with GOD nothing is impossible

No one is limited by the color of his or her skin—and always—we celebrate during this month of Black History (a) the accomplishments of black men and women, and (b) the grace and mercy of GOD, Who made all those accomplishments possible.

Jesus is on the main line; tell Him what you want!

If thou canst believe, all things are possible to him that believeth.
Mark 9:23

February 24, 1991

February 27

Is There a Daddy in the House?

Roughly half of African-American homes do not have a father present, and in another sizeable percentage even when a father is present, he is not active, and the home is still matriarchal.

But the tribal quality of our heritage has already made allowances for the absence of fathers. In our history we have always known the subtraction of fathers through wars, through the machinations of slavery (even long before American slavery), through the hazards of the hunt, etc., etc. And we have known the natural process of bringing into the family structure "father-figures": uncles, grandparents, brothers-in-law, respected village leaders. There have always been male role-models provided for children to see and learn from. So if we didn't have a resident daddy, chances are our relative or neighbor or preacher or principal gave us some guidance anyhow. The ugly side of integration has been the breakdown of the neighborhood where we have separated families from each other, thus making the "father-figure" less available to us. Thank GOD for the black church, where every child can still have some contact with father-figures, even when he or she does not have a daddy living at home.

Yes, earthly daddies have earthly weaknesses. But in the church we can praise a Heavenly Father Who never disappoints, never forsakes, never misleads—always provides, always is available. Hallowed be His Name!

59

Our Father which art in heaven, Hallowed be Thy name. Matthew 6:9b

June 20, 1999

February 28

The Joy of Sorrow

Lent is the six weeks before Good Friday, when Jesus set His face toward the cross. It was a grim forty days during which He prayed much and tried to prepare His disciples for His impending death. His soul was sorrowful He said, even unto death (Mark 14:34). But even as He bore the immeasurable weight of death, He lifted the spirits of His followers. He told them that their sorrow would turn into joy.

What a paradox!

Everybody suffers. We have no option about that. Suffering is the common lot of us all. But we can choose whether to suffer consequences of our own sins or to suffer redemptively as a testimony to the righteousness and mercy of GOD. Jesus knew that death would be painful, but He could impart joy to His followers because He knew He was doing the will of His Father.

So during Lent, we should try to strengthen our "doing-His-will" muscles by beginning to do something that is His will. This is more than a time to give up beer or red meat or sugar. It is a time to give up selfishness, vengefulness, thoughtlessness; it is time to increase prayer, study of GOD's word, witness to His grace in our own life, and to express love for those we touch.

If you try concentrating on GOD's will, two things are guaranteed: (1) Satan will be mad at you, and you will suffer; and (2) GOD will be pleased with you, and you will have joy in the midst of your suffering. It is O.K. to work on your waistline during Lent so you will look great this summer. But it is better to exercise your soul and be strong enough to resist the Devil as he tries to sprinkle sorrow on your joy.

That ye shall weep and lament, but the world shall rejoice: and ye shall be sorrowful, but your sorrow shall be turned to joy. John 16:20

February 17, 1991

February 29

I Could Just Die

There are times when everything that can go wrong does. We are in financial straits. Our wife/husband/girlfriend/boyfriend is doing us wrong, or not showing us proper love/respect. Our doctor tells us that we have serious medical problems. And we misplace our keys. (Add a couple more problems for flavor.) It is time to put the gun-barrel in our mouth.

We may find a ray of light by looking either down or up.

GOD may open our eyes to somebody who has twice as many hardships, but who has a bright and joyous spirit through it all As we look at him/her, we begin to realize that we are not that bad off after all. We don't exactly thank GOD for being broke or abused or sick or keyless; but we do acknowledge that by His grace, things are as well as they are. Looking down usually reveals somebody with more problems than we.

Or GOD may remind us that when we have fallen into deep holes before, and were sure this was the absolute end, He has rescued us and restored us and exchanged our misery for joy. We sometimes have short "grace memories," but it only takes a little reflection to bring to mind that GOD's grace has brightened our lives time and time again. When we look up and see His love for us for as long as we can remember, the grim realities of our present predicament give way to hope that He will step in again, just in the nick of time. Looking up always distracts us from agonies below and helps us to focus on love from above.

Bad day? Tough week? Miserable ten months? Lousy life?

For GOD so loved the world, that He gave His only begotten Son, that whosoever believeth in Him should not perish, but have everlasting life. John 3:16

November 5, 2000

March 1

How Do You Approach the Almighty?

When L. Frank Baum penned his fantasy about a little Kansas girl blown far away by a Kansas tornado, he climaxed it in a wonderful land called Oz, where Dorothy and her friends were ushered into a huge hall from which the Wizard of Oz ruled the country. But when the frightened quartet entered the hall, the Wizard unleashed a storm of fire and smoke and thundered at them in a deafening voice. They, of course, trembled.

You tremble when you come before GOD. But even more than the Wizard, the frightening power of GOD belongs to One Who also exhibits mercy to respond to your needs. Power and mercy—with the Wizard, it was artificial; with GOD, it is real. We ought to appeal to GOD's mercy while respecting His power.

The time will come (or has come already) when you are at the bedside of a loved one on the brink of death. Do you ask GOD to overrule the doctors, or start making funeral arrangements?

62

Jesus showed us how to approach the Almighty in His own prayer in the Garden of Gethsemane. He appealed to GOD's mercy (let this cup pass from me), but surrendered to His power (nevertheless, not my will, but Thine be done). So ask GOD for a miracle; then surrender to His will—do both.

And he went a little farther, and fell on his face, and prayed, saying, O my Father, if it be possible, let this cup pass from me: nevertheless not as I will, but as Thou wilt. Matthew 26:39

April 20, 1997

March 2

To Think about Death

Most of us would rather not. We all know death is inevitable, and we will, when we are pushed, make some preparations for it—life insurance, perhaps the writing of a will. But death is not our favorite thing to focus on.

And yet, all around us, every day, people are being taken from us, gradually or suddenly. A favorite aunt languishes for months with cancer, and we watch her waste away. A friend has a devastating heart attack and dies in the emergency room. Young people leave on a school trip and a drunk driver snatches them from us in ten seconds. We go to a class reunion and are stunned at who is not there, and why. Death is a major theme in the symphony of life.

The Lenten season climaxes with Good Friday. All of the prior weeks of Christ's earthly ministry were spent thinking about His death, forcing His disciples to focus on the meaning of that grim day on a bleak hill outside Jerusalem. He told them that His death would have purpose, would benefit all generations. Strange, that death can be defined as beneficial rather than simply tragic! The value of Jesus' death was determined by the direction of Jesus' life. Had He been just another consumer, scratching for dollars as long as He lived, His death would have been just a local statistic. But He was sent for a purpose, and He fulfilled it completely.

You and I are not Messiahs, sent from Heaven by GOD. But during the final two weeks of Lent, can we not ask ourselves, "What good am I doing day by day? When my time comes to die, who will care?" Live well today, my friend—your death ought to matter.

Verily, verily, I say unto you, If a man keep My saying, he shall never see death. John 8:51

March 16, 1997

March 3

Well, Don't Just Stand There

They had not gotten over their amazement at Him. For forty days He had been with them, showing them what it was like after death. He ate with them, even cooked for them; but He no longer needed food. He walked with them for miles, but had no need of walking; He was capable of suddenly disappearing from one location and being instantly teleported to another. He could pass through stone walls, and yet He urged them to feel the ordinary corporeality of His flesh. They often stared at Him open-mouthed.

Then one day on top of a mountain, a strange little mist enveloped Him, and He began to levitate upward until He disappeared from their sight. Jesus had ascended!

While they gazed up at the empty air two angels rebuked them: "Why stand ye gazing up into Heaven?" The bottom line was: "You know what you are supposed to do—get back to Jerusalem and do it!"

64

Then returned they not then returned then unto Jerusalem from the mount called Olivet, which is from Jerusalem a sabbath day's journey.
Acts 1:12

October 15, 1995

March 4

About Feeding Sheep

Jesus laid a heavy one on Peter. He challenged the loud-mouthed disciple to prove his love for Him by feeding His sheep (John 21:15-17). This should have echoed to Peter, who would surely remember the day when they were surrounded by a hungry crowd and they suggested sending the crowd away so they could feed themselves; but Jesus said, "They need not depart; give ye them to eat" (Matthew 14:14, 15).

He is still challenging us. He knows we are surrounded by the poor, the young, the struggling. And He asks us to this very day not to send them to somebody else to deal with their needs—He wants us to make some effort to help them. (Why else would He give so many resources to us?)

If somebody among us is hungry, or sick, or in prison, or otherwise deprived, He will not allow His church to look to government or to public charities to minister to them. As He provided the power to multiply a child's loaves and fishes, and then dispatched His disciples to deliver the meal, so He has provided to you and me Heaven's power to multiply earthly resources; and He beckons us to the door of the hungry, to the bedside of the sick, to the cell of the incarcerated to deliver His mercies.

65

When we say we love GOD, we praise the Name of Jesus, we worship and adore Him, He says, "Really? Well, show me—see those folks out there, struggling with their pain, crying out in need? Take care of them, and you are loving me" (see Matthew 25:31-40).

So why does a church need to care about the quality of life in the neighborhoods around it? Because Jesus lays heavy stuff on us!

Then shall He answer them, saying, Verily I say unto you, Inasmuch as ye did it not to one of the least of these, ye did it not to me. Matthew 25:45

March 21, 1999

March 5

The King Is Coming

The Lenten series tells the story of the Triumphal Entry of Jesus into Jerusalem (Matthew 21, Mark 11, Luke 19). It is often depicted with all the majesty of a coronation, or a presidential inaugural. That is not a proper image. Jesus was not exalted and applauded by the power system.

He interrupted the power system with a mass of common people. Imagine a miles-long backup of traffic on the freeway. Our Sunday was their first day of the business week—like a busy Monday morning. And here came crowds of people, mostly common laborers and housewives and their children, to clog up the narrow streets among the market-places, to interrupt first-of-the-week business, to create unanticipated congestion and unwanted noise. And they were not celebrating a Roman procurator or a high priest, but a non-descript itinerant rabbi on a donkey whose background was a carpenter-shop in a low-class village far north of Jerusalem!

Five days later, He would be executed by the state.

The lesson we ought to learn from these passages is that GOD does not respect our carefully laid-out agendas, our "five-year plans." He interrupts our schedules with His demand that we hear Him, that we recognize His primacy in our lives, that we define Him as King of kings and LORD of LORDs.

And many spread their garments in the way: and others cut down branches off the trees, and strewed them in the way. Mark 11:8

March 3, 1995

March 6

We Shall Overcome

The tragedy of the assassination of Martin Luther King still causes grief. Nor is it only African- Americans who have been deprived of a major leader; Dr. Martin Luther King, Jr. is still the prophet for all people. His theology of praise to GOD, plus compassion for neighbor speaks to people of every race, every nationality, every faith-structure. His social technique of raising issues of human rights without violence or hatred is universally powerful and still completely disarms those whose primary expression is deadly force.

He emerged during the forties and fifties when discrimination by race was as normal as red, yellow, and green traffic lights. But when he lay in a pool of blood on the balcony of a cheap Memphis motel, he had already made a world aware of the injustice of holding down human beings because they were not Anglo or Protestant or male. In the more than 27 years since he died, we have seen major changes in opportunities for black people. But in the past decade or so, we have watched many of those gains recede. We are moving back into a "neo-segregationist" era without Martin to be our Moses.

But there is good news.

Dr. King was not the basis of our gains. He was the channel. Our gains came from the One Who sent Martin among us. Dr. King is not in Georgia now, but GOD is still in Heaven. And Dr. King always made it clear Who his Boss was. We all knew he considered himself to be a "servant of the LORD." And the same GOD Who sent him is still watching over us, and providing for us, and working to redeem us. He does not take a Moses without providing a Joshua. We can still sing, "We shall overcome!"

O magnify the LORD with me, and let us exalt His name together.
Psalm 34:3

January 14, 1996

March 7

It's Time!

Some things never change. In 1915 songwriter Irving Berlin reflected the attitude of young soldiers in World War I. How different is that from your anger at your alarm clock today?

Oh, how I hate to get up in the mornin',
Oh, how I'd love to remain in bed!
But the greatest blow of all
Is to hear the bugler call:
'You gotta get up
You gotta get up
You gotta get up
This mornin'!
Some day I'm goin' to murder the bugler,
Some day I'm goin' to kill him dead!
Then I'll amputate his reveille,
And step upon it heavily,
And spend the rest of my life in bed!

68

We are still governed by calendars and clocks (and now worrisome electronic devices in pocket or purse or on wrist). How can we escape the slavery of time?

We can't—and shouldn't.

According to a Divine schedule, Christ was born, and lived through a brief three-year ministry, and died just before Passover, and rose on the first day of the week (our Sunday), and is coming back for His church. All of that means we need to use wisely the time we have to praise Him, to witness for Him, to help somebody in His Name—we really don't have unlimited time.

To every thing there is a season, and a time to every purpose under the heaven. Ecclesiastes 3:1

March 25, 2001

March 8

Don't Forget the Turpentine

Zephaniah was the prophet of "the great day of the LORD." His message is, "Repent in a hurry; GOD is going to bring judgment upon Judah."

How did we come to paint GOD as a kindly Santa Claus and sing words like, "Though it makes Him sad to see the way we live, He'll always say, 'I forgive'"?

When in our history did we erase the wrath of GOD and remember only His mercy? Whatever happened to sin and judgment and reaping and Hell?

Remember when we did not have access to medical insurance and HMO's and specialists and antibiotics. If we caught the flu or strep throat or the whooping cough, there were "home remedies," wondrous mixtures or plasters or strange things in little bags hung around our necks. One of the more familiar medications was a spoonful of sugar. The first time we saw it, we welcomed it. It seemed at first a much better resort than the bitter laxatives or the heavy castor oil we expected. But we soon learned not to welcome it. Mama or Grandma or Aunt Toddy had poured into the sugar a healthy squirt of turpentine. And when we opened our mouth to enjoy the sugar, our throat burned with the bitterness of that unexpected fluid. Ugh!

GOD is mercy, and He has forgiveness for the worst of our sins. GOD is grace, and He blesses us when we neither ask for blessings nor deserve them. GOD is sugar.

But GOD is also justice, and He enforces His laws when we violate them. He requires that if we sow the wind, we shall reap the whirlwind; He has a very real Hell for people who take Him for granted and who put off repenting and confessing of their sins. GOD will indeed destroy those who neglect His salvation!

So remember what the children sing: "He sees all you do, and He hears all you say; my LORD is writing all the time." Clean up your act, or expect the turpentine!

So then every one of us shall give account of himself to GOD. Romans 14:12

July 12, 1992

March 9

A Bird in the Hand

"A bird in the hand is worth two in the bush." At first glance, this seems a wise saying! It probably meant to its author that we ought not waste time seeking the exotic when we already have something solid right at home. That is a half-truth. The other half is that if we do not dream of reaching the unreachable star, we may flounder forever on the ground.

Jesus encourages perfection. What a goal! What the Father challenges us to do is to stop whining about our imperfections and reach for divine gold. That is not going for "two in the bush," but for the whole flock in the sky.

The season called Lent is the time when Jesus set a goal higher than any rabbi who wanted to teach the law to his neighbors, higher than any master teacher who wanted to introduce a newer and higher vision of GOD. His goal was to use His own death to redeem every human being who ever lived and every human yet unborn. Talk about leaving behind the "bird in the hand"!

70

Young people should not be satisfied with what their parents have provided for them. They should not stop with a decent income and a nice car. Moody once said, "The world has not yet seen what GOD can do with a person completely committed to Him." Why not be that person? Let ordinary people be satisfied with full cupboards and closets. You are a child of the King. Aim at a crown!

Be perfect, be of good comfort, be of one mind, live in peace; and the GOD of love and peace shall be with you. II Corinthians 13:11b

March 15, 1992

March 10

What Did You Give Up?

This is the season of cleansing and purification we call Lent. For some of us, it is a simple cultural season, like "basketball season" when we go through some traditions like calendaring games, checking out players' statistics, or holding Playoff Parties. Lent for some of us is the time we give up bedtime ice cream. Also, for most of us, we never make it through the whole Lenten season abstaining from Blue Bell. Maybe the problem is that we trivialize the season with "no candy bars until Easter." It is more than probable that GOD is not impressed with our "confections penance."

There are still days left to do some soul-cleansing, to focus on the love of GOD in sending His only begotten Son to die for us, to remember the horror and the heroism of the cross. But why not "give up" something far more significant than carbohydrates?

From now until midnight Holy Saturday, we could give up some grudges and forgive somebody we have been mad at. For the days ahead, we could give up some sleep time and spend a few minutes early in the morning reflecting on GOD's word and talking to Him in prayer. For the remaining days we could tell somebody we have taken too much for granted that we appreciate/love them. It would make spring much more beautiful for him/her/them.

And you know what is the best part? If we didn't eat a single doughnut (chocolate covered) from Ash Wednesday until Holy Saturday, we would not impress anybody, and might not lose 15 pounds. But if we strengthen our communication with GOD and touch somebody with love and/or forgiveness, we bless them and ourselves.

Easter would be a much more triumphant Sunday for us! Think about it.

And walk in love, as Christ also hath loved us, and hath given himself for us an offering and a sacrifice to GOD for a sweet smelling savour. Ephesians 5:2

March 18, 2001

March 11

When Does It Become Too Much?

The medical community has dealt with "crack babies" in recent times. We are told that these unfortunate infants, born to addicted mothers, enter the world with withdrawal symptoms. They are often in pain, they cry incessantly, and sometimes have congenital brain damage that guarantees that they will have learning problems. So are they fit only for society's trash bins?

We have learned some things about these tragic little creatures. With enough good nourishment, some warm hugs, some smiles, even some humming and cooing, they can rally to become healthy, normal children! The best medications cannot do for them what consistent expressions of love can do. Even though you and I were not "crack babies," we also thrive with generous doses of "I love you."

The Bible tells us that the very nature of GOD is love. If GOD is love, surely GOD needs loving—indeed, commands it: 'Thou shall love the LORD thy GOD."

72

It is not too much to say to Jesus, Who came to earth to redeem us, and Who sacrificed His life for us, "I love you." Crack babies need it, you and I want it, and He asks for it.

So, don't wait until a special time to tell GOD you love Him. Every time He lets you see the light of another day, shout it to the rooftops, "I love You!"

Herein is love, not that we loved GOD, but that He loved us, and sent His Son to be the propitiation for our sins. I John 4:10

March 7, 1999

March 12

Beware the Makeup

The Sunday when Jesus entered Jerusalem is called a "triumphal entry." But as we look back over it, we know in retrospect what nobody but Jesus knew in advance—that it was all shallow public celebration. In only five days, some of the same crowd that applauded Jesus as He came into town called for Him to be crucified outside of town.

People who know cars never buy a used car on the basis of its shiny paint job and its clean interiors. An old maxim says, "There's many a wreck 'neath a new coat of paint." And Jesus knows us better than a mechanic knows cars.

There are huge multitudes who flock into churches and swear their commitment to Jesus. They love gospel music and enjoy good preaching as much as good situation-comedy or a close game. They may even have "I love Jesus" on their car bumpers. But there are not huge multitudes who are fully committed to Jesus. GOD is not deceived by our fawning and flattering ways.

We must check ourselves out to be sure we are not just shiny wax jobs, praising Jesus but obeying Satan: How often and how fervently do we pray? What priority do we give to the study of GOD's word? How easily do you volunteer to help somebody? What is our giving like? Do we forgive quickly? Can we love down-and-outers (even worrisome ones)? Jesus does not need more "Hosanna" types; He wants cross-bearers! He said it best Himself:

> *Wide is the gate, and broad is the way, that leadeth to destruction, and many there be which go in thereat: Because strait is the gate, and narrow is the way, which leadeth unto life, and few there be that find it. Matthew 7:13b-14)*

March 24, 1991

March 13

Monkey See, Monkey Do

It is not a compliment at all. It is a derisive way of saying that foolish people imitate the actions and attitudes of somebody else. It implies that we should do what we know is right instead of what somebody else is doing. At first, that sounds like good advice, but how else do we know good actions and attitudes except as we have seen them exemplified by people we respect? We have no option about imitating; we only have choice of models, good or bad.

The best model in history is Jesus Christ.

Jesus saved His life by giving it up. His worth is not measured in assets, achievements, or balance of power, but in the multitudes of generations redeemed because He gave up His life for all of us. In a world of grabbing and holding, what a model!

Lent is the forty days before GOD gave up His life on Calvary. Traditionally, Christians "give up" something for the forty days of Lent: sweets, or smoking, or cocktails. It is a form of respect for Jesus, but it does not model itself after Him.

Tithing is one consideration—giving to GOD the first 10% of our income, plus a freewill offering above the 10%. It sacrifices something very precious to you. Or how about giving five or six hours a week in Christian community service? That costs some golf or TV or fishing time, a bit of a sacrifice. "Give up" something you love very dearly to the glory of GOD. Imitate the sacrificial model set by Jesus and experience the delight found in imitating His sacrifice. And GOD will duplicate for you the crown Jesus wears in Heaven.

Let them sacrifice the sacrifices of thanksgiving, and declare His works with rejoicing. salm 107:22

March 1, 1992

74

March 14

We Come into His House!

Every adult over thirty has had that command barked to him or her at some point in his or her youth. The better-reared youngsters still hear it. In fact, one of the marks of good child-rearing is a periodic demand for accountability: Where are you, who are you with, and what are you doing?

This season is a "come-out-of-the-street-into-the-house" time in the ministry of Jesus. He called His disciples away from the traffic of Judea and Galilee, away from crowds and teaching and miracles, away from public applause or public anger. He needed to spend some time preparing them for His approaching death, just as good parents need to spend some time preparing children for their approaching adulthood.

It is, therefore, imperative that as we celebrate the Lenten season we find time, place, and refuge from traffic to reflect on our relationship with GOD. It is a good time to fast and pray. It is a good time to read the entire book of John. It is a good time to find somebody we need to forgive (since what happened was really their fault—of course, we were completely innocent), and begin to rebuild a bridge between him/her/them and us. We need to retreat from the busy routine that demands our attention from dragging out of bed to falling exhausted into it. And in that retreat, we need to ask ourselves who we are, whose we are, where we are going, and what orders we are following.

It is a time to look deeply into the eyes of GOD.

So whatever we are rushing around trying to do during these weeks of Lent, we need to slow down enough to include some reflection and meditation time to think, to pray, to read, and to savor our love for Jesus Christ and the immeasurable love He has for you.

We have thought of Thy loving kindness, O GOD, in the midst of Thy temple. Psalm 48:9

March 7, 1993

March 15

To Save Our Girls (& Boys)

March places special emphasis on girls. There are always two primary reasons for such an emphasis—one clear as day, the other not so obvious.

We are under Divine mandate to lead girls into a commitment to Jesus Christ, and therefore to push toward the high standard of character which He exemplifies. One primary reason for Girl Scouting is character-building of girls so that we can produce strong Christian (African-American) women.

Reason number two is black boys are an endangered species.

When GOD had put the last coat of enamel on Adam, He stood back and surveyed His magnificent animal, and frowned. "Something's wrong with this model," He boomed in a cosmic basso profundo. "It needs a mate that can add sensitivity to its strength and be partner in transforming individual into family. So We'll turn out a second model to match this one." And He did precisely that; and from that time to this, males have worked well when females were in partnership with them and poorly when females were in conflict with them.

That is not an allegory. That is hard, proven fact.

So we celebrate girls because we want better families, not just more female professionals. And if our girls exert the right influence on our boys, we can produce a better grade of women and men.

So GOD created man in His own image, in the image of GOD created He him; male and female created He them. Genesis 1:27

March 8, 1992

March 16

Going for the Gold

We like whoever is at the top.

So how does it happen that we celebrate the lowly today? How is it that we affirm people who openly admit that they are "not leaders, but servants"? When Jesus instituted the sacred supper we share today, He met with His disciples in a house that had not provided a servant to wash feet. And He astonished (perhaps even embarrassed) them by disrobing, girding Himself with a towel, and taking on the role of foot-washing servant! Then He told them they must take the role of servant, too (John 13:12-15). That amazing descent into servant-hood was the prelude to the first LORD's Supper.

You ought to be the best you can be and strive for excellence in whatever you endeavor to do. But remember that true greatness is not in being at the top, not in gaining the applause of champions. There is a transitory and cosmetic eminence that receives the adulation of humans; but it takes another kind of achievement to engender joy in Heaven. Angels rejoice when we humble ourselves before GOD. True 77 greatness is being willing to serve, even if the people you serve are at the bottom (see Matthew 20:25-28).

Even as the Son of man came not to be ministered unto, but to minister, and to give His life a ransom for others. Matthew 20:28

October 5, 1997

March 17

Pullers & Kickers

Some people are impressed by the high level of education of much of the modern African-American clergy. It is no longer news to find a black preacher with one or more Ph.D.'s or speaking knowledgably about banking and finance or astrophysics or microbiology or quoting easily thinkers from Thomas Aquinas to Ibsen to Blackwood. But every once in a while a pearl of wisdom comes from somebody without a background of international relations or an Ivy League sheepskin or a menu of languages. Some of the most provocative thoughts that drift across Black pulpits still come from the "hot water cornbread" preachers whose breadth and depth of thought has been distilled in the crucible of midnight prayer and tear-stained Bible pages. One such pearl came from the preacher Rev. I.H. Henderson, Sr. Speaking of church squabbles, with factions of Christians lined up against each other like enemy armies, he once said, "I need to give folks a job to do. Maybe we ought to build a building or canvass a neighborhood. A mule can't kick when he has a load to pull."

Half a century has passed since Rev. Henderson dropped that jewel. And many times before and since, that truth has been confirmed. Moses dealt with it when he dispatched twelve spies to determine the best way to enter Canaan as Israel approached the Promised Land. Ten of the spies protested that Canaan was invulnerable and could not be invaded; they opposed Moses' intention to enter the land. Only two of the spies felt that Moses, under GOD, could indeed carry out a successful invasion and that they were willing to share in that effort. Ten kickers and two pullers! That story, told in Numbers 13 and 14, about human nature over 3,600 years ago, sounds so much like human nature today it is frightening.

If we look at external conditions right now, we will be tempted to be kickers. But we must fight drugs, racism, corrupt politics, lop-sided economics, and the breakdown of the family for starters. We can add six problems to that from our own inventory of headaches. What else should we do except scream about whose fault it all is?

The answer is simple: We can remember Who woke us up this morning and started us on our way, Who has made a way out of no way, Who is closer than a brother, and Who is the same yesterday, today, and forever. Then we will not have to be kickers. We will know that we can be pullers, because we are on the side of all power!

> *So built we the wall; and all the wall was joined together unto the half thereof: for the people had a mind to work. Nehemiah 4:6*

July 8, 1990

79

March 18

We Are What We Eat

With monotonous regularity, mothers throw that adage at their children. It is the standard handle to a good parental appeal to vegetables, fruits, meat, and bread before children dive into ice cream, dessert pastries, and candies. And there is a broad universal truth to it.

Dr. S.M. Nabrit, a former president of Texas Southern University in Houston, was a renowned biologist. One of the stories students heard him tell was about a certain sea creature that eats only one kind of sea vegetable—a white, cottony ocean plant. It does not eat any of the many tiny seaweeds or sea creature that float past its shell. It only eats that white plant. But when it is fully satiated, it accepts other white things into its shell—even cotton balls. Until that time it rejects even white look-alikes.

Would that we were that selective about what we put into our minds every day!

80

It is so easy to gobble up the ugly story, no matter how half-founded. How delicious seem the suggestive scenes on television or the lascivious lyrics in popular songs! We devour the insult or the irritation, real or imagined, and build bitter grudges around them. (And may or may not find out that the person we are mad at did not intend to offend us at all.)

If highly developed humans can take lessons from primitive sea creatures, why not learn from that strange mollusk to take in only that which is true, honest, just, pure, lovely, and of good report before we allow neighbors or the media or our own sinful temperament to stuff filth into our souls?

As a matter of coincidental fact, that sounds like Paul's advice to the Philippians. Remarkable!

Finally, brethren, whatsoever things are true, whatsoever things are honest, whatsoever things are just, whatsoever things are pure, whatsoever things are lovely, of good report; if there be any virtue and there be any praise, think on these things. Philippians 4:8

September 27, 1987

March 19

Keep On Keeping On

She was screaming at the lop of her lungs. She was six and just learning to ride a bicycle. For a month, training wheels had provided the necessary security. Then for the past twenty minutes, her Daddy had held her on balance. But now, he had turned her loose, and with no training wheels, she plied a wobbly course alone. A family chorus of Mommy, Daddy, and big brother trotted along beside and behind her, urging her not to slop pedaling, but to keep going. "If you keep pedaling, you won't fall down," they told her.

But she screamed. And she quit pedaling. And she fell down.

After a week, the family had a hard time getting her to come inside for dinner. She had fallen in love with the clumsy two-wheeled vehicle she was so afraid of only days ago.

Most of us have gone through that experience, maybe not with a bicycle, but surely with life. We have learned that if we quit, we fall. So if we have gleaned any wisdom at all from our experience, it tells us that when times get scary (and they do get scary), we need to ask the Giver of strength to pour us out an extra portion to stay in the seat and ride it through.

We can overcome failure, or disappointment, or grief, or sickness, or heartbreak, if we can say "The LORD gave, and the LORD hath taken away; blessed be the name of the LORD" (Job 1:21b). When it seems we cannot pedal another stroke, we should ask GOD for the strength He always provides for those who trust Him and watch our "second wind" come from nowhere. We should not quit being generous because somebody misuses our generosity or being conscientious because too few people appreciate the work we do, or quit forgiving because somebody will not forgive us, or serving because people abuse servants. Our reward comes from a much higher source. If we keep pedaling, even our adversaries will be shocked at how strongly and smoothly we can stay the course through Jesus.

Not that we are sufficient of ourselves to think any thing as of ourselves;
but our sufficiency is of GOD. II Corinthians 3:5

November 11, 1990

March 20

Don't Laugh

A once popular radio commercial featured a young couple talking about what the man did for a living. He said he was reluctant to tell the young woman because she would laugh at him. She told him she would not, and then when he told her he sold "meat insurance," she did in fact dissolve into hysterical laughter. (He sold a meat tenderizer, which "insured" the fresh flavor of the meat.) But he persistently went on extolling the virtues of his meat tenderizer for the listening public.

Like the commercial, spring is always a good time for revisiting, renewing, or making bold promises. It is a time when we (1) remind ourselves of the promises of GOD to save us because we have received Christ and to re-affirm our certainty in Him; and (2) tell the unsaved and the unchurched that the same promise is made to them, if they will but receive Christ as we did. We are salespersons of the greatest insurance there is.

82

The test of our seriousness and commitment is when the world laughs at our story. If we cannot endure rejection and derision, we may withdraw like cowards and refuse to witness—or assume that a good moral life is its own witness, and we do not have to sell. But if we know that rejection is part of the territory, we will arm ourselves for it, set our faces to the streets, and sing a hymn of praise while we are being drowned out in the laughter of the world, for we know that the laughter is a cover for hunger and loneliness. We must tell the world our story, and the derisive laugh will turn to smiles of real joy!

Remember the word that I said unto you, The servant is not greater than his LORD. If they have persecuted Me, they will also persecute you. John 15:20a

March 11, 1979

March 21

LORD, It's Comfortable Here!

Toward the end of His earthly ministry, Jesus took His disciples up to the top of Mount Sermon for a time of prayer. Mark 8 describes a light show to end all light shows, complete with cameo appearances by Moses and Elijah (Mark 8:1-4). Peter was so overwhelmed by the spectacular worship service that he proposed never going home from church—just staying on the front pew and shouting (vs. 5). But GOD told Peter, "Don't get hung up on these two preachers from the Old Testament; your orders come from my Son!" (vs. 7).

And Jesus took them straight back down into the valley of service (vs. 14-29).

Some people think of the church as a continuing variety show, with lights and pictures and bells and whistles, to keep them entertained until the benediction. But the girls we salute today have a theme for their programming: helping somebody. And the man who fills our pulpit today brings a clear challenge to us: Get out of this sanctuary and follow Jesus to the valleys of service.

It is titillating to follow the dynamic preacher and the "on-fiah choiah," but the commission of our Boss is to get out and love somebody as He has loved us.

And his disciples answered Him, From whence can a man satisfy these men with bread here in the wilderness. Mark 8:4

March 9, 1997

83

March 22

He Did It Quickly

You and I look back on some distinguished careers. A dinner is given to honor a community pillar retiring after fifty years of business leadership. Children bring their hand-drawn pictures thanking a principal who retires after many decades in teaching and school administration. We celebrate great-grandmothers, among them my mother who blessed her world for 96 years.

And then there is Jesus.

Only three years? A weak President stays in office longer than that! But in those scant months this wandering Jewish rabbi turned water into wine, healed the incurable, cast out demons from hopelessly deranged people, fed thousands from a child's lunch, stilled killer storms, raised the dead—one person after four days. Should we go on? In those three years this Man from a nothing town in Galilee not only changed the lives of the few hundred who followed Him, but so altered history that the world dates its calendars by His birth. Without a doubt, this Jewish rabbi remains the driving force behind thousands of churches and communities in the most expansive religion on earth. Three measly years!

But His greatest miracle has nothing to do with bread and fish or winds and waves or even corpses in cave-tombs.

The most stupendous miracle He performed is taking guilty and condemned sinners like you and me and without forcing us to become righteous or innocent, redeeming us. The climax of His three years was a horrible nine-hour lynching on a mountain outside Jerusalem. And that lynching erased all our guilt and presented us as worthy before GOD. Remember the Man Who died on a Friday, rose on a Sunday, and wiped us clean!

But GOD commendeth His love toward us, in that, while we were yet sinners, Christ died for us. Romans 5:8

March 23, 2003

March 23

Don't Subtract—Add

Somewhere in the distant past, our worship of GOD took a bizarre turn. Perhaps during the centuries when we blended the Graeco-Roman pagan religions with our own faith, we began to practice negative expressions. We prohibited marriage for priests and nuns, we banned dancing, the theatre, and most popular forms of entertainment. We praised ourselves for the number of things we abstained from, or sacrificed. Maybe we were trying to emulate the sufferings of Jesus. But we lost a great deal of our joy.

Lent is always a time to reflect upon the impending death of Jesus Christ, and it rightly focuses upon the cross. But it is a perversion of that forty-day period to assume it requires a simple amputation of pleasures. You do not reflect on the death of Jesus by giving up desserts or pastas (you may help your diet, but it does nothing for your soul). What should we be doing between now and Good Friday? I'm glad you asked!

We should be concentrating on what Jesus' crucifixion means to us. That means spending time in the reading of the scriptural accounts of the original forty days before His death. It means spending time in prayer that we can dedicate ourselves more fully to doing His will for our lives. It should mean at least one day of fasting—but not just to abstain from eating; to focus on prayer.

85

It is 0.K. to abstain from something during Lent, provided the reason for the abstinence is not just to say, "I didn't eat any red meat for forty days," but to emphasize a positive and pro-active concentration on our LORD, Who died for us, and on the incalculable implications of that death. Lent should not be a morbid season, but one where reflection on a death yields joy, not grief.

He that believeth and is baptized, shall be saved; but he that believeth not shall be damned. Mark 16:16

February 25, 1996

March 24

Winning by Losing

There is nothing like it before or after in human history. Heroes traditionally rescue people through their power, their cunning, their wisdom, or all three. Whether Hercules or Superman, it is expected that the hero, however he (or she) may be challenged by adversaries, will always survive.

We worship a Hero Who died. He could have called down lightning from Heaven and destroyed in an instant all of His enemies. But He did not choose to save us through power or cunning or brilliance. His deliberately-chosen method of rescuing us was to allow those enemies to kill Him.

What kind of Hero is that?

It is One Who knows that millions have died in their sins, and that all who were alive in His time, and all who would ever be born after His stay on earth would have to die, too. The enemy held the keys to death. And the only way He could conquer that enemy and seize from him the power over death and the grave was to die Himself and descend into Hell. He was not into rescuing the fair damsel or the six children stranded on floating wood. He had the task of rescuing all creation, past, present, and future. This is the consummate Hero.

> *Who His own self bare our sins in His own body on the tree, that we, being dead to sins, should live unto righteousness: by whose stripes ye were healed. I Peter 2:24*

March 2, 2003

86

March 25

Let the Redeemed of the LORD Say So

The success of a product or service depends less on quality than on sales. It means little to have a better mousetrap unless somebody tells the world which door to make a path to. People buy what they are persuaded to buy. (Nobody needs a compact disc system, but that's what is in! So we must have one.)

We are responsible for marketing a Savior Who has transformed our lives and Who needs to be introduced to anybody we care about. GOD has not established any other plan for telling the world about His love-act. He has commissioned only His church to sell a dying world on eternal life. That means that if anybody we know dies without accepting Jesus Christ, we may have helped to send them to Hell! If we really tried to persuade them, their condemnation is entirely their own fault. But if we only half-tried (or thought somebody else ought to do it, and did not try at all), then GOD holds us to blame for their "lostness."

Selling is something we have to psych ourselves up to do. Why not work on our zeal and our technique in selling for Jesus? (1) Ask GOD's Holy Spirit to give us boldness and effectiveness. (2) Ask Him to bring together us and somebody who needs our witness. (3) Scour His word to learn the scriptures that tell people how to be saved and how to grow in grace. (4) Then aggressively go out there and talk about what GOD has done for us and what He can and will do for him/her/them.

Silently and powerfully, GOD equips us to be His spokespersons— if we just start!

And He said unto them, Go ye into all the world, and preach to every creature. Mark 16:15

August 14, 1998

March 26

The Treasure of Pain

"What? If there are any two words that do not belong in the same phrase, they are "treasure" and "pain"! There is nothing worth collecting or keeping about pain!

At first thought, that sounds right.

People suffer crushing losses, or lingering illnesses, or setbacks that seem totally unfair. And that grief or disability or the pain of the reverses darkens their day, erases whatever joy they might have known, makes them ill-tempered and sullen even to those close to them. Pain is Hell!

Jesus, facing the certainty of a criminal's death on the cross, prayed an unlikely prayer: "And what shall I say? 'Father, save me from this hour'? But for this cause came I unto this hour" (John 12:27).

Most evangelists work for the crowd to preach to, the largest number of converts coming forward, the transmission of the message to the farthest possible point. Jesus says He came to this world to suffer, not to build crowds or institutions or a great personal ministry. But through His suffering the church came into being.

88

We do not know why GOD allows suffering. But we do know that pain matures, ennobles, increases sensitivity and compassion. Whoever has been hurt is more able to bear pain than the one who has been sheltered from hurt. And further, the fires of sorrow burn up a great amount of shallowness. Sometimes we may be contemptuous of someone else when he needs comforting; he may not have time for his weeping. But when we need a shoulder to cry on, we should look for somebody who has stored in his treasure-house of character some pain. That person will find the time for the person in pain. When we find our true self in pain, we will be nourishment for a brother or sister. GOD makes it so.

Bear ye one another's burdens, and so fulfill the law of Christ.
Galatians 6:2

July 16, 1989

March 27

Praise Him Anyhow

It makes good sermon and song material: "Even when things are not going right, praise Him anyhow." We can shout and clap our hands and rejoice when we hear it, because it is such solid spiritual truth. It just sounds right.

But after the song is sung and the sermon is preached and we face the cold light of life as usual, it does not always apply. We complain because the coffee is cold or the office is hot or the work is not done on time or the bill comes early. We had problems with the town we used to live in and we have problems with Houston. Griping comes easily, and we enjoy even more giving you a piece of our mind.

That is why we need to focus on Jesus during Lent.

The days before Good Friday should have been days when He could complain that He had been betrayed by His Father, Who arranged for Him to die on a cross. If you discovered that somebody close to you had set you up, wouldn't you gripe about it?

And yet the example He sets is awesome. He does not complain. He does not attempt to escape His fate. Indeed, some of His most encouraging words to His followers are during these last days before He is unjustly tried, convicted, and executed. Can I learn from Him how to face bad traffic or sloppy work or unfair treatment or sickness or grief and praise Him anyhow?

Jesus answered, Thou couldest have no power at all against Me, except it were given thee from above: therefore he that delivered Me unto thee hath the greater sin. John 19:11

March 2, 1997

March 28

Top or Bottom

How could it happen? He is the hero today, the victim Friday. How can people be so fickle? How did they so quickly turn against the One they celebrated, and lynch Him?

It is a portrait of the structure of human society. We are not looking at fickle people.

The masses shouting on Palm Sunday must not be labeled hypocrites. Anybody who has lived past middle school knows that human society is layered. At the bottom are the masses who survive from day to day. At the top are the power brokers, often bigger than kings and presidents, who manipulate people and events to maintain and to increase their power. In the middle are people like you and me—sometimes aware of the manipulations of the powerful and the predicament of the powerless, most often not very concerned about either. We have children to rear, bills to pay, personal ambitions to deal with.

90

The folks celebrating on that first Palm Sunday are people Jesus deliberately attracted to His pre- arranged festival. They are poor, nameless, children, and those who are sick, the masses from the bottom of the social structure. They adore Him; they pin their hopes for survival on Him; they recognize Him as Somebody Who might establish a Kingdom where they might have dignity. For them He is LORD.

But in that same crowd, on the edges, were the power brokers. They ran the Temple and the synagogues; they controlled the puppet government that Rome tolerated; they owned the businesses whose profit never went to their employees, but returned to themselves, and on the way back, purchased more power. They did not celebrate. They even feared that these screaming masses might foul up their plans to eliminate this worrisome Jesus. GOD allowed the powerful to crucify Him while the masses slept.

GOD blesses some with money and power—but if He has so blessed you, do not identify

yourself with the power-brokers. Be sure to be among the screaming masses!

And in Thine hand is power and might, and in Thine hand it is to make great, and to give strength unto all. I Chronicles 29:12b

March 24, 2002

March 29

The Flip Side of Death

Death, the least welcome guest in our world, but the most consistent visitor—it comes soon or late to every person who is born into the world. We may hold out for a century or more, but however healthy or careful or righteous, death will find us, will embrace you, will terminate you.

Jesus Himself died.

But His was the first and only instance where the dying was not the victim, nor death the victor. People before Jesus risen from the dead. Jesus not only raised people from the dead, but had also empowered His disciples to do so, as well. Elijah, Peter, Paul—all had raised people from the dead. So what is new about the resurrection of Jesus?

He was without sin and had not earned the wages of sin. But He chose to die, as a ransom for your life and mine. And when He rose, He did not rise as a mortal to die again. He came as a conqueror of death, sin, and the power of Hell. Lazarus rose with working parts; Jesus rose with all power in Heaven and earth. Because Jesus died, He could seize from death its ultimate power over us and transmit to us everlasting life.

91

We all will die.

If we are not in Jesus, death is termination for us, and we are separated from GOD forever. But if we are in Jesus, death is the earth-door through which we enter into a realm impervious to sin or sickness or pain or sorrow. It is the bottom surface of joy without ceiling. We rise through it into an endless "Hallelujah!"

And the dead in Christ shall rise first: Then we which are alive and remain shall be caught up together with them in the clouds, to meet the LORD in the air: and so shall we ever be with the LORD.
I Thessalonians 4:16b, 17

April 19, 1992

March 30

In His Steps

There is a big market in "WWJD" bracelets, necklaces, key-chains, T-shirts, etc., etc. They represent a kind of testimony that the bearer is a Christian, asking before acting, "What would Jesus do?" It is based on a novel written in the late 1920's by Charles Sheldon called *In His Steps*, and it has become fashionable. It may not reflect the wearer's actual commitment to Jesus, but it is a politically correct cosmetic statement for the late 20th and early 21st centuries.

Pope John Paul II, aged and frail, has just ended what he considers the greatest pilgrimage of his life, as he visited last week the land holy to Jews, Muslims, and Christians. He considered the most sacred portion of his trip his following the places where Jesus lived and ministered, as the Pope walked in his steps. He said he can die in peace now.

92

We are going through the final days of Lent. We review scriptures telling us what that seven weeks was like as Jesus approached Calvary. We are struggling not to grab that chocolate cake or that cigarette until Easter. And, if we are serious about our "WWJD" ornament, we are in prayer about displaying a sweeter spirit to those close to us; about being more vocal about what Jesus means to us; about committing more of our time, our skills, our income to GOD.

We don't have to go to Israel to walk in His steps. We don't need to stick our prayer request in a chink in the Wailing Wall. We can become "more and more like Jesus" right where we are. During this Lenten season, as we approach Passion Week and the unbridled joy of Easter we can thank GOD that Jesus lives, that He lives in our hearts, and that with the help of His Holy Spirit, we can display Him in our attitudes and in our behavior. Let's follow in His steps.

For even hereunto were ye called: because Christ also suffered for us, leaving us an example, that ye should follow His steps. I Peter 2:21

April 2, 2000

March 31

Have Thine Own Way

At the turn of the century, poet Adelaide Pollard gave us the lyrics to the old hymn that expresses surrender to the Great Potter. These lyrics invoke the phrase from the model prayer of Jesus, "Thy will be done on earth as it is in Heaven."

Magnificent words, but not as easy to mean as they are to say.

When your loved one is dying, it is easy, even urgent, to plead to GOD to heal him or her. It is not easy to add to your plea, "Your will be done."

When you are facing disaster, it's natural to blurt out, "GOD save me!" But how easy is it to give in to His will, which may not be that you escape disaster?

During these days of Lent, we watch with keen interest the way Jesus handled His own imminent death. He had what we do not—the power to escape death. He had never sinned, and so had not earned death. He had complete power to overwhelm His enemies whenever He so chose, and could have mowed down the entire Jewish establishment, all the Roman legions, every vestige of power lined up against Him. He could have said the word, and no one could have crucified Him. When you and I face disaster, we do not face it armed with such power.

And yet He refused to use His awesome power to save Himself. His response to the impending day of His death was not a show of power, but a simple prayer, prayed while He prostrated Himself in a garden.

He is our Model. We can beg and plead for what we want—can we also say, "Have Thine own way"?

Father, if Thou be willing, remove this cup from Me: nevertheless not My will, but Thine, be done. Luke 22:42

April 9, 2000

April 1

Prepare to Die

Lent is the ancient Christian tradition that says that the forty days before the crucifixion Jesus spent preparing for His death.

So the revelings of Mardi Gras come to a screeching halt at midnight on Tuesday and Ash Wednesday ushers the entire Christian community into a period of sober reflection about the death of Jesus. The "coincidence" of our commemorating His death on first Sundays simply sharpens the shadow of the cross over our world. People willingly sacrifice some pleasure or favorite menu item during the forty (actually forty-five) days before Easter. We identify with Jesus as He makes preparation for the ultimate sacrifice of His life.

So give up your beef or sweets or beverage—but know that those are trivial sacrifices for Lent. A preparation for death requires much more serious sacrifice. We talk about a major financial sacrifice for us selfish humans. How about trying it through March and the first two weeks of April? Or read Romans? Or visit two sick people every week until Good Friday? For Jesus, this was a serious season. Let's make it serious as a time to remember that He died for you and me.

94

And He bearing his cross went forth into a place called the place of a skull which is called in the Hebrew Golgotha. John 19:17

March 5, 1995

April 2

What Shall We Wear to the Funeral?

You've noticed, of course. The widow and grieving family members will deliberately ask for upbeat music and light, humorous remarks. The black outfit and the veil are less common. Perhaps the truth about death is getting through.

It is not the end.

We "funeralize" Jesus as we commemorate His death with every LORD's Supper. And yet the tenor and tone of our worship is not grief, but joy. We accept the ugliness of the crucifixion, and do not find any justification for the crucifiers. But our hallelujahs are more boisterous than our weeping. Bright new clothes have no Biblical basis whatsoever; but at least they are in harmony with the joy of the Resurrection.

Until Jesus was nailed to a Roman cross during the Passover season, death was the stopping point. The soul beyond death was in some eternal confinement with no prospect for liberation. But on that dark Friday when the Son of GOD commended His spirit to His Father, and descended into Hell, He forever crushed the power of death to smother us—provided we believe in Him.

95

You want "death-proofing" that lets you glide through the valley of the shadow of death into everlasting life? Then open the door of your heart and invite Jesus to take over. As soon as you surrender to Him, His victory over death becomes yours. And the good news is that "death- proofing" through Jesus does not begin at your funeral; it begins now, this side of the grave.

So snatch out of the tape-player "Come Ye Disconsolate" and plug in "I'm So Glad Jesus Lifted Me." Put the black outfit against the far wall in the closet, and bring out the whites and pastels. Leave the Kleenex box on the night stand and pick up your toe-tapping shoes. Yes, we will face the reality that Jesus died, and we have to die, too.

But we do not moan—we laugh and praise GOD!

And when they looked, they saw that the stone was rolled away: for it was very great. Mark 16:4

April 3

Death Is Defeated—Jesus Is Conqueror

On March 20, nature announced that spring has come. Throughout the world, spring represents the end of winter, and the revitalization of living things. Jesus rose during the Passover season. Is it possible that GOD deliberately timed His resurrection to coincide with spring-time? When the earth announces the conquest of winter's dead colors and naked branches, we rejoice that His resurrection announces the conquest of death for all believers.

The older we get, the more we face the sobering presence of death. That is why older people ought to rejoice more freely than children at Easter time. Death is a much more palpable enemy for us than for them—and the news that Jesus Christ has overcome death is the best news we could possibly hear.

We celebrate Easter with flowers, bright colors, and rabbits, traditionally identified with abundant reproduction. All of this suggests fresh new life. Of course, these symbols came from a pagan past, based on spring festivals related to the vernal equinox. But we can use them in our worship just as we use government printed money and skills we learned in secular schools. Nothing you have is intrinsically good or bad—what an object is used for depends upon the motives of the user. If you submit yourself to Jesus Christ, then when you bring items from a pagan background to the altar of worship, they are accepted by GOD as gifts from a servant-child.

Easter and spring-time—they are coordinates.

We worship GOD, Whose total righteousness demands death for any who rebel. We know we have rebelled, and we know we deserve death. And we praise GOD, Whose total mercy sent His own Son to die for us, and Whose total power raised Him from the dead.

It is the mercy of GOD that gives spring to the winter-laden world. And it is the mercy of GOD that gives everlasting life to sinners who do not deserve it.

And He saith unto them, be not affrighted: Ye seek Jesus of Nazareth which was crucified: He is risen He is not here: behold the place where they laid him. Mark 16:6

March 27, 1994

April 4

"I Came to Die"

When the confluence of certain days seems too coincidental, that seems a good time to believe that it is a sign of GOD. Maybe that seems too easy, but as African-Americans we know that GOD can make a way out of no way. There are no coincidences, those situations are only signs of GOD.

More than two decades ago today, Dr. Martin Luther King, Jr. died. More than two thousand years ago, the son of Man came into Jerusalem to the chorus of "Hosanna," preparing Himself to die. Both men were major figures who had traveled to a large city, not their home city, to be killed.

These two men were both men of peace. They were both violently put to death by their governments: Jesus by the corrupt Jewish leadership, and Dr. King allegedly the FBI. Yet they were also major prophets, and they enlightened all people about the good news of our GOD.

We recognize them both. Instead of seeing this time as the reminder of Christ's impending death, we remember it as the beginning of our new life in Christ. We see the arrival of Jesus on the back of a donkey as the coming of salvation to the common man. Indeed, it challenges us to bring the blind, the sick, and the unloved to the kingdom of GOD through OUR faith in Him.

When Dr. King spoke of his mountaintop dream, we were able to see it too: a time of love and concern for our fellow man. On this anniversary of his passing, we can claim our role in making the dream come true. Dr. King did not set his sights on great wealth or power, yet his voice was heard by the greatest and the smallest of men. Why did his message carry such weight? Because it was the word of GOD, made manifest in the life of an Atlanta preacher. This time of year is not just the odd coincidence of two events. It is the calendar-recognition of the goals GOD has set for us all.

Here I am; send me. Isaiah 6:8b

April 4, 1993

April 5

Sweet Surprise—Hallelujah!

They had done their job well.

Perhaps they had played a bit on the edge of legality. They had tried Him at night, and legally that is a day process. They had procured witnesses whose integrity was questionable and whose testimony was not altogether in agreement. They had rushed through to a conviction and death sentence without adequate due process, but they had achieved (with a bit of under-the-belt pressure on a weak procurator) a Roman conviction to crucify. It was an artful piece of judicial manipulation, and now He was dead and placed in a dark tomb.

Often, it is dark in the tombs of our lives.

But outside the sun (son) is rising!

98

Eager women are rushing to the place of the dead to finish embalming the corpse. The dawn light gleams in the East on their faces, but it gives no radiance. There is no joy of the morning for them. They carry burial spices and additional winding tapes for the beloved dead man. They do not even see the sunrise. It is not important to them, except as light to go to the grim task they come to do.

And suddenly a light many times more brilliant than the morning sunlight blinds them. They are face to face with an angel of the LORD! In a voice not of this world, the angel tells them Jesus is not in the tomb. There is no use for their spices and tapes. Their task is not necessary. It may be dark in the tomb, but the Light of the World shines forever.

Anyone who has ever had a chocolate-covered cherry is prepared for the bittersweet taste of the outer coating, but is surprised at the tender, pure, fruity sweetness of the inside. Most of us expect the bitterness of life. But isn't Easter a sweet surprise?

He is not here: for he is risen as he said. Come, see the place where the LORD lay. Matthew 28:6

April 11, 1993

April 6

So What's the Big Deal?

Hallelujah! All praise to GOD! The impossible has been done! Never before has such a thing happened!

(Yes, it has.)

Did not Elijah raise the son of the Widow of Zarephath? Didn't Elisha do the same thing for the Shunammite woman? The son of the Widow of Nain, the daughter of Jairus, Lazarus, the brother of Mary and Martha—were they not all raised from the dead?

All different—never before has such a thing happened!

Wait a minute! What is so different? They had all been dead. If there had been medical examiners, they would have been pronounced legally dead! And the prophets and Jesus did the impossible for all of them. So now He Himself comes out of the tomb. Isn't that resurrection number six?

Listen to me. The five before that first Easter all came back to mortal life. All five died again. That is resuscitation, re-animation. Parents and families rejoiced. But most of the world did not. But Jesus rose never to die again, without any of the weaknesses of the mortal body! But the really important thing is—He is the only One who died for others, and rose for others. Those five did nothing for you and me. But because He died and rose, you and I have everlasting life. Hallelujah!

99

But now is Christ risen from the dead, and become the firstfruits of them that slept. I Corinthians 15:20

March 31, 2002

April 7

They Die, and We Remember

GOD sends them to die, but they change our world.

A brighter than average child was born to the Rev. and Mrs. Michael L. King of Atlanta. Rev. King was an aggressive man who hated racial segregation, and taught his children they did not have to live with a "second-class" self image. He changed his name and the name of his son M.L., Jr., to Martin Luther King, Sr., and Jr., but nobody dreamed that this bright child would grow up to challenge racial segregation and to be the catalyst that would open doors of opportunity for African-Americans and begin the struggle for human rights for other minorities, for women, and for gays and lesbians. He made a major impact on the world, and he died.

100

A brighter than average young Indian lawyer lived in South Africa, and wanted to be able to identify with the Christians of that nation. The Dutch Boers closed all doors in his face, so Mohandas K. Gandhi returned to his native India determined never to become a Christian and to fight the segregation of his own nation. His philosophy was non-violent protest, and he grew in stature so that the Indian people wanted to name him Prime Minister. He refused public office, so he was named Mahatma, or Holy Man. His leadership of the protests against British racism overthrew British control of India and led ultimately to the downfall of the entire British Empire. And he died.

GOD always seems to have for all ages a special messenger, a prophet, who will make a significant difference in the age into which he or she has been sent. The classic case was His own Son, who set the standard for Gandhi (although Christian followers disappointed him) and for King (although Christian followers rejected him). He also came unto His own, and His own received Him not. He changed the world forever, and He changed it by dying for people who never knew who He was.

He came unto His own, and His own received Him not. John 1:11

January 13, 2002

April 8

Hallelujah

We usually shout this ancient Hebrew word. We do not even translate it into English. We just say it in Hebrew: "Hallelujah!" It can be translated, of course. It means, in English, "Praise" (Hallel) "ye" (altiy) "the LORD" (Jahveh). But whether you shout it in Hebrew or intone it in English, the command is the same.

And it is a good command.

Adolf Hitler, the World War II dictator who built the Nazi regime in Germany, is quoted as saying, "If you tell a lie often enough, other people begin to believe it. Keep telling it, and you believe it yourself." That is a negative way of saying, "Whatever you keep saying lends to become self- fulfilling." If we keep telling a child he is no good, and will never be anybody, we cripple him psychologically, and he may fail because you have driven it so deeply into his thoughts. But chances are that each of us made it because somebody kept telling us that being poor or being Black need not hold us back, that we could be anything we put our minds to. The boost of that mother or father or teacher or relative or friend made it possible for us to transcend obstacles and to succeed against the odds.

If we keep saying it, it comes to pass.

So when the Psalmist orders us to praise the LORD (with songs, instruments, the dance—everything we have in us), he is helping to strengthen our faith. If we believe GOD is almighty, and we keep telling him that; if we believe His mercy endures forever, and we keep thanking Him for that; if we believe He is able to do exceeding, abundantly above all that we ask or think, and we praise Him for that over and over again—soon our faith in Him is so strong we will not give up. So...Hallelujah!

Now unto him that is able to do exceeding abundantly above all that we ask or think, according to the power that worketh in us. Ephesians 3:20

April 9

Hallelujah! Again

It is one of the two words we never translate from the Hebrew original. (The other is Amen, which means "So be it.") Easter is our most Hallelujah day. Without it, even Christmas would be meaningless. The birth of Jesus was important only because He was unlike any other baby every born. And the difference was that He was GOD's own Son, sent among us to redeem us. Had he died and remained dead, He would have repeated the life story of every sinner: We are born to die.

But He did not remain dead.

On the first Easter Sunday, GOD raised Him from the dead, and gave Him all power in Heaven and on earth. Now He lives to intercede for us who are all born to die and to be condemned. As soon as we accept Him as the Son of GOD and as our personal Savior, we are snatched out of the path toward condemnation, and we are given eternal life with Him.

Hallelujah! (Which means in Hebrew, "Praise GOD!")

102

Every human being, no matter what language he or she speaks, can say Hallelujah! It is a word which belongs to all languages. And every human being, no matter what sins he or she has committed, can be changed from the death of condemnation to the life of redemption.

Again, Hallelujah!

And I heard as it were the voice of a great multitude, and as the voice of many waters, and as the voice of mighty thunderings, saying, Alleluia: for the LORD GOD omnipotent reigneth. Revelations 19:6

April 15, 1990

April 10

The Market Value of Pain

The human animal is the strangest of the species. We are the only animal which avoids what is good for it and craves what is destructive. We might get up in the middle of the night and drive two miles to find a Coke, but fail to drink even a sip of the cold water placed beside our plate. We can be addicted to cigarettes, but dislike most vegetables.

In Lent, we consider what it means that Christ deliberately volunteered to suffer and calls us to be fellow-sufferers with Him. How many folks do we see standing in line to "take up their cross," to volunteer for pain? Every one of us knows that excellence in anything requires some kind of stress, some kind of privation, some degree of pain. And yet we avoid pain as often as we can.

But if we avoid sacrifice, we also deprive ourselves of strength.

One parable heard in a restaurant is worth sharing here: A man saw a cocoon twisting and shuddering as its tiny moth-tenant tried to fight its way out. Moved with compassion, the man took a razor blade and very carefully, very gently slit the underside of the cocoon, and the little insect dropped out, spread its wings to dry, and flew a little bit. But its colors remained pale, never developed fullness and beauty, and soon the little moth died. Part of its strength and beauty should have been developed by the struggle to emerge from its cocoon without help; and when it did not struggle sufficiently, it remained too weak to survive in the world outside.

103

Have you volunteered to sacrifice anything lately? Your strength on the street depends on your pain in the closet!

They that sow in tears shall reap in joy. Psalm 126:5

March 25, 1984

April 11

Praise Him Anyhow

We had followed them with clapping hands, patting feet, nodding heads, and a profusion of "Amen's" and thunderous applause. But we had hardly understood a word they sang. Nineteen enthusiastic young singers, a traveling choir from Zaire, Central Africa, had sung their praises to Jesus in exotic languages like Lingala and Kituba. But we did not care that we could not understand the lyrics. They were clearly praising GOD, and we could catch the electricity in their expressions and in their buoyant tones.

When the program ended, their leader, a university president with all the stateliness and elegance that such a person should have, announced in clear English that the group would close the concert by singing "The Hallelujah Chorus" from Handel's Messiah, and that they would sing it in Kakongo.

But the first word that burst from nineteen throats was "Hallelujah!"—and it exploded on the sanctuary air five times! The audience had thought they were going to sing in Kakongo. What had happened?

When the choir came to "The kingdoms of this world," the chaos of another tongue hit us. That was Kakongo! The word for "Hallelujah" in Kakongo is "Hallelujah." (The same word is in Russian, or Japanese, or Pakistani, or Tagalog. It is always Hallelujah!)

That acknowledgement speaks of the universality of sin (everybody is guilty), and of salvation (Christ died for the whole world). So what else should we expect of praise but that it, too, is universal (every sinner saved by the grace of GOD through Jesus Christ has to praise Him)?

Our tastes in food or music or clothing styles may vary widely. Our economics are different; our political philosophies are diverse; our views of family are not all identical. But grace is grace is grace. And so praise is a universal response to a GOD Who has loved us all everywhere—Hallelujah! (That was in Yoruba.)

And after these things I heard a great voice of much people in heaven, saying Alleluia; Salvation, and glory, and honour, and power, unto the LORD our GOD. Revelation 19:1

May 7, 1989

April 12

"Hallelujah" Day

Every day should be a day to praise the LORD, because we need Him every hour, and His mercy endures forever. Whatever the day is, it is always the day the LORD has made: we should rejoice and be glad in it.

But Easter is, of all days, a day to praise GOD. It is unique. It stands alone among the acts of GOD. It is bigger than creation, more forceful than all the plagues against Pharaoh and all the miracles in the liberation of Israel, more magnificent than Solomon's temple, more profound than all the preaching of all the prophets. It is the day GOD conquered death, the arch-enemy of all living beings.

Had GOD made the worlds and stopped, or issued the Law and stopped, or sent into our world every righteous servant from Seth to John the Baptist and stopped, we would be hopelessly condemned to eternal damnation.

But He did not stop at any of those points. He delegated His own Son to die on our behalf. (Even had He stopped then, we would be on Death Row.) But nearly 2,000 years ago GOD raised Jesus from the dead—and in that one act overturned all the hopelessness and despair since Eden.

105

Now whenever we are tempted to feel we are in a corner, with no way out, we should think about Easter and holler real loud, "Hallelujah!"

This spake he, signifying by what death he should glorify GOD. And when he had spoken this, He saith unto him, Follow me. John 21:19

March 30, 1997

April 13

Touch Me

The deliberately-staged pageantry many years ago in old Jerusalem carries a message that is ever new: The King is accessible.

Jesus, the gentle rabbi Who embraces children and lepers, Who heals blind and lame beggars and forgives adulterous women and corrupt tax collectors, has enraged local leadership by raising a young man four days dead. A price is on His head. If He shows up again in public, He must be seized and put to death (John 11:57).

Jesus, the Anointed One, shocked the establishment by boldly, even blatantly, coming down the main street of Jerusalem, led, followed, and surrounded by screaming crowds, including children. They yelled "Hosanna ('Save now!' Psalm 118:25, 26) to the Son of David! Blessed is He that cometh in the name of the LORD!" And the searched-for criminal Who was thought to be in hiding was in the middle of the crowd, available to limping cripples, mothers holding out babies to be blessed, and children running along behind the Man on the colt of an ass.

106

The good news is that Jesus, the Eternal Word Who was with GOD and Who Was GOD, the Creator of all things Who holds the universe together, comes into the middle of our lives every day. We can bring our sicknesses, our grief, our despair, our limitations of mind or body or resources to Him. We can touch His homespun robe. We can run along behind Him, and no matter how dense the crowd, He sees us and feels our hurt and loves us.

The GODs of antiquity have always been aloof and unapproachable. People did not talk to Zeus or expect love from Jupiter or think Baal cared about their cancer. But Jesus barges into our lives with healing in the hem of His garment and says, "Touch Me!"

He hath sent Me to bind up the brokenhearted, to proclaim liberty to the captives, and the opening of the prison to them that are bound. Isaiah 61:1b

April 8, 2001

April 14

Groaning or Floating

What we feel like after is determined by what one does during.

He partied non-stop for three days and slept a total of five hours? That is why he is exhausted. In the past twelve years he has sucked into his lungs the smoke from 35,064 cigarettes plus the carbon monoxide of city streets? That is why he is coughing up blood. He guzzled two and a half gallons of liquor, combining Scotch, Vodka, and Jamaican rum, since Friday at 4:00? Even extra-strength Tylenol did not wipe out that headache.

He spent the night trying to find a child lost in the woods and discovered her cold and wet, but safe this morning? Of course, he is not sleepy. He prayed fervently for the recovery of his neighbor, and the doctors are amazed that they cannot find the cancer today? Small wonder that he keeps giggling and praising GOD. He gave up your mortgage money to pay the pre-exam fees for his straight-A niece, and she gave a fantastic valedictorian's speech at graduation? Who wonders why he is not upset about the money?

What one feels like after is determined by what he does during.

Jesus taught us to love GOD totally and to love neighbors as we love self. If we spend our energy and our resources indulging ourselves, we create hangovers and regrets and unhappy consequences. If we praise GOD in all things and display compassion and love to all people, we create joy and satisfaction for ourselves. And we develop a kind of aura of peace that permeates those around us, too. If we do the right thing today, tomorrow we will not be dealing with hangovers, but with joy.

For all the law is fulfilled in one word, even in this; Thou shalt love thy neighbor as thyself. Galatians 5:14

June 14, 1992

April 15

You Can't Keep a Good Man Down

The evil one aimed his weapon,
And sent the first shot
Into the heart of a woman,
The mother of all living.
"Now," he chucked to himself,
"Every baby born to mankind
Will be stained the color of sin!"
A light set-back...
A baby born in Bethlehem
Lived a life totally free of sin,
And won an exemption from death.
Had Satan lost after all? But then, of all things, that crazy Nazarene
Volunteered for death...he would come to hell willingly!
All the demons danced through the flames with wicked glee.
The One they had lost was surrendering to them!
He died on schedule, and did indeed drop into the lowest depths
Of the condemned.
They sealed his tomb, and erased his name.
But something happened that had never happened before.
Like a cosmic rocket
He burst forth from hell, and rose!

He is not here, but He is risen: remember how He spake unto you
when He was yet in Galilee. Luke 24:6

April 16, 1995

108

April 16

No, You Really Can't Keep a Good Man Down

We are a minority. Not an ethnic minority—a theological minority. Easter means to most people new clothing, an annual trip to church, a long weekend, candy and colored eggs for the children.

If you are rejoicing because the Son of GOD died for sinners and was raised by His Father so that none of us would ever again face the threat of eternal condemnation—if Easter means resurrection for Jesus, and therefore for us, then you represent a small fragment of the people on earth.

You see, all of us must die. We earned it. And until Jesus, death meant eternal separation from GOD. If you have ever sinned, death is a one-way trip to Hell.

But since Jesus had never sinned, Satan hated for Him to volunteer to die, because the grave could not hold a sinless person. When Jesus died and went to Hell, He carried with him return-trip tickets for all who would believe in Him, admitting them into Heaven. Death had taken millions, and would have taken you and me, too; but Jesus rose, and made death forever a stop on the way to Heaven for all who accept Him as Saviour. You look great on Easter Sunday; but have you taken advantage of the real reason for Easter?

109

And He said unto them, Thus it is written, and thus it behoved Christ to suffer, and to rise from the dead the third day. Luke 24:46

April 7, 1996

April 17

Bow Down to Stand Up

No one knows exactly what happened.

Two machines in two different doctors' offices suggested that something was wrong with the patient. The two doctors agreed that he needed to be hospitalized for more thorough testing. The final test ran a probe through his body into his heart. During all this time he was trembling; and saints were praying. When the probe was taken out of his body, the two doctors, both Christian men, rejoiced that everything was normal.

Did the machines malfunction and give a false verdict? Or is it that, as both physicians and the patient know very well, GOD is more powerful than either machines or sickness? Did the prayers of saints do what the advances of medicine could not?

We foolish earthlings spend a great deal of time polishing our pride. We develop expertise and competency and assume that we can accomplish anything we really want to. That is the essence of the very first sin and every sin since. To try to dethrone GOD and to take His place. The serpent in the garden told the woman that she and her husband would not surely die if they ate forbidden fruit; but "ye shall be as GODs" (Genesis 3:5).

The worst thing we can do is to believe that lie.

Our knowledge, our skills, our achievements are nothing if we do not give the glory to GOD, if we do not let Him direct our lives. As we vow before GOD that we will surrender to Him as servants, we are reminded again that GOD is in charge. Even the doctors and their science belong to GOD. Life and death are in His hands. Only as we surrender to Him can we really stand tall.

According as His divine power hath given unto us all things that pertain unto life and godliness, through the knowledge of Him that hath called us to glory and virtue. II Peter 1:3

October 3, 1993

April 18

We Are Not Worth It

You should pay a bit more for a popular hair preparation, says the lovely model, because "You are worth it." Good mental hygiene recommends a positive self-image; you ought to consider yourself worthy of the best you can do and be.

But harsh realism requires a less rosy picture of yourself.

One Advent candle says that after GOD entered our world as a baby; He entered our sins as the victim of crucifixion. Now, we were the cause of that death because our sin had opened Pandora's box, and brought the penalty of death for all sinners. Only a human without sin could come to our defense, and Jesus Christ was that human. The problem is, a sinless human is exempt from death—but Jesus submitted to death anyway, so that you and I could be redeemed and could escape eternal damnation.

So now we have access to eternal life. But make no mistake about it; we are not worth eternal life. We have it because He, not we, is worthy.

111

Sorry about the self-image thing, but truth is truth, right?

Right. Praise GOD for Jesus, Who is truly worth it!

For all is as grass, and all the glory of man as the flower of grass. The grass withereth, and the flower thereof falleth away. I Peter 1:24

December 8, 1996

April 19

Make Your Pitch

Count-down: T minus 120 hours. The Father, Son, and Holy Ghost had agreed on the precise hour when Jesus must be nailed to a cross: Friday morning at 9:00 a.m. So exactly five days before, on Sunday morning at 9:00 o'clock, GOD the Son was to appear in the streets of Jerusalem in a deliberately-arranged royal procession, on the back of a young ass, surrounded by the masses of law- income working people He had come to be identified with. Nobody except the GODhead knew the precision of the timing, or the reasons for this uncharacteristic display of public affirmation that He was the long-promised Messiah. This was the first "Palm Sunday," and it was His last major public appearance before His death.

What does it mean?

112

It means simply that He had (and now we have) a GOD-imposed mandate to tell the world that salvation is at hand, and that Jesus Christ is the Savior. This story is told in four places in the New Testament: Matthew 21, Mark 11, Luke 19, and John 12. In the Luke account, Pharisees urged Jesus to disperse the noisy crowd. He referred to the GOD-imposed mandate: "If these should hold their peace, the stones would immediately cry out."

GOD wants the world to know that Jesus saves, and that salvation is available now. He wants us to tell the world; to do whatever is necessary to tell the world— to disturb the silence of a cold, secular society; to push against laws forbidding witness; to risk being called crazy or fanatical by our friends. GOD wants us to arrange to get the word out about Jesus. If we neglect or refuse to do it, He will find somebody who will, however radical such "stones" may be. We'd better make our pitch quickly!

And Jesus answered them, saying, the hour is come, that the Son of Man should be glorified. John 12:23

April 9, 1995

April 20

Shouting All the Way to the Cemetery

There are some funerals that do not fit the mold. You loved the one who has passed on. You are hurt by his/her demise. You are prepared for the deep ache of an irrepressible grief, and for sleepless nights in an agony of mourning. But to your surprise (and joy), when family and friends surround you with hugs and laughter, and when you all reflect on the great life your loved one lived, and when friend after friend and even the preacher reminds you that he/she is in glory now, beyond all sorrow and pain and suffering, you discover that the grief is only a brief heart-prick, and the agonies you expected never develop. Is there any such thing as a "good" funeral?

We remember the death of Jesus. It was an ugly death. It was an unjust death. It cut short a life His disciples thought might last forever. And they were prepared for an unending despair.

But they were not prepared for the shock of Easter Sunday, for the deep comforts of forty days spent with the risen Savior, or for the unspeakable joys of the fellowship of the new church born at Pentecost. They knew how to grieve when One they loved so much died at the crazed hands of a hateful mob. But it made no sense that the Stranger on the road to Emmaus (Luke 24) told them that all this was part of GOD's eternal plan, and that they needed to rejoice rather than to mourn.

113

We memorialize a dead Jesus. And we will memorialize a dead Jesus repeatedly. But watch us carefully, and you will notice no tears, no wailing. We laugh like family at the wake of a saint, and praise GOD that He sent His Son to die for us because we know the other side of the story!

Ought not Christ to have suffered these things, and to enter into glory? Luke 24:26

April 2, 1995

April 21

How Oft Is Too Oft?

On first Sunday we take the LORD's Supper and we do it without apology for the frequency of it. We munch thousands of morsels of unleavened bread, and gulp down thousands of jiggers of Passover wine. And to this day, no one has dared to come to the pastor and scream, "This is too much! I can't take any more!"

When Jesus shared the Passover with His disciples, He extrapolated from that ancient observance its bread and its wine and instituted the "new covenant in His blood," which we now call Communion, or the Eucharist, or the LORD's Supper, or the Feast of the Cup. And He mentioned frequency of observance. He did not say it should be taken annually or daily or in any specific interval in between the two.

So we take the bread and wine again. Same scriptures, same prayer, same food and drink, same remembrance. First Sunday number 383. And long after we are in our graves and the world is governed by our children or our children's children, we hope they do not forget the plea of our LORD: "As often as you observe this supper, remember Me."

114

And when He had given thanks, he brake it and said, Take eat: this is my body, which is broken for you: this do in remembrance of me. After the same manner also He took the cup, when He had supped saying, This cup is the new testament in my blood: this do ye as oft as ye drink it, in remembrance of me. I Corinthians 11:24,25

May 7, 1995

April 22

The "Gigo" Syndrome

It has embarrassed the Social Security Administration. They stopped sending payments to a woman they thought had died. Local television consumer advocate Marvin Zindler publicized the mistake to the whole city. It has frustrated tax accountants, who could not trace some error in their calculations and who spent hours manually re-calculating what should have been done correctly in minutes by their equipment. It has attacked you, when you dialed a right number and got the wrong party anyway.

It is an occupational hazard of the computer age.

A wrong entry can throw into disorder thousands of correct entries, or can turn minor errors into ridiculous results, or can tie up miles of traffic lights or hundreds of telephone signals. It is the dreaded GIGO syndrome: Garbage in, garbage out. Errors come out of computers when errors are entered into computers. These marvelous devices are limited by the accuracy or attentiveness of the humans who program them.

115

The greatest computer of all is the human mind.

Of course some good stuff is programmed into that marvelous instrument. We learn to stand upright to walk, to communicate, to make and use tools, to create societies and govern them, to project beyond the physical universe and to worship GOD.

But we allow a lot of garbage in, too.

How much trash do we read, or listen to, or deliberately seek out? How much rotten talk do we allow, as we form opinions about people or events? How many bad habits have we formed by failing to discipline ourselves to eat healthy, to rest properly, to avoid addictive substances and degrading activities?

We know what is good. We know we ought to take in information and develop practices that glorify GOD, that benefit neighbors, that strengthen our own minds and bodies. Cut down on the garbage that you allow into your mind, and you will guarantee more healthy thoughts and actions.

The fear of the LORD is the beginning of knowledge: but fools despise wisdom and instruction. Proverbs 1:7

May 1, 1994

April 23

Anywhere He Wants To

Jesus' triumphal entry into the city of Jerusalem was a strange parade. He arranged his own grand entrance, and timed on the first morning of a heavy business week in the city. The religious leaders considered it audacious, and the merchants did not like it. But the common people loved it!

We used to have a giant in the church. His name was Ernie and he stretched up 6'7" tall, and weighed in at 350+ pounds. All his clothes had to be tailored for him, even his size 17 shoes. One Sunday he squeezed his massive bulk into a pew about four rows back. When asked if he could not get his knees into the little space where he was, the whole front row got up.

When power appears, we make room.

Our life is as crowed and noisy as a Jerusalem street market on the first day of the week. The stalls and booths are packed with neat rows of responsibilities. The noises of competition and conflict with family and co-workers fill the air. The many smells of problems and frustrations swirl between fragrance and stench. And we are pounded and pummeled by the pressures of hucksters selling pride and the greed for power and the hunger for money and the lure of passion.

But Jesus always appears and demands a space.

If we let Him in, we see our flea market become a paradise. If we give Him first place, we marvel as our mountains dissolve before our eyes. If we open our hearts to Him, the still, small voice of GOD speaks peace to our soul, and the clatter and din of the world fades away.

It has been over two thousand years since Jesus intruded into the busy market-places of Jerusalem, riding peacefully on an ass. But He comes to our doorway regularly and asks if He can sit down with us. Let Him! Let Him!

Blessed be the king that cometh in the name of the LORD: peace in heaven, and glory in the highest. Luke 19:38

April 12, 1987

April 24

Who Can Call GOD "Father"?

When Jesus taught us to pray, He told us we could call GOD, Who is our Creator, our Supreme LORD, the Judge of our sins, "Our Father." He was talking to disciples who were all Jews, but the clear implication was that those disciples, who would be sent to teach His principles to all peoples, were to give the message to African-Americans and other Gentiles as well. So when we lift our hearts to Heaven, we feel perfectly correct in calling the GOD of Abraham, Isaac, and Jacob, "Father." And we expect Him to hear our prayers and sustain us.

The most profound of the prophets, Isaiah, comforted an oppressed people with a promise that GOD would prevail over earthly tyrants.

The key clause is "all flesh shall see it together." A time will come when the multitude of religions, denominations, and factions within religions and denominations will see the glory of GOD. His wrath will punish the wicked. His grace will comfort the righteous, and His peace will rest upon all who love and revere Him. In that day, I cannot look down my nose at people who are not American, or Black, or Baptist, or Christian. If I am privileged to call GOD my Father, I am obliged to call all who obey Him my brothers and sisters. His glory is bigger than our divisions.

117

And the glory of the LORD shall be revealed, and all flesh shall see it together: for the mouth of the LORD hath spoken it. Isaiah 40:5

October 13, 1996

April 25

How Tall Are You?

This question is not aimed at deriding short people. It is not really a physical question, but a spiritual one.

Our city boasts a number of nationally renowned athletes—in high schools, colleges, and on professional teams. Among the more spectacular are those who play basketball, because they tend to be taller. They command attention when they walk down the street or into a room. Some of them are also very fashionable dressers. When, for example, an African-American man, velvet black with sculpted features, appears in a $1,500 Swiss wool suit and tailored Italian shoes, the ladies just cannot keep their cool. And the brother is seven feet tall!

But on the professional basketball court, this same handsome imposing figure of a man stoops to common gym brawling with other players and gets ejected from the game, not because he plays basketball badly, but because he cannot hold his temper.

118

And suddenly he is a very little man, setting a bad example for the boys who idolize him.

No matter how we may have dieted and exercised, no matter how much we have spent on facials and hair-styling, no matter what labels we wear on our designer clothing, if we cannot treat other people right, or handle disagreement, or allow for opinions or ideas other than our own, we are not tall enough.

At the end of the Passion Season, the world remembers that Jesus allowed His enemies to crucify Him. GOD, Who always justifies those who are wronged, raised Him from the dead anyway. Jesus did not have to slaughter His enemies Himself. And we revere Jesus as the tallest spirit Who ever lived.

Why not add a few spiritual inches to our character? Look good, and dress fashionably, but most of all, act tall.

Therefore, my beloved brethren, be ye steadfast, unmovable, always abounding in the work of the LORD, forasmuch as ye know that your labour is not in vain in the LORD. I Corinthians 15:58

April 22, 1990

April 26

The Twinkling of an Eye

How quickly changes come!

Daylight Savings Time "saves" an hour so that time appears earlier the day time changed than it did at the same time the day before. We just got accustomed to writing the new year which is also an annual adjustment to be made between 11:59 p.m. every December 31 and 12:00 midnight every January 1. Just last week a child had to stand on a stool, and suddenly the child does not need the stool any more. Did she grow like that over night? And once was a time when we could run a block and not get tired.

It would seem that since the date changes every year, and the time shifts twice every year, and all of us have to adjust to children growing and to ourselves aging, we would be ready to make changes when the times come.

Yet the human animal hates to adjust and seems always to get surprised by changes.

But Paul tells the church at Corinth that this world must prepare for judgment and resurrection. He spends the whole of the long chapter of I Corinthians 15 arguing for the resurrection of the body. That is what Jesus paid for with His broken flesh and His spilled blood. That is why we rejoice rather then grieve over His death.

Change comes. And we need to make preparations for the greatest change of all. If death finds our house today, are we ready to be in that number who will be raised incorruptible? Or are we still writing on the calendar of the unsaved?

We have adjusted to the new year and we adjust to daylight savings time. Now is a good time to make one move necessary to adjust to Eternity. Come to Jesus.

We shall not all sleep, but we shall all be changed. In a moment, in the twinkling of an eye, at the last trump: for the trumpet shall sound, and the dead shall be raised incorruptible, and we shall be changed.
I Corinthians 15:51b, 52

April 1, 1990

April 27

What It Is

Aside from being clumsy grammar, that phrase is a very stylish greeting among the young. Now, if we remove it from the very "live" milieu of black teenagers (it most nearly means, "How are things going with you?"), we can pull it into our own spirit and look at it existentially, from inside.

How are things?

The response to that depends entirely on our personal faith-base. Rain is a problem to golfers, car wash owners, and people on picnics. But it is a blessing to farmers who are four inches short. If our life is in the hand of our boss, the few friends we can depend on, and the Federal Reserve System, we are on slippery ground. Any day can overturn our tranquility. A pink slip, a betrayal, or another bank failure can mean disaster.

But if our life is anchored in GOD and our best friend is Jesus, we are shielded against every mishap; and even tragedy cannot shatter our peace. For most humans, economic breakdown and military buildup, a decrease in family stability, and an increase in violent crime all spell bad news.

Nothing is in the news that prophets have not told us about, or that Christ has not equipped us for. "What it is" becomes for the disciple of Jesus simply a challenge for more effective witness, a re-dedication to be GOD's warriors against a busy Satan (he is supposed to be busy), and a calm acceptance of the promise that GOD will wipe away all tears.

Maybe it is not an ideal today. But it is going to be a blessed tomorrow.

Weeping may endure for a night, but joy cometh in the morning.
Psalm 30:5b

April 26, 1987

April 28

Checking Our Mode

Our age shows in our patterns of speech and thought. It is a clue to when we grew up if "coke" means something one drinks. Some of us may even feel dated when those younger talk about "chilled-out" and they don't mean "refrigerated."

In this age of electronic miracles, we have a new definition of the old word "mode," which used to refer to method (Riding a donkey is a slow mode of travel) or to rhythmic patterns (Dorian was the most valued mode in Greek music). It may still have those old meanings, but if our voice-activated capstan drive microcassette recorder is in "play" mode rather than "record" mode, then we will not have all our data on tape for entry into our terminal. (You understand all that, don't you?)

Have you checked recently? In which mode are you? Are you in "whimper" mode or "listen" mode?

If you begin to list your problems, you soon discover that each one you name brings to mind another you had not thought of. Complaining is a perpetual exercise and it can drive you to the 'coke' you do not drink.

121

Black people have tons of pains to complain about. But if we quiet our whimpers and listen to the still, small voice of GOD, we begin to notice that memories of blessings multiply geometrically. If we put our soul in the "listen" mode, GOD's love washes away the slime of much whimpering. We can always tell when our mechanism is in that mode: Our face lightens up.

I will bless the LORD at all times: His praise shall continually be in my mouth. Psalm 34:1

February 22, 1987

April 29

Let Down Your Buckets

It is a permanent part of our history—the philosophical debate between two giants: Drs. W.E. B. DuBois and Booker T. Washington. Every African-American child should review that debate. DuBois, the urbane and scholarly Harvard graduate, wanted black people to aim at professional positions, political power, intellectual development. Washington urged us to "let down our buckets where we are," develop working skills, businesses within our own community, and property ownership.

Neither was wrong. These aims are in sequence, not in opposition.

Jesus told us to take the gospel to the farthest corners of the earth. But He told us to begin where we are. We would receive power from the Holy Spirit, He promised us in the first chapter of Acts; and then we would begin witnessing in Jerusalem, and from there to the ends of the earth.

122

Missions is a central function of Christians. And as we consider the far-flung witness to the continents and the islands of this globe, we begin by letting down our buckets wherever we are. If we are faithful there, we can be effective in Africa, in Asia, in Europe and Latin America, in the most remote communities of the Third World, and aim at evangelizing Bali and reaching the children of the Kurds. But we must drop our buckets first at home and then work our way outward to the uttermost parts of the world.

For our gospel came not unto you in word only, but also in power and in the Holy Ghost, and in much assurance; as ye know what manner of men we were among you for your sake. I Thessalonians 1:5

April 28, 1991

April 30

Somebody Is Reading You

You've done it, and chuckled softly as you did. You have watched somebody in the car next to you or in front of you acting as though they were alone. They bounced to the music or pitched a crumpled wad of paper out of the window or picked at their nose. And they never knew they had at least one eyewitness.

I was being introduced by a distinguished-looking social work professional, a leader in a major social services agency in Harris County. He was dutifully reading my bio, and then abruptly left his prepared manuscript to say that when he was in high school, he followed me on a civil rights march. (I think we all got arrested, and his parents should have shot me.) Now a generation later, he was a mover and shaker in his field. And the memory of my involvement in his life was still there!

Whether you are bouncing to hip-hop or teaching a class, be aware that somebody may be watching you. Your helpfulness is registering with somebody. Your temper explosion is going into somebody's memory banks. Your off-the-cuff gem becomes an unforgettable axiom today's youth will quote twenty years from now. Your sour expression on a "bad hair" day permanently marks you as a curmudgeon in somebody's book. You are never offstage.

123

The 90th Psalm quotes the prayer of a wise man, who asks GOD in verse 12, "So teach us to number our days, that we may apply our hearts unto wisdom." Veteran TV anchors know never to do at the anchor table what they would not want viewers to see, even when they believe the camera is not running. You and I ought to practice doing and saying only what we would want GOD to see and hear. We ought to assume that we are in a fish bowl, and that somebody sees and hears us—because somebody, somewhere does.

And who knows? Perhaps GOD places them there to see if in private we are the saints we claim to be in public!

Be ye therefore followers of GOD, as dear children. Ephesians 5:1

October 24, 1999

May 1

Christian Grammar

We may have forgotten it by now. But when we were in school, we surely learned how to establish the principle of person in pronouns. Some teacher told us (a good one drilled it into our heads): "First person—I; second person—you; third person—he." And if we were good students of grammar, we knew subconsciously "He and I went to the store" not "Me and him went to the store."

For those still in school, the rules of grammar may be still fresh in their minds. Or maybe, it has been a long time since a mean old teacher stood over us drilling us over "lie" and "lay" and "it's" and "its." Whether it happened decades ago or is still happening, it is important to know that there is another version of the principle of person.

Our first love is not supposed to be ourselves, or our families, or our best friends. Our first love should be GOD, Who made us, Who has watched over us every second of our lives and Who has provided a plan of salvation that makes available to you eternal life. No one loves us more than GOD does, and we should love no one more than GOD.

124

Further, because GOD commands us to love others as He has loved us and to forgive others as He has forgiven us, He measures love by what it does for others. For these reasons, we must consider other people before we consider ourselves. This principle supercedes the world's axiom to "Look out for Number One."

So the proper grammar for a Christian is "First person—'He'; second person—'you'; third person—'I.'"

When we can put GOD first, our neighbor second, and ourselves last, we may be considered foolish by the world. However, we have learned the grammar of the language of Heaven.

Greater love hath no man than this, that a may lay down his life for his friends. John 15:13.

May 20, 1990

May 2

May I?

Funny what age does to your memory. I may not be able to remember what I had for dinner last night, but increasingly I can remember snatches from a childhood more than fifty years ago. There was in our worship service one Sunday a lady older than I am, whose presence helped to remind me of St. Louis in the thirties.

I was her only child, and we lived in my grandparents' home with her sister and her family. Lucille had three girls and two boys. So sometimes we played boys' rough-and-tumble games, and sometimes we had to play girls' games (Ugh!). One game is still fuzzy to me, but one child gave commands to the rest of us: "Take two giant steps forward!" I don't remember how you won that game, but you could not follow the command until you asked the commander-child, "May I?" and he or she replied, "Yes, you may." Otherwise, you forfeited your right to take any steps, and you stayed where you were.

How often have we failed to realize that same relationship between us and GOD. If we ask for His will and wait until He allows, we succeed. If we establish our own agenda and do it our way, we fail. Before you choose a mate or a job or a house, or have to make a decision about even medium or "baby-step" things, go into your closet, talk to the Great Commander, and then don't make a move until you hear the great voice saying, "Yes, you may!"

Who is he that overcometh the world, but he that believeth that Jesus is the Son of GOD? I John 5:5

April 14, 1996

May 3

Some Things Never Change (Should They?)

Some have already done it.

At some point in mid-spring (like now), we realize that we will probably not wear our heavy woolens again for a while. We bring out the cottons, the play clothes, maybe the swimwear, and we put away the gloves and top-coats. It's time to adjust to the season.

But these are outside changes.

We still must care for the body inside the clothes, and that care does not change much. It must be supplied with food and drink, cleaned regularly, perhaps given vitamins or other supplements, and checked or treated for illness. Seasonal stuff for the outside, perennial care for the inside.

So it is with our relationship with Christ.

We can microwave our meals, carry our cell phones with us to make calls from the shopping mall, and watch our favorite show a week after it aired via pre-recorded videocassette. But even in a world of fax machines and laptop computers, there are some things that remain the same always.

We need a Saviour. We need guidance from the Holy Spirit after we have been redeemed. We need constant communication with Heaven through prayer. And we need Christian fellowship with other people who know Jesus, too. Gadgets become outmoded, and last year's styles are obsolete. But Jesus Christ remains the same always, loving us in spite of our worthlessness, leading us upward in grace through His Spirit, empowering us to witness to Him even in our high-tech environments. Some things never change.

Jesus Christ the same yesterday, and today, and for ever. Hebrew 13:8

May 5, 1991

May 4

What Does GOD Want in a Woman?

The commandments He wrote with His own finger, and the Beatitudes Jesus recited in His own words tell us what He wants in males and females. But perhaps the best flesh-and-blood example is the young woman He hand-picked to be the mother of our LORD: Mary from Nazareth.

She loved and obeyed the LORD. She was respectful of her parents, other elders, and the traditions of her people. And she was an excellent wife and mother. (No chance then for her to be a top professional.) Today we celebrate our girls, and the work of those leaders and parents who toil among them to help them become the best examples of reverent, respectful, loving, productive womanhood. Women were designed with all the mentality and resourcefulness of men. They make great CEO's and leaders of government. But they were also designed to do something men cannot duplicate—they were designed to be mothers. (Joseph was a great guy, but Gabriel was not looking for Joseph.) If a woman is to be complete, she must be able to set goals, motivate subordinates to work toward those goals, handle budgets in bullish and shortfall situations, and think her way out of crises. That's the CEO stuff she needs. But she must also know how to sense, to feel, to nurture, to make a child feel wanted, to prop up a discouraged man and send him back feeling capable.

She can get the CEO stuff from a good university and from job experience. She must get the uniquely woman stuff from family, from neighborhood, and from GOD. That's why green is such an important color.

Every wise woman buildeth her house: but the foolish plucketh it down with her hands. Proverbs 14:1

March 10, 1996

May 5

Hold The Formaldehyde

Must every decade bring a spectacle of death before us? The seventies taught us the name of Charles Manson. In the eighties we learned to shudder at the name Jim Jones. The nineties brought us the name of David Koresh. (And unfortunately, the 2000's introduced a new name: Osama bin Laden.) In each case, we are confronted with a charismatic leader who summons his followers to die.

Jesus gave us exactly the opposite image.

He told us that GOD is not the GOD of the dead, but of the living (Matthew 22:32). He never emphasized death, even though He came into our world to die. His constant theme was life. If we believe in the Son of GOD, no one need perish, but have everlasting life (John 3:16).

Every physician has come face to face with phenomena that defy medical logic. Somebody who ought to die keeps living, and there is no better explanation than that there is some mysterious "will to live" that is stronger than the symptoms of fatal sickness. Is there some connection between fervent prayer and this inexplicable "will to live"? There is no scientific evidence that can be subjected to analysis and experimentation, so we are left only with faith, or the refusal to exercise it.

128

We do not have to listen to the prophets of death, preaching the wrath of an angry GOD, calling the faithful to die for Him. Don't allow any preacher, however charismatic, however eloquent, however skillful in twisting the Word of GOD into apocalyptic garbage, divert your attention from Jesus, Who never left a corpse on the slab. Wherever He met a funeral, He raised the dead to life and terminated the funeral service on the spot. His theme was never death, not even His own. His theme was eternal life, and any preacher who does not emphasize that theme is not a spokesperson for Jesus!

So do not play the dirge; cancel the casket; scratch the floral wreath; hold the formaldehyde. Plan to live!

That it may be well with thee, and thou mayest live long on the earth. Ephesians 6:3.

April 25, 1993

May 6

"Mother" Is Just a Word

On the second Sunday in May, the calendar requires that we honor mothers.

What a huge concept is "mother." She is the child-bearer. She is the one who nurtures and shapes in those early years when the direction of our entire life is determined. She is the one who will still accept us when our own actions have made us unacceptable to everyone else. She is the model for the highest, most unselfish love we experience among humans, second only to the unlimited love of GOD.

But that description does not fit every female baby-bearer.

Mothers abort babies or abandon them because they do not want them. Or, worse, they abuse them because they cannot tolerate them. Mothers pass on to their children their addictions, their angers, their bigotries and stereotypes, their laziness, their immoralities. Some persons reading these words have been spiritually crippled by bitter or neurotic mothers.

And yet, those mothers deserve respect, too. (!)

GOD commands us to honor our mothers (fathers, too, guys!). But the reason is not because they are sweet, wholesome, caring Mrs. Huxtable types. The reason is much more existential—so that we ourselves may survive. The family structure is the basic cornerstone of society. When it breaks down, so does the social order—we can see that happening already. If we honor our elders, that social order is stable and long-lived. That is the fundamental and irrevocable law of GOD.

We must continue to try to direct the lives of our girls so that we produce more good mothers than bad ones. We must work at rehabilitating as many of those who go wrong as possible. But on this special day which assumes that all mothers are good mothers, we must re-dedicate ourselves to the law of GOD, which calls for us to honor mothers even had there never been a Mother's Day. GOD made mothers, and called them very good.

For GOD commanded saying Honor thy father and mother: and, He that curseth father or mother, let him die the death. Matthew 15:4

May 8, 1994

May 7

Alma Mater

It is what proud college graduates call the college they attended. It is an old Latin phrase, meaning "nourishing mother" and refers to the benefits a student gets from his or her school. So in May, when the nation remembers mothers everywhere and schools are preparing to confer diplomas on their graduates, we are forced to look at the unique role of mothers—personal and institutional.

From Eve to Mary to our own mother to our Alma Mater, there has been a common thread defining that role. A mother is expected to give birth and to bear the pain and travail of that birth. A mother is expected to provide the basic nourishment and nurture for her offspring and usually provides his or her first taste of love and protection. We may or may not consider our father or our siblings as precious to us. But the peculiar role of mothers, if it is carried out, guarantees a special place in our heart for them.

A twenty-first century tragedy is the deterioration of that role.

130

Because the Holy Spirit mothers the church and the church mothers the followers of Jesus Christ, it is critical that we take responsibility for the restoration of motherhood. No financial opportunity, no rage at fathers, no inconvenience of child-rearing can justify the abdication of the primary role of motherhood. And if the breakdown of that role leads to the breakdown of the social fabric, we cannot blame the mothers. We must find creative ways to undergird them, to affirm them, to challenge them to perform the unique function only they can perform. Giving flowers and candy is grand, but more than that, helping them be Alma Maters is critical.

Behold thy mother. Matthew 12:49

May 10, 1992

May 8

Pretty Paradox

She is faced with a strange and conflicting set of expectations. She must be soft and gentle, yet able to succeed in school as well as her boy classmates. She is expected to have delicate sensitivities, enjoy dressing up, love flowers, and like dolls and cuddly animals more than football and rap—but she should be able to appreciate with her dad or her brothers an impossible three-pointer or a hard- driving 70-yard run. She must prepare to be homemaker and professional, both mother and dad (with credentials as teacher, nurse, counselor, and accountant).

Did GOD really feel Adam was that inadequate?

We salute girls and women—the cute "before," the elegant "after," the real backbone of our social order. (If females went on strike, what would happen to schools, businesses, churches? All the candidates for president might as well quit campaigning!) They make great subjects for jokes and are convenient to blame for the foibles of children. But without them, there would be no families, no societal stability, no civility among humans.

131

The pattern came from Mother Africa. The women would teach the girls the values and skills of womanhood, long before marriage or childbearing age, to prepare them for the usually unfair demands to be made upon them. These girls must accept the radical paradox. They must be soft as foam, tough as leather. They must pamper their men, but stay on their case. And they must be totally aware of the needs of those they love, while totally dependent upon their GOD to supply those needs.

LORD, You really pulled it off with that rib!

Who can find a virtuous woman? For her price is far above rubies.
Proverbs 31:10

February 27, 2000

May 9

Give the Ladies Some Grief

Yes, we males enjoy gently giving a hard time to the ladies. We tease them about being talkative. We kid them about being obsessive shoppers. We stereotype them about a fear of mice or bugs. We josh them about a fixation on "pretty" or "neat," as over against "functional" or "efficient." That is a man thing, to irritate women.

But as we come to celebrate our ministry to girls, Transformation*, we grow serious about the value of "the weaker sex." The real strength of our families has generally been female rather than male. When we have to deal with corruption in business or in government, it seldom points to women—almost always to males. When we have needed to get something done, women would most often accomplish it while men were still writing descriptions and drafting blueprints. It comforts us men to giggle about women's foibles, but in our most sober moments we know who holds together the family, the economy, the social order. It was no accident that when GOD chose to send into the world the Perfect Man to redeem us from our sins, He sent His Son through a virgin woman (Galatians 4:4).

132

It is a tragedy that we have neglected the character-building of boys and have lost generations of males. But it is a greater tragedy when our females are at risk—their easy acceptance of poor grades and generally poor performance, their tolerance of filth and profanity in music and on the screen, their surrender to verbal, mental, and even physical abuse—all of this means we need to offset a crisis among girls and women.

But when the fullness of the time has come, GOD sent forth His Son, made of woman, made under the law, to redeem them that were under the law, that we might receive the adoption of sons. Galatians 4:4-5

February 24, 2002

* Transformation is a mentoring program for teen-age girls.

May 10

The Crown of Creation

There is no real type for "Mother." She is wrinkled and wise. She is young and scared. She models reverence for her children as she prays without ceasing. She shows them what drugs and a string of boyfriends can do to a woman. She is the pillar of strength for the whole neighborhood. She is the pitiable victim of abuse by her husband or current beau. She is there for her children in all their school and church involvement. She is in the street when police and social workers come to pick up her children. She may be 65 or 45 or 15, but one thing is universal—she loves her children.

The stories of great mothers most often come from children who at some time in their lives swore that they would escape her and never emulate her. And even the children who remember their mothers in jail or soaked in alcohol or stupefied by drugs still remember women who loved them, and who wanted the best for them. As you remember your own mother you will probably be part of the multitude who recalls her love for you, and her desire for you to be somebody. Yes, you will recall being embarrassed by her or being ashamed that she was so behind the times or silently characterizing her as the meanest woman in town. But unless you are still six years old, you have found yourself saying and doing things she did and perhaps even looking more and more like her. Whatever your image of "Mother," it includes that one constant—Mama loves (loved) me.

Lost in the infinite mystery of GOD's wisdom is the reason for His institution of Motherhood. The role of Eve and of Mary was also the role of Jezebel and of Herodias. However bad women may have perverted the role of mother, it has remained the same: to nurture us from birth to adulthood. Let us thank GOD that of all of the marvels of His creation, the crown is Mother, through whom He sent His only Son (Galatians 4:4).

...she shall be saved in childbearing, if they continue in faith and charity and holiness with sobriety. I Timothy 2:15

May 12, 2002

May 11

Behold Thy Mother!

This was Jesus' fourth word on the cross. It was not uttered in a setting of carnations, greeting cards and gifts, and the glory of a national holiday. There was pain and brutality and ugly crowds and blood under a sky darkening at midday. Evil men were lynching the Son of GOD. But even in the excruciating agony of His last hours, He remembered to make arrangements for the welfare of His mother Mary as he assigned His apostle John to take care of her after His death.

So you need not give all the credit to Anna Jarvis for the idea behind Mother's Day. Long before President Woodrow Wilson proclaimed the second Sunday in May as a national holiday honoring mothers, our LORD set the pattern of recognizing Mother as worthy of love, respect, and honor.

134

We read or hear much of defective mothers. Their children engage in violence, even killings, or create problems in their schools or neighborhoods. They neglect them in unsupervised homes or locked cars, or lose them to regulatory agencies because they abuse them. Mothers, like the rest of us, make mistakes.

But they are worthy of honor. And we do not honor them because they are all we want them to be. We honor them because GOD demands it in His law.

Honor thy father and mother; which is the first commandment with promise. Ephesians 6:2

May 9, 1999

May 12

Woman—the Finishing Touch

According to the scriptures, GOD fashioned a man in His image and after His likeness. While the Creator has approved light and sky, dry land and water, vegetation and all living creatures with the affirmation "it was good," He did not make such an affirmation about this newest of His creatures. GOD looked at this upright being, with a creative mind to alter his environment and a soul to worship GOD, and declared "It is not good for the man to be alone" (Genesis 2:18). And GOD set out immediately to improve His creation by adding to the man a woman (Genesis 2:21-23). Only after He had complemented the man with the woman could He declare His creation finished and institute the Sabbath.

Today we celebrate humanity as matching sets—"male and female created He them" (Genesis 1:27). Our ancestors set for us the pattern of men teaching boys the best principles of manhood, and women teaching girls the best principles of womanhood, in their "rites of passage" traditions. While Africa is many cultures, many languages, many customs, the practice of rites of passage seems virtually continent-wide. GOD has made a good world—but it was not "very good" until He had topped it off with the woman (Genesis 1:31). This transformation for girls is a declaration that the best in womanhood begins with reverence to GOD. Then they should add being good daughters, sisters, wives, mothers, and successful professionals.

135

And the LORD GOD said, It is not good that man should be alone; I will make him a help meet for him. Genesis 1:18

February 28, 1999

May 13

More Than a Pretty Face

For over seventy years now, Mother's Day has been special on the calendar. It is a time when America (and now, much of the rest of the world) salutes motherhood. Long before it was surrounded by the trappings of a legal holiday, respect for motherhood has approached reverence—our feelings about our mothers the closest thing to worship next to the overt praise of GOD. Whatever her views or opinions, Mother was never wrong; whatever she looked like, Mother was never ugly.

Mother was beautiful because motherhood was sacred.

The biology of motherhood does not explain this near-reverence. A "mother" is defined simply as the female progenitor, whose body produces the infant after fertilization by a male. Periodically, television stations focus on "children having children," females as young as nine years old giving birth to babies. We agonize over abandoned babies, babies born with the symptoms of their mothers' addiction to alcohol or drugs, babies doomed to mental and physical retardation by bad prenatal habits or lack of prenatal care, even babies murdered by abusive parents.

Mothers are not automatically beautiful.

The beauty of motherhood is not in the naked biology of child-bearing. Any homeless dog can sire or bear pups. The real beauty of motherhood has always been a matter of the spirit. Mothers worship GOD and teach the family to serve Him. Mothers have compassion for people and pass it on to her children (even influence their husbands to have it). And Mother had high moral and ethical principles and fed them to us with our oatmeal. They are beautiful outside if they are beautiful inside. We ought to celebrate the deeper motherhood, and pray that it is more contagious as we produce girl-children.

She is more precious than rubies: and all the things thou canst desire are not to be compared unto her. Proverbs 3:15

May 12, 1991

136

May 14

Put Them All Together; They Spell M-O-T-H-E-R

The song is pure sentiment, sugar-sweet, and idealistic to a fault. The writer assumes many things, like "her heart of purest gold." Any counselor at Children's Protective Services can tell you that they must deal with mothers who are not always portrayed by "tears shed to save me."

The entire passage about the ideal mother in Proverbs 31:10-31 makes an assumption, too. It begins by asking, "Who can find a virtuous woman?" Once you have identified a woman with virtue, then you can attach to her the qualities and attributes of the ideal wife and mother.

Mother's Day is not a time to for every female who has given birth to a baby. It is a time to celebrate the GOD-intended role of motherhood. So eliminate the foolish women who thought that having more babies would increase their profits from the welfare system. Ignore the cruel women for whom their children are inconveniences or even nuisances—and who may abandon or abuse or even kill their offspring. These are not the females who are the subjects of the scripture or of the holiday.

137

What GOD intended for motherhood may be more like your own mom—thank Him for her, and good ones like her.

She openeth her mouth with wisdom: and in her tongue is the law of kindness. Proverbs 31:26

May 14, 1995

May 15

The Highest Role

It is remarkable how many opportunities there are for women today. Once they could not vote, make major credit purchases, or hold the top job in companies. Once they were considered as little more than the property of husbands or fathers, subject to the wills of the males who had the power of life and death over them.

You've come a long way, Baby.

Women are in positions of leadership, of influence, of power, in virtually every field of endeavor. They are CEO's and presidents; they run school systems and cities and even states—keep your eye on the White House; one day...

But their highest role is not to make half a million per year, nor to oversee global operations. It is, as it has always been, to be a mother.

Don't lynch me yet.

138

GOD created woman to he a child bearer. All our technology has not conveyed that power to men. (And aren't you glad?) We use terms that hint that the woman is to be the heart of the family—a matrix gives origin or form to something enclosed within it. We call the college or university that produced us our Alma Mater ("nourishing mother"). Even when we speak of the key planet in the universe, we call it (or her) Mother Earth, because it produces all that lives.

We celebrate woman, not as power-broker or even as professional, but as the partner-being who was designed to be the "better half" of the primeval couple, and to be the Alma Mater of the race. Praise GOD for the divine concept of motherhood!

And Adam called his wife's name Eve; because she was the mother of all living. Genesis 3:20

May 13, 2001

May 16

We've Got Backup

When he was a skinny little third-grader, he was always in danger of being pushed around by the "big boys"—fifth and sixth graders. And he was constantly cowering whenever they showed up.

Until my Uncle Ervin came to escort him home.

Ervin was an eighth-grader, and he was thirteen. He seemed humongous—nine feet tall and 400 pounds. When Ervin showed up, the lad could swagger and strut and dare anybody to look at him. He had backup!

Over 40 years ago, the highest court in the land passed a landmark decision that said that African- American children could not constitutionally be excluded from the mainstream of public education. Decision number 347-US-483, Brown vs. the Topeka Board of Education, was rendered by the U.S. Supreme Court on May 17, 1954, the result of the efforts of an under-funded group of black lawyers headed by a man with holes in his shoe. He was NAACP Attorney Thurgood Marshall. The little people had spoken, and an entire nation, like it or not, had to listen.

139

That was because GOD showed up in the schoolyard.

In this age of resurgent racism, of the collapse of every good thing from family to economic opportunity, it is easy to assume that the bullies are winning. But how can we keep forgetting Israel at the Red Sea, or Elisha at Samaria, or the Hebrew boys in the fiery furnace, or thread-bare lawyers arguing for children in shanty school houses? There is always a Big Backup for little people. We do not need to swagger and strut, but we ought to believe!

I will lift up mine eyes unto the hills, from whence cometh my help.
My help cometh from the LORD, which made heaven and earth.
Psalm 121:1

May 17, 1992

May 17

Body & Soul

The nation (and, to some extent, the world) honors mothers. We will by syrupy words, lavish meals in better restaurants, candy, flowers, gifts, and gestures of sweetness we do not commonly make, portray mother in virtuous, almost angelic tones. We may have been upset with Mama yesterday and resume our disgust tomorrow. But on Mother's Day she must be queen.

In the most raw sense, "mother" describes a base biological function. Whatever dying creature is differentiated sexually, male and female, and can reproduce its own kind, can claim some identity with mothering. Female roaches, rats, elephants, and women (saintly ones and rotten ones) can all be mothers. But no one in his/her right mind assumes that Mother's Day celebrates fundamental egg- laying or baby-bearing. We take it for granted that everybody understands what we are celebrating: the soul of a mother who nurtures, who loves, who moulds character, who conveys values. Surely everybody understands that this day salutes the higher spirit of good mothers, not the common function of every promiscuous trollop who looks for a plastic bag and a dumpster to erase her misdeed. We know what Mother's Day is all about!

140

Her children arise up and call her blessed, her husband also, and he praiseth her. Proverbs 31:28

May 12, 1996

May 18

Tell It Like It Is

The physician, the nurse, and the technicians all agree: Something weird has happened here. The patient who should have died did not, and the cluster of praying people in the waiting room are saying GOD saved her. The brilliant lawyer and his associates do not understand. They saw the iron- clad case presented by the prosecutor and saw the jury hardened against their client. He would get the maximum penalty—this one they lost. But some group of women set up a round-the-clock prayer vigil, with people trysting in their homes; and the situation turned completely around. The jury acquitted their client, and both sides were stunned. A well-dressed man stands in a room full of people, identifies himself as Tom, and says he is an alcoholic. And he gives the credit for his three years of sobriety to the "higher power" described in twelve-step programs.

It is politically correct not to call the name of GOD. Laws of separation of church and state have discouraged us from giving vent to our faith in public settings. The ACLU could sue you about prayers or religious music. It is dangerous to introduce GOD into social rhetoric—somebody may consider you a religious nut.

141

But you and I know Who heals the sick and protects the innocent. We understand the real Power that helps us to quit bad habits and form good ones. So whatever is politically correct, whatever is socially safe, since we know Who woke us up this morning, let's praise Him anyhow!

I will praise thee, O LORD, with my whole heart, I will shew forth all thy marvelous works. Psalm 9:1

September 4, 1994

May 19

When the Bit Is In

Modern technology has revolutionized our streets in this century. Seldom do we see a horse now where once they dominated traffic. Even when we do, carrying aloft a proudly mounted policeman, or stately in a procession of trail riders, or sleek in the gates waiting to take our money in 120 seconds at the racetrack, modern technology has immeasurably advanced the way we feed them, groom them, transport them, even clean streets or track behind them.

But at least one thing remains constant: We control the most expensive Clydesdale pulling the decorated beer-wagon in 1990 with a bit in his mouth.

The Holy Spirit, like a seasoned horseman, directs us to follow the leading of Jesus Christ through His sometimes gentle, sometimes forceful pulling of the reins on us.

Often, we marvel at our stubborn adherence to the Great Commission. When the Holy Spirit tugs at the reins, we must make a decision.

If we spend time regularly in prayer-conversation with the LORD, digging through His word and beseeching Him for understanding of it, witnessing for our Christ at every available opportunity and consistently asking Him to direct our paths, then the bit is already in our mouth. We should trust our hunches, realizing that not all our impulses will be Spirit-led, but a good percentage of them will be. No lightning or thunder, no voices in the night—just a gentle tug saying, "Do it this way. It is the right direction." Trust and obey.

Behold we put bits in the horses' mouths, that they may obey us, and we turn about their whole body. James 3:3

June 25, 1989

May 20

Dumb Order? Follow It!

The story is told in John 21. Several of Jesus' disciples went fishing and completely flunked out after fishing all night. A key fact is that they were being led by three professional fishermen: Peter, James, and John. But some time around daybreak the newly-resurrected Jesus appeared on the shore and suggested that they cast the nets on the light side of the boat. Now, Jesus was a carpenter all His life. What would He know about catching fish? Furthermore, nobody cast nets on the right side—all the rigging was in the way. But the ring of authority in His voice pushed them to obey. And in minutes they caught 153 wriggling fish! It was a dumb order from an amateur—but the "amateur" was GOD.

One Sunday School lesson that is another classic in dumb orders speaks about a dozen priests who know the awesome value of the Ark of the Covenant are told by Joshua (a soldier, not a priest) to carry that precious box to the flood-swollen Jordan River and wade into it. But because they believe Joshua is relaying an order from GOD, they risk it. We discover (or have learned) the joy that comes when we follow GOD's orders.

143

He says to believe in Him, Whom you cannot see, rather than in the resources of the world, which you can see. He orders you to respect elders, who are not as smart as you are. He wants us to forgive enemies, rather than attack them. What kind of orders are those?

They are the basis of eternal life.

And he said unto them, Cast the net on the right side of the ship and ye shall find. They cast therefore and now they were not able to draw it for the multitude of fishes. John 21:6

September 11, 1994

May 21

Say "Hallelujah" & Watch What Happens

When you're smilin', when you're smilin',
The whole world smiles with you;
When you're laughin', when you're laughin',
The sun comes shinin' through.

Those lyrics, over half a century old, will not die. They float over the dialogue of movies made this very summer, and the melody to which they were once sung emerges amidst the background music at the shopping center.

They are not literal truth. They are what is called cosmic truth. The world does not literally get better because you have a happy attitude. But in a larger spiritual sense your own perspective of the world is brighter when you are glad to be alive. Your mood affects your environment

So it is with the praise of GOD. You may consider it beneath your dignity to rejoice publicly, to testify to the goodness of GOD, to make praise noises among your peers. But haven't you found a strange cosmic connection between praise and joy? Haven't you noticed that when you tell somebody how good GOD is, it strengthens your own realization of what He is doing for you?

144

You see, GOD responds to praise. The psalmist speaks of GOD as "inhabiting the praise of Israel" (Psalm 22:3). When you praise Him, His power increases in your life, His blessings are multiplied, you actually stimulate impulses of joy. Jesus told a woman at a Samaritan well that GOD is not impressed with church attendance. He seeks true worshippers who will worship Him in spirit and in truth.

Don't restrain yourself from praising GOD. What does it matter if the person in the pew with you or in the pew behind or in front of you looks at you when you shed tears or clap your hands or shout "Praise GOD!" or raise your hands in reverence? Those folks are not the source of your blessings. If you suppress your praise of GOD, you will appreciate His blessings less. But if you give free vent to your praises—in church and outside of church—not only will you find His blessings more real, but the whole world will smile with you.

Give unto the LORD the glory due unto His name; worship the LORD in the beauty of holiness. Psalm 29:2

August 14, 1994

May 22

Where Is GOD When You Need Him?

You are driving 25 miles per hour in a 30-mile-per-hour zone. You are carefully on your side of the yellow line. Your seat belt is on. But, sure enough, there are the blinding reflections of police lights in your rear-view mirror. You circumspectly slow down to allow the squad car to stop behind you, and you are reaching for your driver's license even before the officer asks for it. What are you being accused of?

Your inspection sticker has expired three days ago.

You force a mild expression while the policeman writes you a ticket; and you modulate your voice to keep from yelling at him. The city is full of street crime, drugs, unsolved killings, un-apprehended burglars. Where was this officer when your aunt was mugged last month? How does he have time to notice an expired inspection sticker while people are being killed in the park, in the supermarket parking lot, in their homes? Where are the police when they ought to be available?

We are facing a fusillade of deaths. The human rights we thought we had won in the sixties are being systematically snatched from us. We groan beneath the growing burden of debt, while salaries are frozen and pink slips are multiplying. We are hurting in a multitude of ways.

We need a GOD Who can stop all this pain. WHERE IS HE?

There is no simple answer to that question. The righteous suffer, and we must watch the wicked prosper and ask GOD, Why? Why?

Our finite minds cannot contain the Master Strategy of GOD. Even if He sent angels to tell us why He does not immediately stop all suffering, their infinite language would be babble to us. We will never know why. But we can trust—and He will take care of all we cannot understand now.

I know that Thou canst do everything, and that no thought can be withholden from Thee. Job 42:2

June 12, 1994

May 23

Like a Mighty Army

"...moves the church of GOD." So goes the first line of the third verse of the old hymn, "Onward, Christian Soldiers." A whole body of clever sermons have been put together criticizing the traditional church for not having military discipline and aggressiveness.

But the Reverend Sabine Baring-Gould, who gave us those lyrics, drew them directly from scripture, where Jesus proclaimed that His church would have such an onslaught against the kingdom of Satan that the gates of Hell could not withstand the invasion (cf. Matthew 16:18). The church of GOD is not supposed to be a weekly forum where you doze through dull discourses whenever it is convenient for you to attend. The church of GOD is an equipped and trained army, waging a real battle against principalities and the powers of evil. It is not passive—it must be aggressive, and it must be deadly to the Enemy.

146

All of that means that the church that Jesus established attacks evil whether it is in the seat of government, in the communities, or even in the Temple itself. Yes, it has social services, and counsels the incarcerated and the addicted and tutors children, and speaks out on behalf of the underdog. And all of that is done so that GOD's Kingdom might come, that GOD's will may be done on earth as it is done in Heaven. Ten-HUT!

And said unto them that sold doves, Take these things hence; make not my Father's house an house of merchandise. John 2:16

July 9, 1995

May 24

Surely GOD Knew Better

When a strange man approaches you, be cautious. When someone you don't know calls you, make sure you don't volunteer to him or her any personal information. Lock your doors when you leave, and never leave your keys in your car. Assume that a stranger is dangerous before you assume that he or she is embraceable.

Humans are more dangerous than Bengal tigers.

The Psalmist inquires about this creature called man. Did he have any idea of the kind of humans who revolve in and out of our jails and prisons? Nine hundred years before Christ, could he have possibly conceived of the kind of humans who could kill without remorse while still in their teens? What is man?

Humans are the highest beings in all of GOD's creation. They are the only animals with souls; the only creatures with whom GOD makes covenants; they are the only beings to whom He has entrusted the fate of the created universe.

147

Didn't He know when He shaped the first man out of the dust of the ground how low he would ultimately sink? Didn't He anticipate that even the woman He made to accompany man would be as corrupt as her male partner? Why doesn't He just turn His back on humankind and allow us all to disintegrate to the dirt of which we are made?

Because He loves us. WHAT?

It doesn't matter whether we understand why a GOD, Who knows everything, loves us anyway. He just does.

What is man, that thou art mindful of him? And the son of man that thou visitest him? Psalm 8:4

January 9, 1994

May 25

Seedless = Useless

It was a marvel of horticulture—a 47-pound Hempstead watermelon with bottle-green stripes against a bright Kelly green field. Cameras clicked away at the fruit and its developer, a leather-skinned, bearded, bespectacled A & M professor, as he waxed eloquent about his prize melon. It had taken years of research, costing hundreds of thousands of federal and private dollars, and utilizing the best skills of dozens of scholars and farmers. And they had produced seven of them, this being the largest and finest (four were growth-stunted and useless).

148

In the crowd was an old black farmer who had been harvesting watermelons since he was pre-teen in the rich soil of the Brazos Bottoms. His grandson asked him, "PawPaw, that watermelon doesn't look as good as yours. Why are they talking about it?" The grizzled old farmer replied, "It doesn't have any seeds—they have developed a melon that doesn't have any seeds." "Wow," said the child, "that's cool! So you don't have nuthin' to spit out?" "No, son, you don't have nuthin' to spit out." "Cool," repeated the boy (when you get a good word, you use it repeatedly). "Maybe they will put them in the stores instead of the ordinary kind!" "No, my boy," said the grandfather; "since there are no seeds they cannot produce other watermelons. You only get one small crop of these, and then you have to start all over again." The grandchild replied with a smaller "Wow."

Every once in a while, you ought to think positively about yourself. Work on learning all you can. Work on weight and muscle and skin and teeth and hair. Develop social skills. But don't forget your real reason for being here—you are to pass on to those younger than yourself the ideals, the commandments, the principles of GOD. You are to plant seeds so that others become believers and servants, too. It is great to become uniquely beautiful. But beauty is sterile unless it can be transmitted.

So spit out something that can grow. Seedless fruit is not "cool."

Being born again, not of corruptible seed, but of incorruptible, by the word of GOD, which liveth and abideth forever. IPeter 1:23

July 18, 1999

May 26

Good "How-To" Stuff

It is so easy to become expert on so many things today. An ocean of information is available on world affairs, local and national politics, sports, cars, food, gardening, decorating, etc., etc., etc. In days, or even hours, we can bone up on any subject we can think of. Want the songs Duke Ellington composed? Need the mistresses of Henry VIII? The weather in Bali? Not hours—minutes.

So why is it so difficult to learn to live with a wife or husband? Why are we fighting with our children, or letting them rear us? Why can we not learn to cope with the pressures of everyday life?

Because the information is not on the Internet, or on the special channel for antiques or quiz shows, or in the downtown library. Some wise saints you know in your own family or in your own church are handling life's challenges well. How did they learn to stay married (and still like each other), and rear kids that made them and us proud, and handle life with a smile, and get to be "wise saints"?

Not the newest cybernetic program. We follow an old king from the Middle East who said trust in the LORD with all your heart.

149

Not very new. Not very slick. But for over two and a half millennia, the best expertise you can find anywhere.

Trust in the LORD with all thine heart; and lean not unto thine own understanding. In all thy ways acknowledge Him, and He shall direct thy paths. Proverbs 3:5,6

May 18, 2003

May 27

Glory and Bruises

Any running back will tell you they go together.

The glory of galloping into the end zone, spiking the ball, and doing a bizarre "touchdown dance" comes at a great price. That few seconds in the spotlight costs the ball-carrier the pain of being tackled, piled upon, flesh bruised on the outside, sometimes bones cracked or even broken on the inside. He gets beaten up many times before he gets to do his dance (sometimes he goes through a whole season taking the beatings and never getting to do the dance!). As soon as he catches a pass, his opponents swarm after him—the man with the ball is the target.

That is the law of the field.

150

It is also a major principle in life. If you are blessed with special gifts, you are simultaneously loaded down with special responsibilities. You are a role model, whether you intended to be one or not. You are a target for criticism, you are expected to give direction you may even be the subject of hatred by people you don't even know and have done nothing to.

Dr. Martin Luther King, Jr., was incredibly gifted with a brilliant mind, with eloquence, with leadership qualities, with vision. And our age demanded of him that he lead us out of statutory segregation and toward a dream of unity in diversity; and further, that he pay for that leadership with his life. But we do not feel cheated by the immensity of that sacrifice. We understand that the price of being the Christ is a cross.

So what bruises are you willing to take?

For unto whomsoever much is given, of him shall be much required: and to whom men have committed much, of him they will ask the more. Luke 12:48b

January 16, 1994

May 28

Cost & Value

There is an axiom that individuals must receive by experience. They cannot really absorb its depth by hearing it or reading it: "The best things in life are free."

In a world of net worths and bottom lines, of upward mobility and P & L, we teach even our youngest to be acquisitive, to want the expensive rather than the cheap, to judge people and situations by economic externals (fabulous neighborhood/fantastic house/incredible car/elegant clothes/top-of-the line, state-of-the-art equipment, etc., etc.). We receive the well-dressed con artist and reject the homeless saint because he or she is in rags.

It is easy to talk value but act cost.

But think about how great it is to learn that the lump is not cancer. Or what a thrill to hug the child who lakes four steps before falling down. Or what it does to you when Mama comes out of the coma and starts fussing about your lacquered hairdo. We do not need a Mazerati when you are able to steer your old car out of the way of the drunken driver, nor a mansion when we see home for the first time after a long absence.

If we recognize the Divine Source of all blessings, then you can thank Him just because we awoke this morning—and we could never place a price-tag on His care. Bragging about the cruise to Tahiti is not necessary. Neither is complaining about the lack of finances. Praising GOD we can shift from horizontal to vertical. That is a priceless gift!

Stand up and bless the LORD your GOD for ever and ever: and blessed be thy glorious name, which is exalted above all blessing and praise. Nehemiah 9:5

June 23, 1991

151

May 29

What Would Jesus ~~Do~~ Pray For?

We have considered, during this month of prayer emphasis, the prayer Jesus taught us to pray. We have entitled it The LORD's Prayer, and since He taught it to us, that is not a bad name for it. But the best guide for prayer is Jesus' own prayers. As a pre-teen in the Temple, Jesus showed a wisdom and a grasp of reality far beyond the normal acumen of a twelve-year-old. When He began His ministry, His power over Satan indicated a strong line of communication with His Father. He did not do a standard search process when He called His disciple— He spent all night in prayer. Over and over again, we see the One Who taught us to pray in fervent prayer Himself.

So it would be most instructive if we could eavesdrop on His own prayer.

152

And we can. The real LORD's Prayer is not in Matthew or Luke, but in John 17. Those 26 verses display His priorities, His chief concerns as He prays to His Father. He does not pray for health, or wealth, or success in business. He does not ask that the wrath of GOD shall fall upon His enemies. He prays that His mission as Savior shall be effective, that the Father shall be glorified in Him, and that the church He has established shall be preserved and shall be unified. He prays that GOD's Name shall be glorified (hallowed), that GOD's Kingdom shall come, that GOD's will should be done through the disciples He leaves on earth.

Sound familiar?

Genuine prayer is never appeals for selfish benefits; it is always for the ultimate glory of GOD. Yes, we should ask for daily bread. But even daily bread is not at the top of the list for genuine prayer. Jesus told us that if we seek first the Kingdom of GOD and His righteousness, "all these things" should be added to us. If we work toward the glory of GOD, He will provide us with both what we need and some of what we want. If our prayer-focus is to lift His Name, to affirm His Kingdom, His blessings will pour out on us to the overflowing. Pray right, and live well!

I pray for them: I pray not for the world, but for them which Thou hast given me; for they are mine. John 17:9

October 29, 2000

May 30

Prayer—It Works

I know you never did this. But I have found myself advising people to do what I have not done myself. I was asked by a church which is seeking a pastor to come and talk to them. I heard myself advising them to fast and pray, even suggesting procedures for encouraging the entire church to plead with GOD for His choice of a pastor.

And while I was driving away, patting myself on the back for my wise counsel, I asked myself, "How much do you agonize before GOD when you must make decisions?"

OUCH!

Our model in prayer is Jesus. No one knows as He does how to approach GOD in prayer. A graphic picture is given as He takes His disciples into the Garden of Gethsemane the night of the Last Supper. Mark tells us, "And He went forward a little, and fell on the ground, and prayed..." (Mark 14:35a). The image is not of a polite folding of the hands to bless a meal or to begin a meeting. The picture here is of a man falling flat on his face on the cold, wet ground of the garden, and pleading with, beseeching, begging GOD—PLEASE let this cup pass; but I'll obey Your will, whatever it is!

153

I don't pray like that, unless I am in big trouble. It is so easy for me to pitch a prayer into the air like a clay pigeon, and expect GOD to hit it for me. We have a world in turmoil. We have loved ones who are sick. We have a whole generation of children growing up without values, often without ambition. And we are personally addicted to merchandise and personal comforts. We need to agonize before GOD. Jesus was not praying for Himself—He was praying for you and me.

Who knows the power of prayer? The connection between praying people and GOD has healed the sick, turned lives around, worked out sticky situations, even spared nations in trouble against tyrants. The finest scholars cannot analyze the miracles wrought by serious, fervent prayer. We could accomplish far more, face fewer obstacles, if we lay prostrate before GOD a little more often. As our kids would say, prayer rocks!

If my people, which are called by my name, shall humble themselves, and pray, and seek my face, and turn from their wicked ways; then will I hear from heaven, and will forgive their sin, and will heal their land. II Chronicles 7:14

November 17, 2002

May 31

Beauty from Ugliness

It was a way to make spring rains more bearable. Somebody coined an adage, "April showers bring May flowers." The lesson is good—bear the temporary inconvenience so that you can enjoy the ultimate fruits of it. But while picturesque, it is not quite accurate. Water is not the only thing necessary to developing blossoms. No matter how much you pour water on cut flowers, they will not last. May flowers depend on rich soil and also on death. The mulch or fertilizer in the soil is critical to the production of blooms. So what is watered by April showers is a sprout rooted in dirt which contains decaying matter. Without something dead and decaying, we have no roses, no zinnias, no lilies (no fruits or vegetables, either).

Our faith is based on redemption through the death of our LORD. Had He not made Himself available to die for us, we would have been destroyed long ago. In fact, all life depends on death. We live because medicine can kill the microbes that invade our bodies. And that beef or chicken or seafood we enjoy means that some creature has given its life for us.

154

In the same way, the strength and security of our nation exists because of the millions of men and women who died on hundreds of battlefields in the defense of our people. We may be violently anti- war and feel that the military is a corruption of proper society. But Jesus told us that there shall be wars and rumors of wars (Matthew 24:6)— we will never outgrow war. And be sure that had we lost World War I or II, this would be a very different world. So thank GOD that the deaths of many and the sacrifices of all have helped to make beautiful the blossom of democracy, despite its faults.

...whereby the dayspring from on high hath visited us, to give light to them that sit in darkness and in the shadow of death, to guide our feet into the way of peace. Luke 1:78b-79

May 27, 2001

June 1

Beware the Hot Spots

Hurricane season begins today. Weather experts say most hurricanes are spawned in the African deserts as "hot spots," huge masses of super-heated air that move eastward into the ocean (most weather moves westward) and begin their ominous journey toward the western hemisphere. The hot spots are not dangerous in themselves. But, say the meteorologists, when they get over the water, they create a low pressure area that attracts high pressure winds which begin to swirl around the low pressure heat zone in a swift, counter-clockwise funnel, and a tropical depression develops in the ocean. Depression swells to storm, and storm grows into hurricane. And a little hot spot becomes a destructive monster with winds that can crush whole neighborhoods, destroy years of careful cultivation, and snatch away lives in miniseconds.

James says the tongue likewise is a destroyer.

We should not let a little offense begin to move toward vindictive feelings and attitudes. They swirl around some thoughtless action or badly-phrased statement and remind us of a thousand ways to strike back and before we can say, "I forgive you, as GOD has forgiven me," we have a fury that can destroy years of friendship in seconds and leave behind a wilderness of bitter feelings. If we can't say something kind, we should just keep quiet!

155

Even so the tongue is a little member, and boasteth great things. Behold, how great a matter a little fire kindleth. James 3:5

August 6, 1989

June 2

Can You Keep a Good Man Down?

If ever a man should have been defeated, Jesus should have been. He was born homeless, to transient parents, with a price on His infant head as a king tried to slaughter all boy-babies, and was forced to be fugitive before He was old enough to know He was in any danger. He grew up in a despised town, citizen of an oppressed nation, and started His ministry being hated by the rich and powerful. He was accused and convicted to be executed by the state, and even His few friends left Him unsupported. He walked to His execution surrounded by crowds, but utterly alone.

Was that bad enough? Not quite.

Not only did He face death without friends or supporters, He had the sins of all the combined populations of the world laid on Him—and He had never committed a single sin! But all our sins weighed Him down to the deepest Hell.

156

His Spirit really should have been crushed by this pileup of negatives. He had every right to curl up in a fetal position and tell His Father to shove it. But you and I both know that He considered the cross a form of glory (John 19:23-32), and accepted unquestioningly whatever the Father laid on Him (Luke 22:42).

Because of His unwavering obedience to His Father, GOD reached into the bowels of Hell, lifted His Son back to a glorified new life, and through Him redeemed all of us. Any wonder why we shout about a grim and ugly cross? It is because from that cross came the ultimate victory over all our problems forever! Jesus beat Hell and the grave! Hold my mule…

Jesus saith unto her, Mary. She turned herself, and saith unto Him, Rabboni, which is to say Master. John 20:16

December 13, 1998

June 3

GOD Likes Kids

Funny how we can advance and fall back at the same time. The twentieth century gave us modern industry, transportation without animal power, communication via wires or air waves, more income, shorter work weeks, and marvels like television and the world of computers. It provided us with better medicine and conditioned air and access to a universe of information at the roll of a mouse. We have advanced geometrically since 1900.

But as we got more sophisticated technically, we somehow backslid socially. Our toys made children less necessary. When our food came from the supermarket rather than from the farm, we did not need sons and daughters to milk cows and plow fields. Children became inconvenient, then an unbearable expense, then downright nuisances. Some who were rich, if they did not abort them, farmed them out to nannies and day care centers. Those who were poor struggled with them (like my folks), or at worst abandoned them. Second cars were status symbols—second kids were a blunder and a burden.

Because kids are GOD's favorites even when they are not ours.

The first ten verses of Matthew 18 gives you an idea of how He feels about children. Not only does He dare us to hurt one, but even says that these little inconvenient, overly expensive, noisy, always hungry creatures are the essence of the Kingdom of GOD!

We don't need to build a more sophisticated technology in this new century. We need to rebuild the family structure we abandoned in favor of the new toys. Find a child, hug him or her, and tell that child GOD loves him or her, and you do, too!

Whosoever therefore shall humble himself as this little child, the same is greatest in the kingdom of heaven. Matthew 18:4

May 21, 2000

June 4

Children—Ugh!

Why do we waste time and concern on kids? They do not add to the household income, but each consumes food enough for three adults. You search for the shoes they prefer, and in six months they have outgrown them. They give you grief about your old-fashioned clothes, your outdated sound and video equipment, your ignorance of the newest rap artist—but they want to drive your car. They take all manner of abuse from their running-buddies, but if you so much as ask them where they have been, they sulk for a week (or two).

Surely it would be more peaceful if you were in a monastery in the mountains of Tibet, where there were no children, no young people, not even dogs or cats.

But, let's face it; very soon you would be miserable.

158

Societies which do not bear and rear children soon die. At some point, we became sufficiently self- centered so we did not want to have big families. And we are indeed small-family people (or even childless people). We have fewer mouths to feed, but we are watching a dangerous trend with the amputation of young people and children. The strength of this church has been its families, including its noisy and expensive children. GOD loves kids, however noisy and expensive they are. The Bible tells us to "take heed that ye despise not one of this little ones"; for, Jesus tells us, "in Heaven their angels do always behold the face of my Father Which is in Heaven" (Matthew 18:10). A quiet neighborhood with no children is a dying neighborhood. A stately and elegant church with no children is moving toward extinction. Kids are the essential wealth of any institution, any neighborhood, any community. Fuss at your kids—O. K.! But love them as GOD does.

And Jesus called a little child unto Him, and set him in the midst of them, And said, Verily I say unto you, Except ye be converted, and become as little children, ye shall not enter into the kingdom of heaven. Matthew 18:2,3

July 14, 2002

June 5

Pigeons & Parents

You see it almost daily—somebody has been swindled out of their money, or has been duped into a scandalous situation, or has been deceived by someone he trusted but should not have. The perpetrators are called scam artists, and they deserve punishment. But we have little respect for the victims, who are called "pigeons," because we have labeled them as naive, as gullible, as foolish. You do not usually give major responsibility to a known "pigeon."

So why do we glorify GOD? This Being of all power, Who created the universe, placed in charge of it His highest creatures, two humans. They defied Him. He could have terminated the species, but did He? Nooo! He put into operation a plan to save them. He sent a perfect law—humans violated it. He sent generations of prophets—humans killed them. Had He learned His lesson? Would you believe He then sent His own Son among them? And they crucified that sinless Son! What is wrong with GOD? Is He naive? Is He stupid?

No, He is a father.

"Pigeons" succumb to scams because they are gullible. Parents keep working with children because their love is greater than any disgust they may have for the bad things their children do. GOD knows I am a sinner—but He keeps trying to redeem me because I am His child.

> *...but wait for the promise of the Father, which, saith He, ye have heard of Me. Acts 1:4*

March 24, 1996

June 6

The Year of the Boy

"Where will I find a good man?" she asks, innocently. "I have been reared in a Christian home, and I have committed my own life to Christ. I have finished school and I have a good job. I want a home and children. So where do I go to find nice Christian young men with standards, principles, and aspirations?"

The wise old pastor wrinkled up his brow and looked at the floor. He could tell her how to find Christ, or good insurance, or a job. But the answer to her question was not easy. "Well, daughter," he began, "we have to eliminate some first. We must eliminate those who are in jail or on parole; then those who have already dropped out of school; then those on drugs or addicted to alcohol; then those who are gay. Cut out those who have no ambitions and finally slice off those who do not share your faith in Jesus. If there are any left who are not already married, they are your prospects."

We ought to work to make that description less accurate. We should dedicate to GOD the best skills we have toward raising the standards of African-American males. We have been entrusted by GOD to be stewards of all He has given us—and that includes doing a better job of rearing boys. It is not good that we push our girls to succeed and to rise above poverty, ignorance, and crime and fail to push our boys likewise.

We must hold our males to these same high standards. Then when our girls ask, "Where can I find a nice man?" we can say with honesty (and with justifiably inflated chests), "Our community is full of them!"

O man, what is good; and what doth the LORD require of thee, but to do justly, and to love mercy, and to walk humbly with thy GOD? Micah 6:8

September 2, 1990

160

June 7

Out of Gear for GOD

We have all had the experience. Your car has had to be pushed. Maybe the battery went dead, or the starter wouldn't turn over. Maybe you were at the car wash, and the tires needed to be sprayed, so the wheels needed to be rolled a half-turn. But for some reason pushing by humans had to replace locomotion by engine. And somebody has called out to the driver, "Take it out of gear!" You moved the gear shift from Drive or Park into Neutral. And with a few grunts, human pushers moved the car from point "A" to point "B" (even if it is just a few feet).

Automobiles are made to be moved by their own engines, and the driver determines movement by engaging the car's transmission. But if for any reason the car needs to be moved by a force external to its own engine, whether pushed by humans or towed by another vehicle, it is necessary to disengage the transmission. The gears which help the car to move when it is moved internally become a hindrance when it must be moved externally. All drivers understand this. (To non-drivers, this is incomprehensible gibberish.)

So it is when you want to be directed by GOD.

161

You are built to determine your own direction. You are a magnificent machine, and your mind is the transmission that moves you. Your natural inclination is to establish your own goals, your own style, and your own pace. But if you want to be the best you can be, you have to ask GOD to direct you. Now, that requires a surrender of that mental transmission that tells you when to go forward, when to back up, and when to park. He has a powerful Pusher called the Holy Spirit. That Pusher can move you slowly or swiftly, forward or backward, even tell you when to stand still—but only if you put your transmission into neutral. You cannot determine what job you will do, or who you will associate with and who you will reject. You cannot select comfort as over against hardship. You cannot even drive toward profit as over against scarcity. But when the Holy Pusher is behind you, you cannot go too far or too fast or in any wrong paths.

Solomon counsels the wise to trust in the LORD with all your heart and lean not unto your own understanding. In all your ways, acknowledge Him, and He shall direct your paths.

So take your ego out of gear; let go and let GOD!

Trust ye in the LORD for ever: for in the LORD JEHOVAH is everlasting strength. Isaiah 26:4

May 25, 1997

June 8

"I'll Make Me a Man"

Those are the words of GOD, according to James Weldon Johnson's familiar folk poem, "The Creation." Johnson, portraying the picturesque language of the old slave preachers, describes GOD as musing over His creation, finding it not quite complete and deciding that as the crowning feature of that creation, He will fashion from the dust His finest creature—a man.

But the sixteen-year-old who has just been hustled into the booking area of the County Juvenile Detention Center, dirty, sullen, and bloody from the knife fight that left dead the elderly man he was trying to rob, hardly looks like what Johnson depicts. A middle school dropout, functionally illiterate, mentally bruised by cocaine addiction, and here for the third time, he seems hardly more than one of GOD's lower animals.

Our mission is to restore him.

162

So we talk about missions, not with deserving residents of the nursing home, or with truly needy children in the projects, nor even with cancer or AIDS patients who are innocent of any crime, but with the unlovely, the guilty, the disposable, "undesirable" part of GOD's creation—boys who need GOD's redemption just as they needed GOD's creative hand.

Today is more than a day to editorialize about how awful racism is, or how inefficient our government or our system of education is, or even how ashamed ought parents of such boys to be.

Any day is a good day to confess that we are either part of the solution, or we are part of the problem. It is a time to stand up to be counted for GOD and for this and for all bedraggled black males for whom He sent His Son to die.

This is a time to say, "I can help to restore at least one broken black boy. And I will."

Thou madest him a little lower than the angels; Thou crownest him with glory and honor, and didst set him over the works of thy hands.
Hebrews 2:7

September 30, 1990

June 9

Tommy Did It

He was the only boy in a house of three girls, and he was the baby. So it was an unwritten rule that almost anything he did would be frowned on by somebody. It was not just that he was curious, energetic, quick to explore, and 100% boy. It was that he was the most handy person to blame when something was broken or spilled. Tommy was a male.

The tragedy is that this situation is more often grim reality than cute joke in the black community. We seem to have a built-in inclination to downgrade and demean the black male, to push our girls to achieve and to succeed while we let our boys slide as though they should not be expected to do well anyway.

We are challenged to develop strong Christian men.

Because GOD blames males, too.

His first human creature was a male, and He laid upon Adam the responsibility for sin. It did not matter what Eve did. GOD punished not the woman, but all human beings because when heads of families go wrong or become weak, then all society suffers.

Why crime and delinquency? Why corruption everywhere? Why injustice and brutality? Because fathers have not put GOD first and their own families second. Why the deterioration of the social order? Why the breakdown of family values? Bad mothers must take some blame. But mostly GOD charges absent, weak, or sinful fathers. Let's work on human rights and economic advance, but first, we need to work on Tommy.

Hear, ye children, the instruction of a father, and attend to know understanding. Proverbs 4:1

September 13, 1987

June 10

You Need Your Daddy

Every large urban city has such a scene. A large luxury car—Cadillac, Lincoln, usually a bit bruised and battered, but still running—is parked on the sparse grass outside a shanty. It looks so incongruous, since the driver of the car does not even own the shanty and may be behind on his rent. (The driver is usually male.)

It is a grim parable of the priorities of the times.

We have developed such sophisticated tastes that nobody is without color television or expensive athletic shoes or at least one designer garment. We rear children in advanced school systems that feature computers and well-equipped sports programs, where pre-school day care has replaced grandmas and play aunties, and even the pre-schoolers are unchecked by profanity in movies and on television.

164

But our Cadillac of twentieth century sophistication is parked in front of a run-down family structure, most often with the father or father-figure either absent or inactive. We blame the media or the withdrawal of prayer from the schools for our problems of crime, teen pregnancy, and poor school performance. But the real problem is that we have not honored GOD's blueprint for the social older.

GOD made the first human a male; then created a female as a mate for him and commanded them to begin families. He still demands that men serve as fathers or father-figures, not as predators after money, women, other men, or all three. When men return to the task of fathering, then many of the disorders of our society will be corrected. That does not require higher taxes or more prison-beds. It requires solid homes before the Cadillac.

And GOD blessed them, and GOD said unto them, Be fruitful and multiply, and replenish the earth, and subdue it: and have dominion over every living thing that moveth upon the earth. Genesis 1:28

June 16, 1991

June 11

Let's Lift an Image

The irony of it is that a day meant to glorify is a day that brings pain to many. The image of "father" is positive in many communities of the world. Our history has marred that image, from the male slave forcibly separated from his mate and children to the shiftless modern black male who impregnates but does not support.

And yet, we can look beyond the black male who did not function as a true father, to the One Who is indeed a true Father. If your own daddy did not do well by your family, send up praises to GOD, Who always has been, is now, and always will be, the absolute best Father you can imagine.

So if you have or had a good daddy, thank GOD for blessing your family with him. It is common in the African-American community to "diss" black males, whether fathers, husbands, sons, boyfriends, or "n——" in general. We do it with a certain gentle humor, but we tend to give brothers a hard time. Let's shut down the "dissing"; let's encourage young black males to look at good role-models, and to commit to being good husbands and fathers even before committing to being rich and powerful.

165

GOD has shown us how he can use flawed fathers. Abraham, Isaac, and Jacob; Moses, David, and Solomon all had serious problems being good fathers. But GOD took those daddies with clay feet and made them a blessing to us all. He can take that black male who spent too little time with his children, who abused his wife and showed too little tenderness for his offspring, whose drinking or gambling or philandering made him the subject of neighborhood gossip, and pass on through him some good genes or an example of hard work or a bright mind. He can make even shaky daddies a blessing to their children and to those who follow them.

But now, O LORD, Thou art our Father; we are the clay, and Thou our potter; and we all are the work of thy hand. Isaiah 64:8

June 17, 2001

June 12

Be a Man

When a boy hears this admonition, he understands what is being expected of him. He should be strong. He should be able to stand stress and not buckle under pressure. He should be willing to face without fear, an adversary, and to do battle in sport or in combat, and win (or, if he loses, give a good fight). He must not be soft—a man is tough.

But if he wants to be a Christian man, his Model is One who shows some other qualities.

Jesus had more courage than a multitude of normal men, but He was soft enough to respect women, to embrace children, to respond to the outcast. Soft? He did not call us to win—He called us to love!

In fact, Jesus loved us—and even a person of feeble mind could tell that only a patsy would love proven sinners. He loved us enough to die for us and to receive unto Himself us who had rejected Him.

You want a boy to be a man? Then tell him not to copy the athlete or the street fighter. Tell him to copy The Man.

166

Let this mind be in you, which was also in Christ Jesus. Philippians 2:5

February 18, 2001

June 13

Fathers Are Custom-Made

We are blessed that GOD designed daddies. Moses tells us in the Genesis creation story that after GOD had made all things, He wanted somebody to manage them, so He fashioned Adam and Eve to run His universe. And His first order to them, even before charging them to "subdue" and "have dominion" over the universe, was to bear children: to "multiply and replenish the earth" (Genesis 1:28). Parenting preceded sacrifices and temples.

Your father living or dead? Present with your family or absent? Loving or abusive? No matter—somebody played a father-role for you. Your real daddy? Uncle, grandparent, principal, teacher, coach, neighbor? If he is living and you have access to him, you ought to tell him you are thankful that GOD put him in your life. If he is no longer living, or you do not have access to him, you ought to praise GOD today for him anyhow, and you ought to try to guide some child as your father or father-figure guided you.

"Father" is not a twelve minute act that produces a baby—it is a life of shaping somebody's character, of producing another person who lives by principles and values. It's O.K. to wear a Superbowl ring or to become CEO or to exhibit a Grammy. But men ought to strive to become a good daddy to somebody—their own children or those of others—and to counterbalance the pain caused by men incarcerated or guilty of abuse or addicted to substances. GOD made boys to become men and men to become daddies and daddies to mold children into strong and productive Christian citizens.

167

Like as a father pitieth his children, so the LORD pitieth them that fear Him. Psalm 103:13

June 16, 2002

June 14

You Are Wonderful—I Love You

These words are powerful. They can produce adults of astounding strength. They can turn out super achievers. They can generate people who demonstrate genius in complex fields, superior leadership among strong peers, wisdom beyond academic learning, compassion reaching deep into the underclasses. All of that can be stimulated by a few words of affirmation, repeated over and over again.

Somebody said these words to us, and we achieved.

I saw a moving story of Siamese twins, so conjoined that they were one body with two heads—one arm and one leg belonging to one body, the other limbs to the other. There were two hearts beating in this double body, now eight years old. The two heads were pretty blonde girls each with her own personality, but working in such perfect coordination that they/she ran, rode bicycles, swam, played softball as though they really were one rather than two!

168

The beauty of the story was not these physical accomplishments, but the fact that they accepted themselves as normal, and were confident they could do anything any other child could do (except cartwheels, they said). Their parents never told them they were sideshow freaks or needed to hide from society. They said to them, and to the television interviewer, that they were wonderful and that they loved them.

Just as it made us do our best when somebody told us that we were wonderful, and they loved us, so we can impact the lives of children (or other people) by giving them strokes in a world which often discourages and impedes. Hug somebody. Tell others they are wonderful—not just once, but repeatedly—and watch them rise to heroic levels of performance!

And ye are complete in Him, which is the head of all principality and power. Colossians 2:10

March 26, 2000

June 15

Today Daddy Is King

For yesterday and tomorrow, he can be once again a bum, the butt of jokes, the scapegoat to blame for whatever has gone wrong. But on the third Sunday in June, we honor fathers. The strength of families depends on them. The breakdown of the social order can be traced to their absence or to their weakness. GOD deliberately fashioned the family so that it would be headed by a male and a female. Neither can provide complete parenting alone. Fathers are a key ingredient to the properly functioning family, and properly functioning families are essential to the building of character, the development of ideals, the growth of a work ethic, even a healthy faith in GOD.

We can laugh at daddies. We can "diss" daddies. But we need daddies.

GOD, Who is not a sexual being, is commonly called "Father" and sets the example for perfect Fatherhood. A society without fathers becomes a sick society (check out what is happening to our own even as you read these lines). Since GOD is the model for daddies, we ought to teach our boys to pattern their behavior after Him, long before they become fathers.

169

Find a daddy to hug—and thank GOD for daddies!

And [He] will be a Father unto you, and ye shall be my sons and daughters, saith the LORD Almighty. II Corinthians 6:18

June 16, 1996

June 16

I Want to Know, Do You Love My Jesus?

There is a direct relationship between what you love and what you talk about. Does money figure prominently in your conversation? Then you cannot deny that dollars turn you on. Are you constantly chattering about cars or music or clothes or sports? The topic indicates your preference. There is a grim indication in the conversation of a child who never mentions Mama or whose child- talk never talks about Daddy. Now, be honest with yourself. How often does Jesus come up in your casual conversation with non-church contacts?

It is normal to reflect on our mandate as the church of Jesus Christ to tell the world about Him. And we spend thousands of dollars on missions and on the needy, and regularly pray for hundreds of people. A few of us even go to the streets to proclaim Christ as LORD and Saviour.

170

But the real proof of our love for Jesus is in our daily, informal conversation. If we can learn in fifteen minutes that we love our mate and children, Bill Cosby, Whitney Houston, and fishing, then Jesus should be in that series (and not behind fishing). Our talk ought to periodically bounce back to Him.

"Missions" is not an enforced duty. Telling the world about Jesus is the natural effect of a personal relationship with Him. When we got that special autograph, or won that trophy against tough competition, or bought the best house on the block, we broadcast it excitedly to friends and strangers.

You love Jesus? Glad He has purchased your redemption with His blood? Feel His blessing coming through day by day? Then get excited about it. Tell the folks at lunch; mention it to the office staff (carefully); bring Jesus up to the friend who asks for advice. Tell it wherever you go!

And that repentance and remission of sins should be preached in His name among all nations. Luke 24:47

May 29, 1988

June 17

Ingredients of a Man

If a boy-child survives infancy, early childhood, and adolescence, and reaches the legal age of adulthood, he is officially called a man. There is nothing qualitative about the term "man." Police blotters may make it a matter of cold gender: "suspect, now in custody, is a seventeen-year-old man." This distinguishes a male robber or killer from a female one.

But we define "man" as more than "male." We want to see a boy live up to the highest of all standards—what GOD intends in an adult male. And GOD has made it crystal clear what He wants adult males to be. His mandates are in the Shema of Israel (Deuteronomy 6:4-7), in the Commandments He gave through Moses (Exodus 20:1-17), and in the directive He gave through His prophets (cf. Micah 6:8). But just in case we did not get the picture clearly, He sent a Model to show us what a real Man is.

171

The Boys' Rites of Passage Program* is rooted in the ancient traditions of Africa, but is not limited to teaching them what good African or African-American manhood is. We want them to know what are the ingredients of the best in manhood. So we look at the Shema, and we revisit the commandments, and we marvel at the succinct pronouncement of the prophet; but we focus on the Model, the perfect portrait of the ideal Man GOD wants us to emulate.

We teach our boys reverence for GOD and love for His word, respect for elders, a sense of their history, exaltation of their women and protection for children, a strong work ethic, and fundamental integrity. We want them to have the best ideals of African-American manhood. But most of all, we teach them the message of a line from an old Negro spiritual: "I want to be more and more like Jesus."

And GOD said, Let us make man in our image, after our likeness.
Genesis 1:26a

February 20, 2000

---

* Boy's Rites of Passage is a character-building program for 11-16 year-old boys.

June 18

Everybody Has a Daddy

GOD makes no mistakes. Whatever He creates, ordains, or allows has a purpose. It matters not whether we understand its purpose. There is one, and it fits into His own master plan for the ages.

He designed the human race to be headed by adult men and women. The father figure was deliberate, intentional, and based on divine wisdom. With all respect to feminists, GOD obviously intended for one of the adults to be the head of the family and to establish the principles by which the children should be reared. That, properly, is the father-figure. The other adult was clearly intended to provide the nurture and the higher sensitivities by which the children would be elevated to compassion, truth, and faith. That logically is the mother-figure.

172

Now, many millennia after GOD established these roles, the family is corrupt, broken, and confused with conflicting roles. A large percentage of the world's families have no father present in the home at all; another huge chunk of the world's families have weaker impotent fathers. This situation forces mothers to attempt to play both roles simultaneously; and often they play neither role well.

The father-figure is not expendable. We cannot have a fully effective family when the father is either absent or weak (Yes, mother-headed households have done miraculously well, but they have not been what GOD intended originally.)

However, GOD's Will will be done.

So He compensates for the absence or the weakness of fathers by strengthening mothers, or providing father-figures from elsewhere (Uncle Jake or Principal Smith or Reverend Johnson or Daddy Sweetback). If we do not get our principles from a father who sired us, who provides for us, who loves us, who disciplines us, and who challenges the best in us, then we will get our principles from someone else—a strong mother who must father us as well as mother us, or misguided peers who will pull us down rather than up. There is no option about having a father; there is only an option about who that father will be.

Get wisdom, get understanding: forget it not; neither decline from the words of My mouth. Proverbs 4:5

June 17, 1990

June 19

Remember—And Tell the Kids

There is a Texas anniversary called "Juneteenth." It commemorates the day, June 19, 1865, when news reached Texas through Galveston that the slaves had been emancipated by Presidential proclamation two and a half years before, on January 1, 1863. Slave holders simply withheld the news from slaves and abolitionists here in Texas, so they could get out one more crop before Union soldiers showed up in Galveston with the proclamation and its order to release all slaves. So while most African-Americans celebrate Emancipation Day on January 1, Texans have been celebrating it on June 19, Juneteenth.

So who cares? Who needs to commemorate slavery?

GOD ordered Israel to remember their deliverance from slavery and to hold a solemn feast every year. Even wealthy and pampered Jews observe Passover.

We do not need to be morose or melancholy; but we need to remember (a) the pains of our forebears in slavery and Jim Crow and (b) the goodness and power of GOD, Who was the real Emancipator. Move forward, but do not forget from whence we came!

173

Then beware lest thou forget the LORD, which brought thee forth out of the land of Egypt, from the house of bondage. Deuteronomy 6:12

June 23, 2002

June 20

Sunshine & Storm

It was an odd contradiction—a "pleasant funeral." The lady who had died was one of those rare souls loved by everybody. She was gentle, sweet-spirited, unfailingly cheerful, and deeply compassionate. One might have expected uncontrolled grief at her memorial, as friend after friend eulogized her. But it was as though her spirit hovered over all the congregation, whispering comfort and encouragement to every person who was tempted to weep.

Every once in a long while somebody lives among us who warms the chill in our society, who brightens the somber moods of our pain-filled days. And he or she impacts our lives, even when we do not realize it. We left that funeral uplifted, not because of the eloquence of the speeches or the beauty of the music—but because her aura of peace had caressed us and quieted our troubled hearts.

174

Remember the old story about an argument between the sun and the wind about who could affect people the most? Each claimed that he could remove the cloak of a traveler below. The wind blew into a mighty tempest, and the traveler's cloak flapped violently, but he held it more tightly and would not let it go. Then the sun shined rays of warmth on the traveler; and as the sweat beaded his brow, he loosened, then removed, his cloak. The sun had won. Warmth had triumphed over power.

How many titans and tycoons and potentates have died unmourned, despite their wealth and influence? How many celebrities have had crowds at their lavish funerals, but few if any who really felt close to them? And yet you know somebody whose sweet spirit, whose sunny disposition, whose GODly compassion makes them far more precious to us than the rich or powerful could ever be.

Ask yourself how you affect those around you. Are you power or warmth? Do people see in you one who achieves much or one who loves much?

Ye are our epistle written in our hearts, known and read of all men.
II Corinthians 3:2

July 8, 2001

June 21

How's Your Tilt?

Today is the first day of summer. That means that today is the longest day of the year. The length of days, we were told in school, is determined by the way the earth is tilted toward the sun, and by whether, in our oval orbit, we are closer to or further from the sun. So today we should be tilted just right and close enough, so that we get maximum exposure to the sun.

And our day is longer.

The writer of Proverbs admonishes us to trust GOD with all our heart. He even tells us how to lean: "lean not unto thine own understanding." If we acknowledge GOD in all our ways, he continues, GOD will direct our paths.

If we are properly tilted toward GOD, we will ask for His direction in every decision we make. We will depend upon Him for a job, for a mate, for guidance in child-rearing, for a choice of house or neighborhood or business partner. And if GOD helps us to make decisions, our days will be longer, and more sunny.

Trust in the LORD, and do good; so shalt thou dwell in the land, and verily thou shalt be fed. Psalm 37:3

June 26, 1994

June 22

How to Become an Eagle

The wide-eyed fifth grader dreams of doing it some day. She gazes at Venus and Serena Williams overpowering every opponent on the tennis court. He is spellbound as Tiger Woods strolls across the green defeating the finest golfers in the world. How can he or she become the best, too? What he or she does not see is the hard work that is not televised. How many hours, weeks, months of practice and exercise and study go into the spectacular game that leads to the trophy? What is the daily routine that makes the difference between a beginner and a champion?

The key is "daily."

Rain or shine, cold or hot, feeling great or lousy, every day demands eating right, plenty of water, strenuous exercise—and all that before you pick up the racquet or the clubs! There is no guarantee that if you go through a rigorous daily routine you will be a world celebrity; but there is a guarantee that if you do not spend the hours, the weeks, the months of practice and personal discipline you will never rise above mediocrity. The best requires hard work every day.

Would you believe that the same thing prepares you for the stresses of life?

How do some folks face crises with such strength, such wisdom, such spiritual power? They have a daily regimen of plugging into the Omnipotence of GOD. You and I may be devastated when grief strikes or an unexpected sickness floors us or the job we gave so many years to is snatched away from us. But those with a daily discipline of prayer and feeding on GOD's word and praising Him just because He is worthy can renew their strength; they can mount up on eagles' wings; they can walk, even run, and never tire. Isaiah says it—and you can take it to the bank!

> *...the GOD of Israel is He that giveth strength and power unto His people. Blessed be GOD. Psalm 68:35*

October 13, 2002

June 23

Choose Your Sweat

One day your life changed forever. You may remember it as though it were yesterday. It was clear, it was graphic, it was dramatic and traumatic; it is frozen in time—no time before or since like the day you accepted Jesus Christ as your Savior. Or you may have no clear picture of it at all. One day when you were eight, or ten, in Vacation Bible School or Sunday School or at Youth Camp, you went forward with two or six or ten other kids to give your life to Jesus and tell the preacher/teacher/sponsor that you wanted to join the church and be baptized. No lightning. No fireworks. Not even a day and month and year emblazoned in the heavens. You just came to Jesus.

However it happened, it changed you forever. You were instantly qualified for Heaven, and could have risen that very moment to be forever in that bright realm of eternal joy. You needed no other qualifications than that you gave your life to Jesus.

But you did not rise that instant. You are here amidst the corruption and the war and the injustice and the poverty and the miseries of this side of the Jordan. Why did GOD qualify you for Heaven and leave you in Texas (or Illinois or Louisiana or New Jersey)?

The answer is simple: There is a job for you here—on this side of Jordan.

GOD needs you to work among children. Or young people. Or senior citizens. Or the addicted. Or the incarcerated. Or the aristocratic. You can select your place of service for Christ. The one option you do not have is idleness. Your growth in faith depends on your working somewhere. "Use it or lose it" applies to your spiritual muscle as much as to your physical sinews. You have to work, because you have given your life to a working GOD. So browse through the smorgasbord of opportunities for Christian service and labor, find one that fits your own gifts, and roll up your sleeves. That is the reason you're still down here.

My Father worketh hitherto, and I work. John 5:17

October 14, 1990

June 24

Keep Moving

It was a minor detail in the news story—and long after the incident it reported it hit me. It was a parable about life with Jesus Christ.

Rescuers had found the young people on the side of the mountain, over five thousand feet up. The temperature was far below freezing, and three of them were stranded in the snow. They had been there almost three days when the rescue helicopter arrived. Two of them had serious frost-bite and could not use hands or feet. But one seemed to have resisted the damage of the icy cold weather and showed surprisingly little damage to his extremities.

How could he have survived that long in those temperatures without significant freeze-damage? I read the question of the medics, and his answer, but the significance of both the question and the answer was slow seeping through this dull brain. He said, "I kept dancing and clapping my hands. I couldn't let myself sleep because I knew I might freeze."

178

What an object lesson!

Are you in danger of freezing spiritually? Are you too Still and passive, so that the frigid air of soul- lethargy is numbing your sense of praise and dependence upon GOD and joy in His service?

Then don't just sit or lie there! Praise GOD in private and in public. Talk to Him every idle moment you have, thanking Him for His blessings, seeking His guidance, interceding for folks you know and issues you know about. Witness about His goodness to you every opportunity you get to include Him in your conversation. Don't be a "pew warmer"; find a place where you can serve in the church, in an institution or in your neighborhood. Keep moving and you will stay spiritually alive.

...the life which I now live in the flesh I live by the faith of the Son of GOD, who loved me, and gave Himself for me. Galatians 2:20b

January 28, 2001

June 25

The Person You Love to Hate

Good television has it. Fine opera features it. Award-winning movies (even animated cartoons) make it a point to include it. Great plays write it into their scripts.

Scripts have to have a bad character.

Somebody has to oppose or frustrate the good folks, and he or she may even be murderous. But we pay our money to go to see the tension between the heroes and the villains—even when the plot is convoluted so that the line between them is fuzzy.

There have been people in your life you once hated; and now you respect their memory. They were the stern parents, the tough teachers, the relatives and neighbors who would not let you get away with sloppy behavior. At the time, they may have been monsters in your mind. They pounded you with demands for excellence over and over and over again. You got sick of their rejecting your mediocre efforts and pushing you to do it again, or to do it better. But now you reflect on your mathematical skills or your writing abilities or your championship trophies, and you are glad that teacher or that coach or that parent kept pushing.

179

Any good commercial writer knows that repetition sells products. So even that villainous daddy or monstrous biology teacher who was your worst enemy, now you see him or her as a good friend.

You ought to push yourself to read the New Testament. Listening to an old, old story, repeated hundreds of times over the last two thousand years, you may find a new quality coming into your life, a new maturity that helps you to deal with the daily challenges you must face. It may seem a villainous task when you start; but you will look back and remember how you were helped to grow as you were pounded again and again by the force of the Word of GOD!

My son attended unto my wisdom, and bow thine ear to My understanding. Proverbs 5:1

April 24, 1994

June 26

Pushoff Is Critical

At the Olympics, dozens of hard-muscled young people are given last-minute pep talks by coaches speaking in dozens of languages. And they pound home to their young charges almost the same message, whatever the language: "Make sure you have a strong start!" What happens when you spring from the board or take the first steps of your routine or push off from the starting blocks may determine whether you bring home gold, or silver, or bronze, or disappointment. The very first movement can give you the edge or cost you the victory.

How faithful a son or daughter of GOD will we be this year? How hungry and thirsty for GOD's word? How constant in prayer? How responsive to the needs of a neighbor? How good a role model for the children who watch us daily? We can begin to determine how "good and faithful" a servant we will be by starting today as we praise Him with fervor, as we remember Jesus and suffering in the LORD's Supper, as we pray for those who will be baptized this evening, as we quietly resolve to spend more time with GOD and be a better mate or parent or son or daughter or sibling or co- worker or friend.

If we have a powerful pushoff today, we can have a dynamite year!

180

No man, when he hath lighted a candle, covereth it with a vessel, or putteth it under a bed; but setteth it on a candlestick, that they which enter in may see the light. Luke 8:16

September 1, 1996

June 27

I Was Sick & Ye Visited Me

In one of the most remarkable vignettes in all of literature, Jesus paints a picture of the final courtroom session in history. This dramatic glimpse into the future makes Jesus the supreme judge, and all humankind is on trial to determine whether we shall be acquitted of our sins and admitted into the Kingdom of Heaven or found unredeemable and sent into eternal punishment. Tune in to the courtroom drama in Matthew 25:31-46.

The viewer quickly notices the absence of some criteria for Jesus' favor. He does not judge us on our church attendance, or our love for scripture, or our generosity in giving to the church, or the years we have invested in church, or the position to which we have risen over those years. None of these is mentioned as credit-worthy.

The basis of acceptance into His kingdom, according to this powerful courtroom vignette, is how we have treated those who suffer.

If you have never suffered in your life, you will not understand the agony of those who are passed by in their suffering. But if you have ever felt the compassion and the caring of somebody who spent time and energy helping you when you suffered, then you know how valuable that caring is. And since you know how important it was to you to have somebody to visit you or to minister to your needs, then you know why Jesus considered such compassion a critical qualification for His kingdom.

181

Next time you learn about somebody who is sick or hungry or in trouble, think about which side of that courtroom you want to be on when Jesus takes the bench!

When the Son of Man shall come in His glory, and all the holy angels with him, then shall He sit upon the throne of His glory. Matthew 25:31

June 29, 1997

June 28

He Couldn't Mean It

You know, you cannot take literally everything the Bible says. There has to be some common sense balance between direct obedience and interpretation before obedience. Yes, the Bible says that if your right eye or your right hand offends you, you should gouge it out or amputate it (Matthew 5:29, 30). Now you know Jesus does not mean that! We are told, by Jesus, that it would be easier for a camel to go through a needle's eye than for a rich man to enter into the kingdom of GOD (Luke 18:25). You have to give a common sense interpretation to that statement. Of course, Bill Gates is welcome in Heaven!

So when Jesus says that if we fail to feed the hungry or clothe the naked or visit the sick or the incarcerated, we have failed to feed, clothe, or minister to Him (Matthew 25:41-46), we should nod politely and realize that He is speaking figuratively. You simply cannot take literally all these Jonah- and-the-fish statements.

182

Or can we?

When was the last time I visited somebody who was not personally close to me? How often have I provided food or clothing for people other than my family or friends? (This does not include the bags of castoffs for DAV or Purple Heart when you needed to clean out your closets.) How responsive am I to people who cannot do much for me? How open is my door to those who are not only needy but nuisances? Could I have dealt with such people as the men who broke through the ceiling to get their friend to Jesus, or the woman with the issue of blood who grabbed His clothing while He was trying to get to a dying girl, or the thankless lepers, only one of whom turned back?

We had better take literally His words: "Inasmuch as ye have done it unto the least of these my brethren, ye have done it unto me" (Matthew 25:40). Our blessings are tied up in our treatment of the hungry, the sick, the criminal, the outcast!

I was a stranger, and ye took me not in: naked, and ye clothed me not; sick, and in prison, and ye visited me not. Matthew 25:43

September 30, 2001

June 29

GOD Has the Last Laugh

When I was a little boy, there were two things that were certain. I had to go to church, and I was going to get punished for laughing.

The old-fashioned Baptist church was full of funny stuff. The preacher reaching third gear with a staccato "HOCK!" punctuating his sentences, and his tobacco spit-can at the foot of the pulpit. The proper schoolteacher with her pinkie extended as she waved her lace handkerchief while she primly praised GOD. The hefty soprano who hit her highest note when the beetle flew in the open window and swooped under her choir robe.

How can any normal boy keep from breaking up with that much comedy?

And not all the laughable events were on Sunday in the little sanctuary. One of the hardest backhands I ever got was at the bedside of an elderly deaconess who had been diagnosed with cancer. We children had no idea of how crucial was the prayer-circle that was formed around her bed. And when the praying got loud and the "Hallelujahs" made the dogs bark and feet on the floor created weird snare-and-bass patterns, I felt the giggle well up from stomach-pit and erupt in contrast to the prayer-chain.

I got up off the floor whimpering, and thinking I ought to pray— that GOD would strike me dead with lightning.

Later I learned that the deaconess had been told the doctors could find no sign of her cancer and that they marveled at her remarkable recovery. And when I became a man, I remembered—and repented— that I laughed at the fervor of the prayers of the saints, without understanding their warfare. Now I appreciate the power of GOD when the symptoms are grave.

Symptoms do not determine outcome. GOD does. And He waits for our fervent faith.

Now unto Him that is able to keep you from falling: and to present you faultless before the presence of His glory with exceeding joy, To the only wise GOD our Saviour, be glory and majesty, dominion and power, both now and ever. Amen. Jude 24, 25

September 23, 2001

June 30

Faith Is

If someone prays for rain, he should already have his umbrella. That old Indian adage fits times of doubt and uncertainty. There is a boldness that is absolutely essential in receiving miracles. Jesus often said to the sick, "According to your faith, be it unto you." He scolded His own disciples for being unable to cast out a child's demon "because of your unbelief." And He claimed that a portion of faith as tiny as a grain of mustard seed would make possible the re-location of a mountain (Matthew 17:20). Every hospital has marveled at some case where all medical evidence pointed to death but somebody lived on anyhow because of the stubborn faith of themselves and their praying friends.

Ever notice the "present tense" attitude of GOD? His Name is "I Am that I Am." Jesus is without age: "Before Abraham was," He says, "I am." Examine His prayer at the most spectacular of all His miracles: "Father, I thank thee that thou hast heard me. And I knew that thou hearest me always" (John 11:41b, 42a). GOD does not mourn the past nor fear the future, because He controls an eternal present. When we are locked into that control, we can depend upon an eternal present. We can say, "By His stripes I am healed"; "I am saved by the blood of the Lamb"; "I am a child of the King." That is far better than saying, "I am somebody" because it rests upon resources infinite, eternal, and unmovable.

184

We are saints—not after we die—right now. We claim the privileges of sainthood. We tell GOD what we want. Even if He does not choose to give it to us, we stay locked into His love and power and know that He is our Father and we are His child. Whatever His will for our situation, it is an expression of His love for us. The basis of faith is a certainty that we are tightly locked into the love and power of GOD.

Now faith is the substance of things hoped for, the evidence of things not seen. Hebrews 11:1

April 7, 1991

July 1

Make It a Habit

I cannot cook. I mean, I really, really cannot cook. But once I could—at least a few things. My mother taught me, when I was a boy (a couple of hundred years ago) to make cornbread and fix breakfast foods. I even learned to bake steaks and pork chops. But I could never learn to fix a mess of greens or beans, or prepare a turkey, or bake a cake. Now, of course, all that is pre-packaged or frozen or maybe even pre-cooked, needing only to be popped into a microwave (Abe Lincoln and I did not have microwaves).

The problem was, I didn't have, and couldn't get, a recipe that would make it taste like hers. When I asked her how much of what she put in, she would use words like "a pinch" or "a dash" or "until it tastes right." How in thunder do you fix a gourmet meal with pinches and dashes? And the Betty Crocker cookbook did not turn out a proper mess of greens with ham hocks!

She learned as her mother and her grandmother learned—by doing it over and over and over again.

185

In a world where so many things get on your last nerve, and so many days are "bad hair days," and between too little money, too little respect, and too much racism, and you feel like cussing all the time, there must be some way to have a good mess of joy.

There is.

The psalmist says, "I will bless the LORD at all times: His praise shall continually be in my mouth" (Psalm 34:1). That means he practices over and over and over again rejoicing in the goodness of the LORD, until the bad hair days become fewer and fewer and the "Thank you, Jesus" days become a matter of habit. I don't know how much praise per hour you put in—just a dash ought to do it.

I will praise thee with my whole heart: before the GODs will I sing praise unto thee. Psalm 138:1

May 7, 2000

July 2

We Don't Invent—We Discover

I sit here pecking away at this thing that looks like a TV set with a typewriter keyboard, and stop to marvel at what I am dealing with. Thanks to this little box with all its circuitry and a brain whose memory dwarfs that of an Einstein (it can solve problems much more quickly and much more accurately than the brilliant physicist), I can misspell words which it will correct before I notice them, and I can ask what I wrote two years ago in this same space, and in milliseconds it regurgitates for me exactly what and when it was.

I am surrounded by examples of this remarkable box—at the store, in my car, even in my pocket; computers are everywhere, some smaller than the credit cards we cannot live without. Who do I credit for the electronic marvels of this age?

Some say I should thank the team of Bell scientists who developed the transistor in New Jersey in 1947. Others say it belongs to old Albert, whose $E=mc^2$ formula blew away the world of science in 1903.

186

But if the real guts of the computer miracles are the tiny chips of silicon, without which computers would still be the size of your refrigerator, then neither Bell Labs nor Albert Einstein deserves the credit. They depended on an element GOD built into creation: a crystal, element number 14, next to oxygen the chief constituent of the earth's crust. So when GOD created the first humans, He was sifting through stuff He had already made abundant in the dust of the ground!

Before we break our arms patting ourselves on the back about things we think we achieved with our own brains, before we call Mama silly for praising GOD when she is struggling to pay her light bill, let's remember Who is really holding this old world (with all its new-fancied toys) together. Is He worthy of praise, or what?

Praise ye the LORD. Praise ye the LORD from the heavens: praise Him in the heights. Psalm 148:1

August 27, 2000

July 3

Independent Free

It has been many years since the colonists issued the document that declared their independence from England and from King George III. It was the beginning of the best-known democratic government in modern times, and in these years this nation has grown from thirteen weak but determined colonies to the most powerful on earth. Now when new nations emerge from colonial yesterdays, they will generally look to the United States to be their model of government. They look up to us as a model of independence.

Should we be proud of ourselves?

Only if we know who we are. The political independence we celebrate must be viewed in the context of the sacrifice of Jesus. This sacrifice symbolizes the redemptive plan of a GOD Who loves us so much that He would send His Son into our sinful world to pay the ultimate price for our sins. We are not "free," despite the majestic lyrics of our national anthem. Under GOD, we do not have "inalienable rights"—He has final control over us and determines health or sickness, life or death. We are not our own; we are bought with a price. And the price is the blood of Jesus Christ. We were condemned and could not appeal the condemnation. We were slaves to sin and on our way to destruction.

We are made free by the broken flesh and the spilled blood of the only human ever to be completely sin-free. No Congress can grant that freedom. No document, however stately and eloquent, can convey it. Only if we surrender our wills to become bondslaves of Jesus Christ can we experience true freedom. (Jesus avoided the use of "bondslave," John 15:15, but you and I know who we are, and we are totally subject to Him.) So you and I are not independent, but we are free!

If the Son therefore shall make you free, ye shall be free indeed. John 8:36

July 1, 2001

187

July 4

Free for Slavery Selection

Today, our nation celebrates another birthday with yellow ribbons and waving flags. We are ostensibly at peace. We do not have a formidable enemy that we need be worried about. Famous last words?

What a time to rejoice!

But we are slaves to foreign oil, to trade balances, to unhealthy alliances with dictators and shaky governments, and to a world-wide drug market. And where once families, schools, and churches set our value systems for us, those value systems are now set by the media with its powerful advertisers, by government with its potent lobbyists, by local power structures with their profit-oriented priorities.

What a time to mourn!

Independence is a misnomer. Nobody is independent. Everybody is dependent on somebody or something. The only option we have is on whom we choose to be dependent. Depending on whom we select as our master, our life deteriorates; and ultimately, we self-destruct. First, we surrender our beliefs and values; then we watch our institutions wither; finally our family structures decompose; and by that time, our social order has crumbled.

188

Paul very proudly calls himself a bond-slave of Jesus Christ. That means he is free in the truest sense of the word, because only in Jesus has the truth made us free.

Stand fast therefore in the liberty wherewith Christ hath made us free. Galatians 5:1a

July 7, 1991

July 5

So You're "Independent"?

Yesterday our nation commemorated the document that declared our independence from England, the beginning of our pilgrimage to become a free nation. Many years ago a proud group of colonists agreed to sign a document that affirmed that thirteen "united colonies are, and of right ought to be free and independent states." Their declaration was based on "self-evident truths" that they were "endowed by their Creator with certain unalienable rights." The language was noble, proud—and wrong.

At some time in your childhood, you got too big for your britches. You began to glory in your blooming adulthood (probably long before you were an adult). And when you were head-high and ready to challenge whoever dared to cross you, some Mama or Daddy said, "Boy/girl, I brought you into this world, and I'll take you out!" Somebody reminded you that you have to be accountable to somebody.

189

The truth is our Creator did not give us "unalienable" rights—rights that no one can take away from us. Jesus tells a story of a man who did well in business, on the stock market, even won the Power Ball jackpot. He said he would buy his own bank in the Cayman Islands and retire to white beaches, good liquor, and bad women (Luke 12:16-19). Why not? It was all his, and he had gotten it with his shrewdly brilliant money management. He didn't even care what Alan Greenspan did with interest rates. He was filthy rich and could chill forever.

But Luke 12:20 says to this brother, and to Thomas Jefferson, and to you and me, that we have nothing that is "unalienable." GOD said to the blue-chip man, "Fool, I brought you into this world, and I'll take you out—tonight!" (Please excuse the free translation of Luke 12:16-20.)

You and I are servants, not free agents. We work for GOD or we work for Satan. Choose you this day whom ye will serve. And give up the "independent" bit—somebody pulls your chain!

...and not using your liberty for a cloak of maliciousness, but as the servants of GOD. I Peter 2:16

July 4, 1999

July 6

Constitution: Wrong
Bible: Right

Our Constitution carries in its First Amendment a principle of separation of church and state. The government is not to interfere with the church, and the church is not to manipulate the government. They drew a hard line between the sacred and the secular.

GOD ignores our hard line. When Jesus rode into Jerusalem, He was proclaiming Himself not chief priest or senior rabbi, but King of all sinners—and that designation fits every one of us (Romans 3:23). There was no area that belonged exclusively to the business community, no humans who did not need redemption, nobody who was outside the divine law of GOD. "The earth is the LORD's, and the fullness thereof," says the word of GOD—"the world, and they that dwell therein" (Psalm 24:1). Thomas Jefferson and the scholars of the Enlightenment in the 18th century could theorize all they wanted about a separation of church and state. But Jesus marches in as absolute Sovereign over church, state, the seas, the wilderness, all time and all space. Our little fences do not matter to His redeeming agenda.

So while we respect the laws of the land, we consider them subordinate to the Higher Law that allows GOD to judge whatever we do, wherever we are. We are not our own. We are bought with a price— the price of His blood, shed for all people!

190

But now the righteousness of GOD without the law is manifested, being witnessed by the law and the prophets. Romans 3:21

April 16, 2000

July 7

Anchored or Free-Swinging

On July 4th, our nation celebrated over two centuries' years of independence. (For anyone "just an American" their forefathers declared it; for African-Americans, their masters did. But whichever the case, we all received the benefits and responsibilities of this independence.)

This tremendous principle of government by, of, and for the people makes it possible for us to choose or reject our leaders, to rise from peasantry to wealth and power, and even to burn our nation's flag if we are unhappy with her policies. Few places on the earth have such privilege. But with all privilege comes the challenge of responsibility. So actually there is no such thing as "independence." Freedom of choice demands some choices; and all choices come with consequences. Not being dependent upon government means being dependent on oneself or somebody else; and because man is a social being, he is in reality interdependent, tied inextricably to his fellow human beings, their thoughts, and their actions.

But even more tightly, he is tied to GOD.

191

He is never independent either of people or of GOD. Either he is gregarious or he is anti-social. He is helping to build his community, or he is helping to destroy it. He is part of the solution, or he is part of the problem. Whatever he does, he does in the context of other human beings.

And he is never independent of GOD. Either he reveres GOD and is blessed, or he rejects GOD and is punished. He obeys or resists and is sustained or pays the price. No one is "free, black, and twenty-one." Someone may be Black, and he may have survived to become twenty-one, but he is not free. His choice is simple: to be dependent upon GOD or to be dependent upon the enemy.

Imagine the consequences of a wrong choice.

So whatever Thomas Jefferson and his friends meant by "independence," they could not have declared us really independent. The best they could have said was that we would no longer be subject to the King of England. But even that involved a choice. Now, we would be subject to the will of a local electorate.

We either choose our master, or one will be chosen for us.

...for of whom a man is overcome, of the same is he brought in bondage. II Peter 2:19b

July 1, 1990

July 8

What Holds You Up?

When I was a boy, I admired muscles. Some day, I would look like Tarzan. I liked the story of Samson in the Bible and Superman in the comic books. One of the favorite art pieces for me was the graceful yet powerful marble of Atlas, holding up the earth. Here was somebody even stronger than Superman!

Later, in high school, I learned the myth of this Greek figure. I was told that the earth was supported by Atlas, that Atlas was supported on the back of a huge elephant, and the elephant stood on the massive shells of four turtles, and the turtles stood on...

That illustration told me that nothing is truly "independent." That everything depends on something or somebody.

Independence Day, 1776, celebrates the breaking away of the colonies from the power of the English monarchy. But they immediately established a principle of dependency. They would depend on the collective will of the people—the government would be directed by the consent of the governed. If the people did not like a party or a leader, they would divest that party or leader of power.

Not one of us is here because of our brains or our skill or our connections. We stand on the shoulders of our elders and predecessors, and they stand on the legacies of those who went before them. And all of us, even the turtles, stand on the grace of GOD.

"Independence" is a concept, not an actuality.

The GOD of my rock; in Him will I trust; He is my shield, and the horn of my salvation, my high tower, and my refuge, my savior; Thou savest me from violence. II Samuel 22:3

July 5, 1992

192

July 9

You've Come a Long Way, Baby

Mama tells her daughter how to make biscuits from scratch and shares with her the age-old skills of one who has done it a thousand times. Daughter listens, but thinks, "That is too yesterday. I'm gonna show her the coolest method!" So the child checks out the food channel and the Internet and runs to the gourmet store for more sophisticated ingredients. The result is a disaster and she tearfully begs Mama to tell her again how to do it right.

Women have been doing that for a long time. GOD created Eve with a strong partnership role, to supplement the role of Adam. Her daughters have gone through many changes since then—they have been dominated by men. They have pulled away and become a separate community. They have competed with men, even trying to out masculinize them. All of these have resulted in disaster. Now they are asking GOD, "What do you want us to be?" And GOD points to the original format for Eve before she consorted with the serpent. They are the female half of a whole human unit, equally a servant of GOD.

193

Praise GOD for women, who do best when they ask GOD, "How do you want me to do it right?"

There is neither Jew nor Greek, there is neither bond nor free, there is neither male nor female: for ye are all one in Christ Jesus. Galatians 3:28

March 11, 2001

July 10

He Is Worthy

It is hard to understand at six years old. But Big Mama is teaching Chrissie an adult lesson. She has given the child a crisp $20 bill, and she is taking her to the mall to help her buy a gift for Mama's birthday, just two days away. Chrissie's eyes grow wide at the DVD's and video games, but Big Mama gently shoves her past them. There are shoes to die for and silver tank tops. Big Mama silently shakes her head and pushes her along. When they get to the pretty scarves and sparkling earrings, Big Mama tells Chrissie this is the place. But nothing costs less than $10 here. Chrissie asks with the blunt honesty only a six-year-old can display, "Why should I spend most of my money on a gift for Mama?"

Softly but firmly the older lady responds, "Because she is your Mama."

The holiday season approaches, with opportunities for trips, gifts, fun events. We spend more in the final two months of the year than we spend in all of the other ten. And the Holy Spirit, like some firm Big Mama, whispers to us that we ought to give the first fruits of our income, the best of our time, the cream of our talents, to GOD. We need houses and furniture and cars and clothing—and fun. Why should we give our best to Somebody Who needs none of those?

Because He is GOD.

He does far more for us than Mama can. He created, He sustains, He provides, He heals. He rescues. He protects, He comforts, He encourages...He woke us up this morning, while some family was calling the funeral home. He is everything to us; and He provided 10/10ths, 100%, all we have. Know any realtor or car dealer or clothier who does even 1% of that for us? He is worthy. Do we need more reasons?

...worthy is the Lamb that was slain to receive power, and riches, and wisdom, and strength, and honour, and glory, and blessing.
Revelation 5:12

October 20, 2002

July 11

You Oughtta Be Ashamed!

I'm practicing. It's a tough discipline, but I've got to learn it.

I've got to learn to thank GOD for a, b, and c. Oh, I do it all the time—in public. After all, I'm a preacher, and preachers have to be thankful. It's like automatically smiling when you meet somebody. But it's funny how little the smile—or the public thanks—reflects the real you. As this is being written, I am sitting in a hospital room. I have visited this hospital and comforted and prayed for other folks for over forty years; but today I am a patient. I have to be stuck and probed and medicated. I cannot grab a cold drumstick from the refrigerator or dash out to run by the church. I cannot even change the temperature if I am too warm or too chilly. After four decades as a visitor, free to come and go, I am a prisoner in a white cell!

But while I waited in a hall for a test, orderlies rolled a comatose lady past me. From somewhere west of my room, there is a constant groan of somebody in great pain. No, I can't grab a cold drumstick, but when my meal comes, it is a full tray of well-prepared food, not the bland liquid of patients critically ill. And there is no sign on my door keeping out all visitors. I am healthy enough to walk the halls to visit other patients who cannot walk the halls. My family and friends give grief to the staff, while on the same floor someone languishes alone and unvisited. And I dare to gripe about the absence of Dial soap!

So I am practicing.

LORD, you have been so much better to me than I deserve! You have given me the people who enrich my life; the health and strength that belies my age; the comforts that millions would die for; and above all, salvation that I did not deserve, but that Jesus has provided. Help me to thank You for a, b, c, d…

195

Give thanks unto the LORD, call upon his name, make known His deeds among the people. I Chronicles 16:8

June 30, 2002

July 12

Big Brother Is Watching

When George Orwell added that sentence to the national vernacular in his novel *1984,* he was predicting our current information age with its impact on our privacy. But in a real sense, that sentence is a Biblical term, Jesus Christ being our Brother, allowing us to call His Father our own. He watches from the Father's right hand in Heaven, making intercession for us every time we mess up—and we do that daily.

But I hate it when He uses kids!

Once I was driving the van for the Board of Mental Health and Mental Retardation, with a dozen or so Hispanic children from the Austin State School. It was nearing lunch time, and we stopped at a hamburger restaurant to feed them. The bill came to a little less than fifty dollars. I handed the young woman at the register a $50 bill, but I didn't count the change; I was trying to herd the kids to seats to eat. (I am a bit clumsy with a large group of high-energy kids.) Then I noticed that one of the bills I had crumpled up was a twenty-dollar bill. I stared at it blankly, not really thinking. Then I heard a little voice behind me, saying, "She gave you too much money. You are going to give it back, no?"

Smart-aleck kid! Challenging me to act like a Christian! How dare she?

So I took the twenty to the young woman at the register, who would have had to make up the shortage out of her meager wages at the end of the work day. I wanted to feel proud of myself, but I could not. I was pushed to do right before I had time to decide to do it on my own.

GOD always has somebody watching what you say and do. Be sure you keep your witness consistent and according to the principles of Jesus Christ. Some smart-aleck kid may be His agent to check up on your behavior!

Suffer the little children to come unto me, and forbid them not: for of such is the kingdom of heaven. Mark 10:14

196

July 13

Why Do I Need to Praise Him?

He was a kind of idol of mine. I was six or seven, and he was a 'big boy,' probably fifteen or sixteen. He could drive, and he could drink beer, and he could cuss. All us kids wanted to be able to do the things Creighton did. We also wanted to be free like him. He didn't have to go to school any more, and nobody made him go to church. What a life!

He said some really cool stuff, like, "You don't have to go to school to learn. You can learn in the streets;" or, "I don't have to hang around all those shouting women; I can be religious out here." Wow, man, cool!

Now I look back on him and remember him homeless, panhandling pedestrians on Tenth Street, dead of cirrhosis of the liver before he turned thirty-five, with nobody to mourn his loss. And he doesn't appear so cool. His problem was not his drinking or his cussing—not even his dropping out of school. His problem was that he had no need of GOD.

197

There are thousands of Creightons out there.

When you realize that you need GOD for every breath you take, every second of every hour of every day; when you reach up to praise Him as the LORD of your life; when you tell people about His goodness to you, you guarantee an inner joy (even when there are obvious problems). The psalmist says that GOD inhabits the praises of Israel (Psalm 22:3)—that means that if we send praises up, blessings come down. I have learned long ago that not only "shouting women" need to praise GOD; we super-cool dudes need to, too.

The more you think about GOD, the stronger you become to say "yes" to the right things, and "no" to the wrong things. We praise Him just because He is worthy of praise; but praise of GOD pays off, too—big-time!

I will call upon the LORD, who is worthy to be praised. Psalm 18:3a

March 15, 1998

July 14

Where Are Your Children?

If you are married or have been, and have sired or given birth to children, you might expect such a question. You know where they are, what they are doing, and they have made you proud or ashamed. You are happy to talk about them, or you would rather change the subject. You are glad or sorry they are where they are, doing what they are doing.

If you are single and/or childless, you will immediately opt out, since such a question clearly does not refer to you.

The ministry to children is unique. It is not part of the program of a school district, nor a profit- making business providing remedial education for a fee. It is the offering of a church because some people volunteered to do it, at the expense of their own time and convenience. Some of them have biological offspring. Some of them do not. But all of them recognize their GOD-mandated responsibility to offer positive

influence to children in a world where negative influences abound. They have children, even if they never sired or bore them, because GOD has made it possible for them to navigate the hazards of childhood and to become adults, still alive, not behind bars, not fugitives from justice, not mentally destroyed by drugs or alcohol. Through many dangers, toils, and snares, they have already come, and they accept their responsibility to look back and help those youngsters who follow them. They have children.

So do you. If you have already reared yours, you have others. If you have never been a biological parent at all, you have children. Every child who passes through your life, in need of a word of counsel or encouragement from an adult is an assignment from GOD for you. Offer yourself to help some child somewhere. That's your kid!

The rod and reproof give wisdom: but a child left to himself bringeth his mother to shame. Proverbs 29:15

May 24, 1998

July 15

Family—A GOD Thing

Something about July makes it the traditional month for family reunions. Perhaps because school is not in full session, and vacations can be scheduled, and the weather makes travel more pleasant (if your air conditioning is working), July is a logical month. But whether in July or January, it is one of the joys of our existence to gather families to celebrate legacies. And one of the common components of family reunions among Aunt Hagar's children (ask one of your elders who that is) is to gather on Sunday in a church.

That is a significant thing.

It is significant because even family members who do not regularly worship know full well that GOD has sustained them, and makes it possible for them to take the next breath. But aside from His love for us even when we do not recognize or thank Him for it, the church of GOD is a peculiar institution. In a world where institutions of government or education or commerce dominate, the church survives and thrives while governments topple, schools close down, and businesses go bankrupt. How can Pleasant Valley Missionary Baptist Church still be here for 110 years, still surviving on fish dinners while Soviet Communism and Chinese Maoism fade away, while Enron and WorldCom and Arthur Andersen fizzle like wet Roman candles? What does that little cluster of poor Christians have that the federal government does not?

199

They are not "corporation." They are family.

The church is not, nor ever has been, based on products or clients or a constitution. It is based on a relationship with GOD, through His Son, through people who have come to know His Son through billions of witnesses, one at a time. Families fuss but hang together and reunite at Mama's funeral. GOD wisely established His church as a family. We will fuss, but we have to agree: GOD loves us through His Boy!

For as many as are led by the Spirit of GOD, they are the Sons of GOD. Romans 8:14

July 21, 2002

July 16

Love 'Em, & Tell 'Em So

This season of the year is uniquely oriented toward family. It is the time when we salute mamas and daddies. It is the time of promotions and graduations when we praise or challenge our children, and when we shift from school routines to summer programs. GOD loves family. That's why He used that model for His church.

We are thankful for Mama if she is still with us; we honor her memory if she is not. Whatever Daddy's failings are, we are blessed if we have one, living or deceased. And as much as we chide or scold children, during this channel between Mother's Day and Father's Day, when schools of all levels come to the terminus of their year, we can be proud of our kids; or if they need help measuring up, we can focus on their potential. In all cases we ought to praise GOD for family—even for that errant uncle or that nosy aunt. And whether with flowers Mama does not especially want or a sport shirt Dad will seldom wear or with gushing compliments that embarrass the graduate or the honor student, we ought to tell family—especially at this time of year—that we love them.

200

An award dinner for a local citizen ended with a thick glass plaque for him and the usual mandatory standing ovation. This tough business man had achieved great success in a tough urban market. Two things made that award dinner stand out: excellent food that was not built around a bland chicken breast, and a tribute by his four adult daughters. Most of us ribbed him, and so did his daughters. But they ended their jibes with a remarkable statement about him. These four young women, who now had children of their own, said to a hushed audience that in all their combined lives they had never, ever heard their father, this tough, high-achieving businessman, speak an unkind word about anyone. (Pause to start breathing again.)

GOD blesses us if we honor parents—and if we encourage and lift kids to right goals.

He that followeth after righteousness and mercy findeth life, righteousness and honour. Proverbs 21:21

July 9, 2002

July 17

Boss   Go to Work
Choose Your ~~Seat~~ & ~~Sit Down~~

Since last November, the definition of Democracy has shifted considerably. It is less a government of, by, and for "the people," and more a government of, by, and for the powerful. Minorities, women, and businesses and institutions outside the good ole boy network are not players in the power strategies of the late nineties. For some, this is a good reason to weep and mourn, or to rebel and lash out.

This is a time to read again the powerful narrative of the Exodus. The book of Genesis ends with a great picture of a liberal government that celebrated diversity, inclusiveness, and affirmative action. Under Joseph, Hebrew outsiders were given a good land and plenty of opportunity to prosper in Egypt. But when the Conservative Right took over, the Egyptian Supreme Court decreed that these Hebrews needed to be suppressed, and the Egyptian Congress passed laws that pulled the carpet from under them.

201

But the Hebrews did not need power coalitions or wealthy patrons to plead their cause. Somebody higher than the Pharaoh came to their rescue. Right now we may think money or politics has the answer for us. But the best course for us is not freedom from bosses, but submission to the best Boss of all. We can be independent of England, but dependent upon GOD.

And the LORD spake unto Moses, Go unto Pharaoh, and say unto him, Thus saith the LORD, Let my people go that they may serve Me. Exodus 8:1

July 2, 1995

July 18

Am I Guilty?

Did you know that you can be arrested and fined (or even imprisoned) for having knowledge that could save lives and not sharing it? One of the defendants in the case involving the bombing of the Murrah Federal Building in Oklahoma City is a man not accused of planning or carrying out the bombing, but who knew of the plot of McVeigh and Nichols. His crime? He did not warn authorities. Consequently, the deaths of 168 people are partially his burden.

The main reason Jesus established His church was not so that we could sit in an audience and be inspired/entertained—it was so that we could be empowered to witness to His saving grace. Our task is not to listen attentively; it is to tell everybody in every nation in the world about Jesus and the redemption He has wrought through His death and resurrection. Witnessing is not always convenient. It is often ignored, even spurned. Therefore it is easy for us to stop witnessing. Why keep taking gifts to people who don't appreciate them, right?

Wrong.

If we fail to witness, and somebody goes to Hell because we never shared our faith with them, we are as guilty as the man who did not warn the people of Oklahoma City that dozens of them might be killed. The prophet Ezekiel has a powerful passage about "the watchman," and his responsibility to see danger coming and warn the people inside the walls (Ezekiel 33:1-9). If he warns them, and they ignore him, they are responsible for their own fate. If he fails to warn them, GOD blames him for their fate.

Somebody will be condemned because he does not surrender to GOD. That is inevitable. But nobody ought to be condemned because we failed to witness to him about possible salvation through Jesus Christ. GOD is watching us to see how faithful we are on His watchtower.

Then whosoever heareth the sound of the trumpet and taketh not warning; if the sword come and take him away, his blood shall be upon his own head. Ezekiel 33:4

May 31, 1998

July 19

When in Doubt, Pray

At 3:00 a.m., people who are still awake are pretty honest in their thoughts and words. (Of course you can be a hypocrite at 3:00 a.m.!) We listened to people in an all-night prayer meeting as they talked about how GOD had helped them. An interesting thing developed— a common thread emerged among these testimonies. Their experiences differed widely, but they were saying essentially the same thing: GOD responds to us when we are really in trouble, and we turn to Him in prayer.

He provided healing for somebody who was sick. He made available money to keep a child in school or to hold onto a house that was about to be foreclosed. He gave just the right answers to questions on a bar or medical or accounting exam, and the nervous candidate passed. You have surely experienced some of this. Maybe when you are trying to impress your friends and associates, you will claim that you have overcome because you are naturally sharp. But in the middle of the night, you know deep down inside that you've come this far by faith, leaning on the LORD.

203

Since you know that GOD cares about you, listens for you, waits for you to ask for His help, responds to you when you finally do—why not turn to Him more regularly? Jesus says we ought always to pray and not to faint (give up). Paul says we ought not to take sabbaticals from prayer, but should pray without ceasing. David knows how critical is the presence of GOD: If GOD withdraws Himself from him, whither shall he go?

So don't pursue the job opportunity without asking GOD's counsel. Don't get into the relationship without prayer. At 3:00 a.m. and at 3:00 p.m., stay in touch!

If ye abide in Me, and My words abide in you, ye shall ask what ye will, and it shall be done unto you. John 15:7

May 19, 1996

July 20

When the News Is Bad

The media portrays African-American males as violent, likely to be in trouble with the law or actually in jail, subject to alcohol and drug abuse, prone to impregnating but not marrying. Some of that is exaggeration, and the media should be ashamed of itself for such exaggeration.

But too much of it is the truth.

An old adage from Confucius reminds us: "It is better to light one candle than to curse the darkness."

We should turn from ugly news statistics about African-American males and toward the beauty of programs that shape strong Christian African-American men who will not drop out of school, who will not engage in neighborhood violence, who will not father children they cannot rear and support, who will not go to jail, who will be gainfully employed, and who will become role-models for the younger boys who follow them. While we will not deny the truth of negative stories about our boys, we will celebrate the equally-valid truth that some positives do exist.

204

Good citizenship and high standards are important, but they do not guarantee strong character. Some programs have taught boys to love GOD before they love America or Texas or Houston. But we must not give up on our boys. They need to be part of a system where strong men stay on their case until they mature into strong young adults who demonstrate that even against heavy odds, African-American males can become credits rather than embarrassments to their communities.

Even so it is not the will of your Father which is in heaven, that one of these little ones should perish. Matthew 18:14

February 14, 1993

July 21

Bundles of Joy?

Whoever called children "bundles of joy" probably never had three pre-schoolers all crying at once, or tried to keep twenty-eight second graders quiet for fifteen minutes, or faced the cost of groceries, clothing, school supplies, medical costs, and the electronic game that "every other kid in the world has except me." Children have inspired all manner of pain from Excedrin headache #46 to custody battles and are the real basis for the phrase "my last nerve." How can anyone be so naive as to call them, as expensive as they are, as exasperating as they are, as inscrutable as they are, "bundles of joy"?

If maybe we could see with the eyes of GOD, we would understand why He did not complete the task of creation until He had given the first orders "Have kids" (a free translation of Genesis 1:28). Maybe we would know why He gave up on the first generation of adult Israelites and allowed only their children to enter the Promised Land (Numbers 14:29-32). Perhaps, we would comprehend why Jesus was so protective of children (Matthew 18:3-10). What does GOD see in our little monsters that we cannot see?

205

Maybe it is not so much what He sees in children; maybe, it is what He does not see in us. Children are only reflections of the adults around them. They learn selfishness from us. They learn cruelty from us. They pick up our bigotries and prejudice and learn to spout stereotypes and epithets better than we can. So if we have a generation of kids who are too materialistic, have too little respect for elders, no reverence for GOD, and not much confidence in themselves, we must take much of the blame ourselves. They were not born with these weaknesses; they learned them from us!

We can escape responsibility for children easily enough. They can try our patience, to be sure. But GOD has made us responsible for what they learn, for what they do, for what they ultimately become. We can obey His commandments and produce a bright generation of outstanding young people; or we can ignore those commandments and be destroyed by the very children for whom we are responsible!

And these words, which I command thee this day, shall be in thine heart: And thou shalt teach them diligently unto thy children, and shalt talk to them when thou sittest in thine house and when thou walkest by the way, and when thou liest down, and when thou riseth up. Deuteronomy 6:6-7

May 16, 1993

July 22

Down with the Prophets

The elegantly-dressed chairperson (is that an automatically sexist title, guaranteeing that the subject is female?) called the honoree's name, asked him to come to the dais, and with a smile that would have illuminated the Baytown Tunnel, told the audience why he was receiving a plaque: He was respected in the community. Did anyone see him grimace? Was his groan low enough so no one could hear?

What that dear lady meant as a compliment hit him right between the eyes. It was less a compliment than an indictment, when he matched his calling with his reputation. We are not called to be "respectable." We are called to bring the messages of GOD to a stiff-necked and stubborn generation. Surely, no one called Amos up to the stage for a plaque (Amos 7:12-13). Jeremiah was not remembered for being "respected in the community" (Jeremiah 26:11). And if Jesus had only generated smiles and applause at banquets, He would have had to beg somebody to crucify Him!

206

Each one of us has the assignment GOD had given to the prophets: to broadcast the message of GOD to all the people of the world. We cannot endorse the sins of the world. We cannot wink at the corruptions of government and the market-place. We cannot ignore the shabby lives of the leaders of the church. But if we are twentieth century prophets, we will not get plaques and awards. We may not be asked to preach the city-wide revival or to chair the annual banquet. People may not consider us "respectable." But Somebody more important than an elegantly-dressed chairperson will say to us,

"Well done!"

His LORD said unto him, Well done, thou good and faithful servant: thou hast been unfaithful over a few things, I will make thee ruler over many things; enter thou into the joy of thy LORD. Matthew 25:21

April 26, 1992

July 23

Loving the Unfaithful

The six words constitute a miracle: "For GOD so loved the world." The world is fickle, unworthy, completely unlovable. GOD is everything the world is not: holy, righteous, completely free of sin, even unable to allow sin in His presence. And yet, through some cosmic reversal of the normal celestial dynamics, GOD wraps Himself in the flesh of sinful humans, immerses Himself in a human environment, and makes Himself available to die on behalf of humans who did not appeal to Him for redemption, who did not attempt to protect Him from the lynch mob which crucified Him, and who consistently ignore Him to this day.

A few hundred people, mostly poor and uneducated people, hailed Jesus as He rode into Jerusalem on a donkey nearly two thousand years ago. But it was hardly a hero's welcome. He understood its real meaning if those who shouted "Hosanna" did not—He had offered Himself to people who would cheer today, but curse or be absent Friday. He could have snapped a finger in disgust as He looked at the fickle crowd, and whispered to His Father, "Beam me up!" But not Jesus. He, His Father, and the Holy Spirit were in perfect accord about His task now. Man deserved extermination. But GOD did not want that for humankind; and despite our unfaithfulness, despite our callous disregard of GOD and neighbor, GOD—Father, Son, and Holy Ghost—would meet at the cross to lift us from our death row and open for us the door to everlasting life.

207

Yes, you have experienced unmerited favor. You have escaped some punishment you should have suffered or been given some advantage you did not have to work for. But there is nothing in your experience, nothing in all human history, that is anything like the miracle of this King, leading His own parade to His death, representing a consummately holy and righteous GOD, on behalf of totally unworthy and undeserving sinners: "For GOD so loved the world."

He raiseth up the poor out of the dust, and lifteth the needy out of the dunghill. Psalm 113:7

April 5, 1998

July 24

"Gimme a Lift"

A convention participant walked into an office at the Christian Education Conference and nearly stumbled over an object not normally found in an office. It was a bullet-shaped cylinder about four feet tall, nearly a foot in diameter, with a complex arrangement of shuttle-cocks and gauges at its summit, and a finger-sized spigot pointed at the ceiling. "What in thunder is this?" he demanded. (He was the president and presidents can bark like that.) The ladies in the office looked at him with compassion. Obviously, they had to phrase their answer with patience, since their president was too clueless to look at the label on the cylinder, printed in large letters, "Helium—Balloon Baron, Santa Maria, California." But the ladies gently informed him that there was to be a reception with balloons.

Now, a strange contradiction is apparent between what this ugly missile looks like and what it produces. It is ungainly and heavy and is painted a badly-smeared dark brown. But its helium breath makes wrinkled sacks become bright, fat globes of joy, and gives them such a lightness that they float toward the ceiling. When we marvel at the bobbing bubbles of red and gold and blue and green, it is hard to remember that they received their beauty and lightness from such a brown bomb.

We may be neither beautiful nor rich nor brilliant. But we can transmit a word, a deed, an example, that lifts and beautifies. The Spirit of Christ is in us. We should let it out whenever we relate with people and offer them a lift.

Now the GOD of hope fill you with all joy and peace in believing, that ye may abound in hope through the power of the Holy Ghost. Romans 15:13

July 21, 1985

208

July 25

Precious: Family

GOD developed the family in order to implement His purpose: "Let us make man in our image, after our likeness...so GOD created man in His own image, in the image of GOD created He him; male and female created He them" (Genesis 1:26a, 27). The bottom line is that GOD is not an individual. He is a community—Father, Son, and Holy Ghost, all in perfect unity and harmony. When He established family, He intended plurality, not solitude. His first order was to "be fruitful, and multiply, and replenish the earth" (Genesis 1:28b). When families love and support each other, they are most like GOD. When families bicker and break up, they are least like Him.

Think about the relationships in your family. How are you doing with your role of being GODlike? It is so easy to take parents, children, siblings, relatives for granted, to overlook their hurts, their joys, their needs. And all too often we allow oversights to become coolness, and coolness to refrigerate into coldness, and coldness to cause member to break off from member. Somebody has not spoken to somebody who is close blood kin for years because they disagreed about a wife or husband or girl or boyfriend.

209

The word "family" occurs many times in the Old Testament, but only once in the New Testament; and the one time it occurs, Paul uses it to describe both the triune GOD and the earthly families. It takes work, but anything worthwhile does. And it is worth everything to come closer to the Model after Whom we were fashioned!

For this cause I bow my knees unto the Father of our LORD Jesus Christ, Of whom the whole family in heaven and earth is named. Ephesians 3:14-15

July 15, 2001

July 26

Aim at His Hat

It was a grim blend of the fascinating and the repulsive. During the John Gotti trial in 1992, the television interviewer questioned the Gambino hit man. The quiet Sicilian, who admitted to assassinating twenty-seven people with deadly efficiency, on assignment for the Don, described the method of aim that accurately located and penetrated the heart of his helpless victim. "I don't aim at his heart," he drones without emotion. "The bullet arcs, so I aim at his hat-band or his hairline; and I seldom miss."

Ugh!

The interview was grisly, but the principle is applicable to much more positive situations. Life arcs. GOD intends for us an upward path, but Satan pushes it downward. Aiming for mediocrity is fruitless; aiming for the top is admirable. Even if adversity pulls downward against us, a high mark (if not the stars, still the mountain-top) is still possible. We ought to be without sin. Jesus tells us to be perfect. If we aim at sinlessness, we will do more good. If we aim at total devotion to GOD, we will reduce our selfishness quotient. If we try for increasing prayer, we may not make it sixteen hours a day, but we will spend less time in mean or idle thought.

Want to hit heart-felt religion? Aim at the head of GOD.

But when that which is perfect is come, then that which is in part shall be done away. ICorinthians 13:10

March 22, 1992

210

July 27

You or a Rock

What a challenge! Jesus said that if we who follow Him refuse to praise Him, "the stones would immediately cry out." That goes back to the most primitive thing GOD created. On the first day, He made light—an energy. On the second day He made space and water—the earliest matter. On the third day, He made "the dry land," which includes stones—the first solids. There was no life at all until the fourth day—and then only plant life. The final and climactic creature was man, in GOD's image and after GOD's likeness. This marvelous creature was given a soul and favored status. Both man and woman were made to praise GOD. Stones were just made to provide material for the ground on which man would live.

But if man does not fulfill the praise-purpose for which He was created, GOD will make the rocks function as though they had souls and voices!

We spend a great deal of our time providing for ourselves, pampering ourselves, protecting ourselves, promoting ourselves. How much priority do we give to praising the GOD Who made all that possible for us? The week yields 168 hours. One-tenth of that should be spent in worship or study or offering help to somebody in GOD's Name. Does GOD have "dibs" on the first tenth, plus an offering of that $15,000 a year (or measly $150,000) salary? Have those same talents and skills used in making a living been offered to GOD?

No lousy piece of sandstone ought to do our job! We must do what we were built to do! Praise GOD.

To the end that my glory may sing praise to Thee, and not be silent. O LORD my GOD, I will give thanks unto Thee for ever. Psalm 30:12

January 12, 1992

July 28

Play It Again

It is in our home (and maybe in our car, our office, even our purse or briefcase). It is a tiny library—66 books. But it is the most remarkable library ever assembled by human intelligence. "Human intelligence"—we will think about that.

Our little library, called the Holy Bible, is the work of fifty or more authors, writing over a span of 1,500 years, from locations stretching from Babylon on the east to Rome on the west. Not a one of them knew he was writing something to be included in a Holy Bible. Most of them did not know each other. And yet, because it was assembled by much more than "human intelligence," this mini- library is uncannily unified in scope, in content, and in emphasis. Our Bible is unlike any other body of literature in history.

What is even more remarkable is that while we could read it in a week, we cannot drain its contents in a lifetime. No matter how often we re-read its stories, its songs and statutes and prophecies and letters, we discover at each reading some gem of wisdom and inspiration we had not seen before; we have to study the Commandments repeatedly. We have to delve into prophecy continually. We cannot dismiss the Sermon on the Mount with one reading or digest the rich implications of the parables by knowing the narratives alone. This indescribable little library, small enough to fit into our glove compartment, is so big we will never ever exhaust the rich store of truth that pours out of it each time we examine it again.

The best part is that we do not have to interpret it by human intelligence, either. The same Holy Spirit Who wrote it through all those authors makes it clear to us as we read. So play it again, Holy Spirit—we love it!

212

All scripture is given by inspiration of GOD, and is profitable for doctrine, for reproof, for correction, for instruction in righteousness. II Timothy 3:16

November 10, 1991

July 29

Pretty Is as Pretty Does

I had heard this statement repeatedly since before I could remember. It never made any sense to me. Ladies usually quoted it, and they usually said it to girls. Even when our mother said it to our sister, it never occurred to us to wonder why she never said it to us boys. Maybe "pretty" and "boys" belonged to two different dimensions, and nothing we could do would make us pretty.

But now I look back over the thousands of people I have known through the years and I remember that some people with handsome features and arrogant attitudes still looked ugly; while other folk, plain as cornbread but sweet as honey, would have an inner glow that made them beautiful even without satin skin or silky hair or perfect teeth. I understand that "pretty" is not cosmetic, but spiritual.

Wonder if you could swap words in that proverb, and say "Christian is as Christian does"?

It is the time when Christians celebrate the birth of our LORD. We have said we love Him and want to live for Him. We are Christians. But if, at Christmas-time, we are to show our love for the Baby Jesus, how do we demonstrate it? Not by putting up a lavish manger scene in the yard, or by attending three Christmas masses on Christmas or by joining a "Messiah" sing-along. We show our love for Jesus by passing His love on to His sheep (John 21:15-17). Expensive gifts for your own family and friends do not express that love—but a kind act or a cup of cold water to somebody who is neither family nor friend may. Is there a child in your neighborhood or that you know about who needs shoes or a sweater or a doll? Love that child. Is there a lonely senior who could stand to have a phone call or a hug? You should provide it.

213

A pretty person is a person with a pretty heart. A Christian is somebody who acts like one.

And let us consider one another to provoke unto love and good works.
Hebrew 10:24

December 16, 1990

July 30

Good Stuff to Sell

Your best times in life may not be at the party or at the casino. You know that deep joy you feel when somebody whose life has been all downhill comes to Jesus because you persuaded him or her? Don't you feel the thrill when he or she, now in clean clothes and sober for a month, walks (trembling but determined) down the aisle to join a church? You can't equal that feeling when you finish 2 under par! Remember how good it felt when that dying person you visited called to thank you for spending that time with him or her? Can you match that feeling by landing a ten pounder on the second cast? Missions is the core component of the church of Jesus Christ. He never told us to build buildings or to exceed last year's budget. He told us to tell the story of GOD's redeeming love through Christ.

You can't tell the story of GOD's love too often. How often does one furniture salesman tell you he "really will save you money," or another throw his hand in your face because a great sale is "at your finger"? Can you imagine no one yelling about fantastic car buys or the best cell phone on earth?

The world sells its stuff with maddening repetitiveness, interrupting your show, popping up on your screen, hiding the sunset with its billboards. You cannot get away from aggressive sales techniques telling you why Target is better than Sears. We have the greatest product on earth to sell—salvation and the love of GOD for whoever is hurting. How can we not try to persuade a lost world to try Jesus?

214

Go ye therefore, and teach all nations, baptizing them in the name of the Father, and of the Son, and of the Holy Ghost: Teaching them to observe all things whatsoever I have commanded you: and lo, I am with you alway, even unto the end of the world. Amen. Matthew 28:19-20

April 28, 2002

July 31

When All Else Fails...

"...Read the instructions." So goes the tongue-in-cheek advice to people who must struggle with gadgets, devices, and systems. In our increasingly technical age, all of us must struggle with new devices. But the newest and most complex gadget is simple compared to the problems of everyday living. How do we learn to handle a marriage? How do we put together a solid friendship? What is the best method for rearing a child in today's risky environments? What is the technique for dealing with too much sickness or too little income? Quite often, people learn to operate a super-collider more easily than they can pick up the most effective ways to handle such challenges as those.

But, fortunately, we are not given such complex problems without a thoroughly-written instructions manual. Its sixty-six sections tell us about the history of some slaves who became GOD's priest- nation and shares with us the system of commandments and worship which governed them. It lays out for us GOD's plan of salvation for us and tells us precisely how to benefit from it.

What a book of instructions we have!

We can struggle with illness or frictions or unhappiness in relationships or on jobs—and keep making mistakes. Or we can develop the habit of reading GOD's word, always praying for His leadership in the complicated business of trying to be a good mate or friend or employee or parent. When all else fails...

215

For the commandment is a lamp; and the law is light; and the reproofs of instruction are the way of life. Proverbs 6:23

July 28, 1991

August 1

So Who Is Worth Helping

There is no argument that we should have compassion on abused children, widowed women left with meager assets, victims of tragic accidents and acts of GOD. We leap to the aid of people left homeless by hurricane, flood, or fire, or to multitudes starving in lands ravaged by drought.

After all, their plight is not their fault.

But recovering alcoholics? Recovering drug users? Didn't they have the power to just say "No"? It is easier to blame them than to offer help to them (especially if your particular sin is not alcohol or drug abuse). But the story of the adulterous woman in John 8:1-11 has an interesting twist to it. Jesus does not defend the woman's adultery. He simply invites any accuser who is sinless to begin the punishment. The bottom line is crystal-clear: We are all addicts, recovering or still chained to our addictions. Your closet and mine may not yet have been searched; but be assured that we all have to deal with skeletons.

216

So since we are a community of sinners, all offered salvation by grace, it is best that we extend the same accepting love to other sinners that GOD extends to us—that we take seriously the challenge to prove that we are Christians by our love (cf. John 13:35).

Somebody, at some time, gave you a helping hand, a word of encouragement. Perhaps you would not have made it otherwise. Now that you and I have an opportunity to give an encouraging boost to somebody who is trying to overcome his/her problem, let's remember that—and reach out for that person!

But all these things will they do unto you for My name's sake because they know Him that sent Me. John 14:21

October 26, 1997

August 2

Spiritual Boomerangs

When you're smilin',
When you're smilin',
The whole world smiles with you.

You want evidence that I am old? I remember when that song was popular. As a youngster, I just thought of it as a nice toe-tapping ditty. Now, as I gaze backward across years by the score, I hear in its words wisdom beyond their simplicity.

If you want people to respond to you with good cheer, you must convey good cheer. If you would like kindness, you prime the pump by being kind. When you are consistently met with sour faces and cold (or no) conversation, don't judge everybody else as negative until you check your own aura. Are you gentle or sharp-edged? Do you find virtues to commend or faults to criticize? Do you smile or growl most easily? What comes back to you often mirrors what you project.

217

So when I get ready to face the world, I have to remember more than to brush the few teeth I have and to wear matched socks. I also have to put on a friendly face if I want to face pleasant countenances today. If I put on my "get-out-of-my-way" frown, I have to expect dour expressions. And I have to put in my pocket a handful of compliments, if I want somebody to be glad to see me. If all I have is complaints and criticisms, complaints and criticisms boomerang right back to me.

Wonder if Jesus knew that song when He said what He did in Luke 6:31?

And as ye would that men should do to you, do ye also to them likewise. Luke 6:31

November 9, 1997

August 3

Why Can't We Just Be a Church?

We have urged contributions of money or food or clothing or toys for the indigent. We have beat a political drum urging registration and voting. We have become the place of asylum for many people needing an advocate. We are a gathering place for recovering alcoholics and addicts. We are acquiring property, not for a larger sanctuary or for rental income, but to establish other ministries to people who are not now, nor are likely to become, contributing members of our congregation. Our buildings and grounds are a mecca for children of all shapes, sizes, and flavors. What does all this have to do with praising GOD and preaching the gospel of Jesus Christ?

Our model is not other churches. Our model is Jesus Himself.

The major criticisms of Jesus was that He identified with people who were not acceptable to the Temple—publicans, sinners, lepers, prostitutes, even non-Jews. But He did not consider His ministry to be limited to the synagogue on Friday evenings. He said He had been sent to the underclasses (Luke 4:18, 19), and in turn He commissioned His new church to spread outward to impact every nation on earth (Acts 1:8).

If we limit ourselves to Sunday or to our own congregation, we will fit in well with thousands of churches throughout the world. But we will be out of synch with Jesus, Who did not come to strengthen the synagogue system, but Who came that we might have more abundant life (John10:10). You see, it all depends on what we define as "the church."

218

He that hath an ear, let him hear what the Spirit saith unto the churches. Revelations 3:6

October 19, 1997

August 4

"Winning Isn't Everything"

That was part of a quote from legendary football coach Paul "Bear" Bryant. The other part was "Winning is the only thing." At first blush, that sounds like the sentiment of a poor loser. But anyone going into competition ought not go into it just to be on the field. He ought to play to win, and he ought to push his teammates to do 110% until the final buzzer sounds. There is always room for those who get defeated but there is not much sympathy for those who do not try hard. That is the code of the best athletes.

Paul understood that code—the most conscientious athletes carry it into all their other endeavors. He told his friends in the church at Philippi that a Christian cannot be concerned about substandard equipment or a slow start or sloppy teammates; he or she has to push hard toward the finish line.

So you are the descendant of slaves. Do your best anyhow. So you are a woman in a male-dominated environment. Aim for the highest achievement. So you do not have a Yale or Harvard degree. Do better with the education you have. Jesus says that those who hunger and thirst after righteousness shall be filled. The bottom line of that promise in the Beatitudes is that you do not have be righteous to be blessed of GOD. You just have to break a leg trying to be.

219

Brethren, I count not myself to have apprehended: but this one thing I do, forgetting those things which are behind, and reaching forth unto those things which are before, I press toward the mark for the prize of the high calling of GOD in Christ Jesus. Philippians 3:13-14

September 21, 1997

August 5

Step One: Praise

What do you do when everything is falling apart, when it seems you have been targeted for pain, and when there is no apparent reason for your troubles? Job's wife had one answer. Since GOD could prevent troubles, but seems not to have, she told Job to curse GOD. Job considered that suggestion stupid (Job 2:9-10).

Another approach was that of two men jailed unjustly and illegally. In fact, Paul and Silas were thrown into the worst part of the prison. But when everything was horrible, they chose not to curse GOD, but to praise Him. And afterwards, not before they praised Him, He sent an earthquake to free them!

It is not hard to praise GOD after He has healed you or your loved one. We can always tell GOD we love Him after He has sent to us a fat infusion of cash. No problem in shouting "Hallelujah!" after GOD pushes you into a great job. Praise is easy after the blessing. But the best time to praise GOD is before.

220

The words of the Gospel song are, "When the praises go up, the blessings come down." Well, there is not a simple vending machine relationship between praises and blessings: 75 cents in, a Coke out. But if we developed a continuing pattern of praising GOD, the first benefit is, it makes us sweeter and happier persons. But an ultimate benefit is praise really does unleash a cascade of blessings. If it doesn't happen in ten minutes, don't stop praising—He may not come when you want Him, but...

And at midnight Paul and Silas prayed, and sang praises unto GOD: and the prisoners heard them. Acts 16:25

October 12, 1997

August 6

It's a Great Life Anyhow

In a world of negatives, it takes conscious effort to be positive. There are enough days of bad weather to make you forget how many good days you had before it got cold or rainy. One or two ugly experiences with a sales or desk clerk can make you stop using the store or hotel without reflecting on how fair the prices or good the quality of the establishment. Notice how many years you have remembered the car wreck that caused you to have a broken leg or arm—and how easily you take for granted the ten years before and the two years since when you have not even had a flat tire?

The air is full of complaints about pain or inconvenience or lousy public officials or inconsiderate mates or children or friends. It is easy for gripe-itis to rub off on you.

But think about that person with a sunny disposition who lights up your day every time you meet. If you really knew the inner pains he or she bears, you would rush to console him or her. But he or she has learned an important lesson from Paul:

"The peace of GOD"—that's what your sunny friend has! How do you get it?

If you force yourself to remember good times, to thank GOD over and over for all He has done for you, to find the good even in the irritating, then you become like your friend, shedding sunshine into a complaining world!

Be careful for nothing; but in everything by prayer and supplication with thanksgiving let your requests be made known unto GOD. Philippians 4:6

April 7, 2002

August 7

Divine Leverage

It was awesome.

The paunchy, sixty-ish man with the almost snow-white cap of wooly hair stood like a rock, bare feet firmly planted on the hard floor of the Ron McNair Activity Center (named for the astronaut), his deep voice obviously fully capable of a window-shattering roar, but at the moment a well-modulated near-whisper as he instructed young Karate students in the control of an "adversary situation." He called for a volunteer opponent to attack him. While a muscular, flat-bellied instructor strode toward the older man, he continued to croon advice to the class. "Your worst enemy is the strength of your opponent," he intoned. "But your best friend is his weight. Don't fight his strength; use his own weight against him." And in a sudden cat-like, lightning-fast move, the elder man flipped the powerful young instructor onto the mat. The class gasped. The older man never stopped talking. "His weight is your ally; the bigger he is, the more your advantage."

That is a principle far bigger than Karate.

222

It is the one GOD used when Moses was sent to confront Pharaoh in Egypt. It is the principle of Joshua and his rag-tag Israelite army looking up at the walls of Jericho. It is what helped Gideon and three hundred hand-picked men defeat tens of thousands of Midianites. And it is how GOD is using the weak and inefficient and the corrupt to turn the world upside down.

We can come even closer to home than that.

At some time in our own lives, we have faced insurmountable odds. The powerful or the vested or the insiders have had a definite advantage. And because we were poor or black or an outsider (or all of the above), we thought we were defeated.

But GOD opens doors in spite of the power or wealth or connections of somebody else. We find an unexpected blessing where there were only troubles. Or we experience victory after we had already marked "Game lost" on the situation.

Then we know that somebody else's strength is not the guarantee that we will lose. In fact, it may be that precisely when we face Goliath or the lions' den or the fiery furnace, we can proclaim that "GOD is able."

I can do all things through Christ which strengtheneth me. Philippians 4:13

August 23, 1992

August 8

Are We On?

How our world has changed since somebody invented the first handheld wireless telephone (Motorola says it was one of its engineers, Dr. Martin Cooper, in September, 1975; but the U.S. Patent office says it was a brother, Dr. Henry Thomas Sampson, an engineer in Aerospace Corp. in July 1971—we can research it). Now wherever you go, people are holding tiny instruments to their heads, or talking into wires hanging over their ears. Ever answered somebody you thought was talking to you, only to discover that they were holding a conversation with a party on the other end of a cellular line? Surely you have been annoyed in a concert or a worship service (or at dinner) when a squeaky version of "The William Tell Overture" announced to all present that somebody was getting a telephone call. The little gadgets are outside buildings with smokers, on elevators with passengers, in rest rooms with—whoever is in rest rooms.

They have made it possible to "be connected" everywhere at all times. Except...

I was being raked over the coals by a friend in another city because he couldn't reach me. I assured him I had my cell phone with me all the time. As his voice moved up the scale in exasperation, he yelled at me the critical question: "Do you have your phone turned on?" I was glad he couldn't see the shame on my face. I was holding this sophisticated instrument that could receive calls from thousands of miles away without paying long distance, that could instantly connect with dozens of persons preprogrammed into the phone with the press of a single button, that could identify the caller and tell me whether I wanted to answer at all, and I didn't have the blamed thing turned on to receive his call—or that of anybody else!

GOD never stops trying to reach us. He has equipped us with marvelous receiving equipment to know right from wrong, to hear His voice 24/7. Are we "on"?

For the promise is unto you, and to your children, and to all that are afar off, even as many as the LORD our GOD shall call. Acts 2:39

July 28, 2002

August 9

It's All a Matter of Balance

I tried to ignore him. He must have been eleven or twelve, a skinny little kid with an Olajuwon shirt. But he was hard to ignore. He was showing off on a somewhat battered bicycle—rearing up the front wheel, doing circles while riding free-hand, even climbing to a seat-stand. People on the street stopped to stare, and I was almost impelled to applaud this showy little boy. He was good!

Riding a bicycle, even without the tricks, is a matter of balance. You have to learn it. After I got over my initial fascination with this young man on his biped, I began to mull over the importance of balance.

Hundreds of thousands of children return to school in August. Their purpose is to learn how to control their own destiny. But the nature of school is such that they are surrounded by peers who influence them to copy the peers. Their clothing and shoe styles, their vernacular, their taste in music, even their love or distaste for learning is influenced by their peers. The most important lesson you can ever learn is how to balance yourself between outside influences and internal principles and ideals.

224

The people of Jesus Christ can help.

We have to strengthen the inner muscles of faith, self-confidence, work-ethic, and sense of responsibility in our children. Then when they are bombarded by peer influences, they can stay on balance without being tipped over. If we can keep our balance, we can ride forever on our faith.

Be not overcome of evil, but overcome evil with good. Romans 12:21

August 20, 1995

August 10

Divine Reciprocity

You've heard it all your life, in one version or another. "Smile, and the world smiles with you." "You can catch more flies with honey than with vinegar." "You want 'nice'? Then give 'nice'!" Jesus put it very well when He urged us to be generous in order to receive bountifully.

How generous a measure of your time and money have you planned to give to GOD? If you are too busy to offer yourself to someone who needs you in His Name, how can you expect Him to rush to the emergency room when you cry out to Him? If you have already spent every dollar He has helped you to earn on your own housing and transportation and clothes and recreation and cannot possibly give Him the first tenth of your income, why should He work the financial miracles you need when you cannot make ends meet?

Paul says that those who sow sparingly shall reap sparingly, but those who sow bountifully shall reap bountifully (II Corinthians 9:6). There is a Divine reciprocity that sends back to us what we commit to GOD. You cannot demonstrate it mathematically—you have to try GOD to see it work.

But it does!

Give, and it shall be given unto you; good measure, pressed down, and shaken together, and running over shall men give into your bosom. For with the same measure that ye mete withal it shall be measured to you again. Luke 6:38

September 8, 1996

August 11

Don't Turn the Other Cheek

This is not an atheist article. This is not a hostile attack on our LORD, Who has told us that "whosoever shall smite thee on thy right cheek, turn to him the other also" (Matthew 5:39). This is not even a trick phrase. It is deadly serious.

There is an adversary we cannot be genteel with. There is an enemy with whom we can neither negotiate nor compromise. If you are a follower of Jesus Christ, you are at war. You didn't declare the war, but you have enlisted in the armed services from the moment you dedicated your life to Jesus. Your opponent is Satan, and he does not take prisoners. He comes to kill, to steal, and to destroy (John 10:10). If he can persuade you to blaspheme against GOD and die, he will do that. If he can twist your arm to violate the law and fall into its punishment, that will be his strategy. If he can do neither, then he will push you into self-destruction by getting you to pervert yourself, amputate your family and friends, and prostitute your own name.

The one thing he wants you to do is to get on the wrong side of GOD—and he will do anything necessary to accomplish that.

You can not pray, "Father, forgive him," because he knows exactly what he is doing. You cannot ignore him and assume he will get discouraged and slink away. And you cannot fight fair with him.

He is totally corrupt. He has no redeeming features at all. He must be fought tooth and nail, day and night, with cosmic weaponry which only GOD can supply. Don't hit above the belt, or let him get up. Drive him away with constant prayer! Do not—repeat—do not turn the other cheek!

Rejoicing in hope; patient in tribulation; continuing instant in prayer.
Romans 12:12

November 4, 1990

August 12

This Vehicle Has Cruise Control

All cars have wheels and engines and brakes and steering wheels. Most cars in Houston have radios and air conditioning. But the more expensive cars have something called "cruise control," which is excellent especially on long trips. A driver can set it on the speed he wants to maintain and drive 55 or 60; then he can take his foot off the accelerator and just let the car accelerate itself, staying at the pre-determined speed whether uphill or downhill. He just steers and listens to good music or good conversation. The cruise control keeps the pace constant.

Each of us needs to develop a spiritual cruise control.

When you are continually reacting to circumstance, you get mad or disgusted or scared or excited. Your mental state is jerky and inconsistent. But Paul admonishes us to think on "whatsoever things are true, whatsoever things are honest, whatsoever things are just, whatsoever things are lovely, whatsoever things are of good report" (Philippians 4:8). And, he tells us, if we set our spiritual cruise control on positive stuff, we will have peace.

227

So if we want to keep a steady pace of calm and a deep sense of joy, we should not respond to insults or offenses with anger or let loose talk sour our opinions of people or have jerky reactions to imagined problems or conditions. We should set our minds on blessings we have received, good opportunities we have, the beauty of the grace of GOD in our life, then take our foot off the panic- pedal, sit back and listen to the melody of GOD's unfailing love for us, and coast at the steady speed of peace.

Those things, which ye have both, learned and received, and heard, and seen in Me, do, and the GOD of peace shall be with you. Philippians 4:9

June 9, 1996

August 13

Mold Clay While Soft

We have better educational technology, more knowledgeable psychologists and counselors, and an ocean of information through media and computers. We can teach our children the contents of all the major encyclopedias, a multiplicity of languages, the great literature of the western and eastern worlds, even techniques for doing everything from building complex machines to profitable investing in world markets. We can help our children perform like geniuses.

But something is terribly wrong.

The highly-publicized school shooting sprees are not even the tip of the iceberg. Every school, every neighborhood has stories to tell of children and young people out of control. They may not kill anybody, or even attack anybody, but they disrespect their own parents and therefore all other adults. They are selfish and expect to have their own way without regard for others. What have we done to produce so many problem children and youth?

We have ignored the word of GOD.

It tells us to teach them His commandments constantly (Deuteronomy 6:4-7). It tells us to begin when they are young, so they will stick with it in later years (Proverbs 22:6).

It tells us to teach them to obey modeling before them "the nurture and admonition of the LORD." We do not need to abuse them, but some tough love is essential to teaching obedience and respect. (A whack on the rump of a preschooler is necessary—too late when he or she is a high-schooler.)

So don't waste time and money on more expensive toys. Spend some adult love on them while you can mold them. They are worth the trouble!

The just man walketh in his integrity: his children are blessed after him. Proverbs 20:7

July 11, 1999

August 14

Don't Forget the Center Stripe

It's tough to drive on a brand-new road when the pavement is fresh and black and the center stripe has not yet been sprayed on. We may not appreciate fully how critical that yellow or white line can be until it's missing.

Everybody has seen the clever poster with the lettering running into the right margin that says, "Plan Ahead." But if we have to lay out any kind of design or graphic, we know how important it is to pre-measure what we are laying out and then to give ourselves some form of guidelines to follow the pre- measurements.

Where there are no guidelines, accidents and mistakes are inevitable.

When we remember the sacrifice GOD made for our redemption, we return to some important guidelines. We are reminded that our lives have to be directed by the life and commandments of Jesus Christ. Most of the moral tumbles we take, most of the dumb things we do to ourselves and to each other are the results of either not seeing guidelines or not following them. We have to return regularly to the example of GOD, Who loved us so much that He sacrificed His best to save us; and the even more understandable example of GOD-made-flesh, Jesus Christ, Who was the sacrifice. This love-act reminds us that we are not intended to live for profit or for pleasure or for power over those weaker than ourselves. We are made to glorify GOD and to pass on to those weaker than ourselves, to our peers, and to those stronger than ourselves, His love, His compassion, His forgiveness.

229

So today, we check again the faint blue lines of His life—before we return to work the next day.

And we need to begin laying the lines down long before we turn the traffic loose on the road. We need to teach those guide lines to our children before we send them off to the schools.

Shew me thy ways, O LORD, teach me Thy paths. Psalms 25:4

November 5, 1989

August 15

Stay in Line

We have seen it over and over again. Thirty or forty children of pre-school age, three to five years old, among crowds of tourists or shoppers, or on a busy thoroughfare. They seldom get lost, never get hit because they have been trained. Their teacher or leader (the one in the bright red jacket or the white baseball cap) is their focus, and they hold hands in a squiggly but definite line. They keep their eyes on that jacket or cap and their hand joined to the hand of the next child. As long as they do those two things, they can go through the long corridors of the government building or the shopping mall or can cross the busy thoroughfare while all traffic pauses to let them by; and they arrive safely back at their point of origin.

They are learning structure and discipline before they learn that 2+2=4. The Boy Scout program represents one model of structure and discipline. Boys who wear cub or scout uniforms must one day deal with a world of professional demands, where they will advance providing they have learned to organize their lives and work within a system of rules and guidelines. That is why, should a boy rise to the level of Eagle Scout, he is virtually assured success in college or in the professional world. He has learned how to focus on a mission and to work hand-in-hand with other people.

So it is with their faith. While their adult leaders are teaching them safety in the wilderness and how to set a task and finish it, they are also teaching them about the GOD Who created and sustains a universe according to well-defined laws and principles. They must learn those laws and principles just as they must learn to tie a sheep-shank knot.

You and I serve a GOD Who has established a universe of structure and discipline; and if we follow His laws, we prosper. It pays to stay in line!

230

This is a faithful saying, and these things I will that thou affirm constantly, that they which have believed in GOD might be careful to maintain good works. These things are good and profitable unto men. Titus 3:8

February 11, 2001

August 16

We Need to Be Reminded

It is so easy to forget. Sometimes we drift into the notion that we are supposed to be an audience. We get lulled by the constancy of music and preaching and somehow identify with listening. And we forget that Jesus did not commission us to listen, but to witness. We were not called to something passive, but to something active. Today, we are reminded that the primary agenda of the church of Jesus Christ is not receiving something, but giving something. We are missionaries to aggressively market the love of GOD through Jesus Christ and to persuade the uninterested to buy.

Perhaps, you thought that church people were above substance abuse? WRONG! The entire inventory of human sins is represented in the church of Jesus Christ. That is what is miraculous about His church—that sinners are turned around by other sinners who have been saved by grace! So people who have fought with addictions and won when they let GOD fight their battles now testify to people who are still fighting that battle. Their testimony: "When I quit trying to govern my own life and surrendered to Jesus Christ, He overcame the drives that had controlled me. He will do the same thing for you."

231

Don't turn off because alcohol or drugs is not your sin of choice. You and I have our own addictions, and we need Christ's power just as much as do people whose problem is substance. And you and I must hear and obey GOD's command to go into all the world and sell GOD's amazing grace.

So don't just sit there like an audience. Put on your armor and fight.

By the word of truth, by the power of GOD, by the armour of righteousness on the right hand and on the left. IICorinthians 6:7

June 30, 1996

August 17

Keep It On

We are all trying to adjust. In this new world of lap-tops and world-wide paging and Web sites and flip-phones in ladies' purses, we are trying to adjust. Take flip-phones. Call a phone number and a recorded voice indicates the user is unavailable or has traveled outside the area. See my friend and ask him why he couldn't be reached by phone, he laughs and says, "Oh, I turned it off—sorry!" Some of us are just getting used to a phone sitting on the restaurant table with no wires, and now he says he can turn it off! We never "turned off" phones in our house or office! We could unplug them, or if we did not pay the phone bill the company would turn them off—but we didn't have a "talk" button that we could use to disable the thing! What kind of communication can we maintain with a turned- off telephone?

That leads me into a sermon.

232

GOD is always trying to communicate with us. But if we don't hear from Him, it is probably not because He is silent, but because we have turned off our own receiving system. We can get preoccupied with our families, our jobs, our favorite recreation, even with trash from the media or from friends' gossip, and shut down so that He cannot get through. Check your "prayer" button, and be sure your spiritual antenna is extended. Make sure your Holy Ghost-powered batteries are good. Be certain you are not in the "off" position when GOD wants to talk to you.

Peace I leave with you, my peace I give unto: not as the world giveth, I give unto you. Let not your heart be troubled, neither let it be afraid. John 14:27

August 11, 1996

August 18

The Danger of Freedom

The dream of every child is to become a grown-up. Few children have any inkling of what adults have to bear. Their image of being grown up is being free of the restraints of parents and school and church. Unless kids have changed drastically since you were one, they want what they are sure adults have—not age, but freedom!

Unfortunately, all of us learn that what we thought adults had, they don't.

On this weekend when the nation commemorated its declaring independence from England, we should have reflected on the high price of that independence. Freedom demands responsibility and that is a costly quality. When we throw off restraints, we become dangerous to ourselves and to others. Real independence does not exist. Everybody is accountable to somebody or something. You cannot call yourself truly free if you are a slave to your appetites, to your emotions, or to your greed. True liberty is the right to choose a master; and you must choose. You are a servant of GOD or the bondslave of Satan. Don't make the foolish choice of the prodigal son. False independence puts you in the pigpen. Listen to the wise challenge of Joshua (Joshua 24:15) and volunteer to be the servant of the Shepherd who loves you.

233

And if it seem evil unto you to serve the LORD, choose you this day whom ye will serve. Joshua 24:15

July 3, 1994

August 19

24/7, 365, & Whenever

Before there was a United States, Governor William Bradford of the Massachusetts Colony decreed a day of thanksgiving and prayer as July 30, 1623.

So do we thank Bradford, or Washington, or Lincoln, or Clinton for the idea? Not quite! Nearly a thousand years before the birth of Jesus, the Psalmist sang.

This is the impulse of true thanksgiving—not nailed to a calendar date like a dance poster, not in July or November, but continually. We don't pause just before the first bite of a feast to spit out a hurried thanksgiving for all the months since the last thanksgiving. When we wake up, we praise GOD for allowing us to see another day, for the ability to climb out of bed, for whoever we have to love, for good times when we can rejoice, for tough times when we can grow, and above all for Jesus, Who has re-opened the door once closed by our own sin and given us free access to GOD and to eternal life. And then after having thanked Him in the morning, we thank Him all day for the day's sunshine (or rain), for safe passage through the streets all our lives, for the taste of food, for the tasteless refreshment of cool water, for the clarity of mind to know that there is a GOD and that we belong to Him, etc., etc.

Thank Him on Thanksgiving Day, to be sure—but that should be just one of thousands of times we have to thank Him, Whose mercy endures forever!

234

From the rising of the sun unto the going down of the same the LORD's name is to be praised. Psalm 113:3

November 22, 1998

August 20

Think It, & It Is

It is remarkable what profound effect thought has upon life. The wise sage tells us in Proverbs to "keep thy heart with all diligence; for out of it are the issues of life" (Proverbs 4:23), because "as he thinketh in his heart, so is he" (Proverbs 23:7). Ever notice that when you are unhappy, everything around you seems wrong? The great seafood you normally enjoy doesn't taste as good. The sitcom that usually breaks you up just isn't very funny. Nothing wrong with the snapper or the show—your own attitude has affected them both.

Physicians and health care professionals are well aware that healing is only partially a matter of the body and medications or therapies applied to it. It is largely dependent upon inner attitudes. People who are cheerful, people who accept the bad with the good, people who pray are much better candidates for healing than sour-faced, complaining, faith-weak and prayerless people. Just as a bright attitude makes a bright day, so "the prayer of faith shall save the sick, and the LORD shall raise him up" (James 5:15).

235

That's why you should work at being content, at accepting with joy the blessings you have. If you can wake up and say, "This is a great day!", it is surprising how much better your back or your joints feel; how much nicer people are; how much better that blackened snapper tastes, especially with the crabmeat spread. If you lie there and breathe a prayer of thanks for waking up; if you get out of bed and thank GOD your legs can swing around and get your feet to the floor; if you move toward the bathroom and praise GOD for walking; if you look in the mirror (forget the morning look) and say "Hallelujah for sight!"—if you can begin counting blessings in that first few minutes, the remembrance of more and more will cascade into your mind. Before you realize it, you are happy to be alive.

And just watch how right Louis Armstrong was: "It's a wonderful world!"

Commit thy works unto the LORD, and thy thought shall be established. Proverbs 16:3

March 19, 2000

August 21

What Goes Around Comes Around

This is surely not a proper analogy for Christian commentary. But if we keep putting money into a slot machine, it will sooner or later pay off. (I read that in a book.) We may lose the rent money and endanger the utilities money, but the odds are that at some point we will find cash coming back to us.

O. K., so sue me for the tainted analogy. But I have a point.

You recommended him for a job, and he got it. But he never thanked you or even credited you with the recommendation. She was in desperate straits and needed $700 to keep from being evicted. She would repay you Friday. You struggled and strained to come up with the money, and she stayed in her apartment. It has been three months, and she will not return your calls. You shared with him highly sensitive information, and he promised on a stack of Bibles to keep your confidence. You heard your secret being laughed about at the barber shop; and he denies (on a stack of Bibles) that he told that loud-mouth anything. Sound familiar?

So you are at the point of promising yourself never to help anybody. Don't do it!

Your reward does not come from unreliable human beings. The One Who does send rewards does not send one each time you do a good deed. But scripture promises that bread sent out on the high tide will return on the ebb tide (free translation of Ecclesiastes 11:1) and that what you plant is what you harvest (Galatians 6:7). Or, to put it in casino terms, keep dropping in quarters and pulling the lever—a shower of coins comes to the persistent.

Don't give up because I disappoint you—over and over. You don't have me to depend on for recompense. Somewhere the great Sender of payoffs is watching you!

Be not deceived; GOD is not mocked: for whatsoever a man soweth, that shall he also reap. Galatians 6:7

236

August 22

Good & Bad Bangs

A rupture in a gas line—deadly fumes fill a closed space—workers totally unaware of the danger—a spark—a powerful explosion rocks the entire east end of the plant—three are killed, many are injured—the plant, nearby buildings, the surrounding neighborhood are thrown into chaos—police and firefighters seal off the area, while construction workers rush to cut off the gas flow to the plant and begin the tedious job of restoration.

Houston and its surrounding communities representing more than four million souls, most of them depending on a complex network of streets, freeways, and highways carry on business as usual, stopping just long enough to hear or read the news story of the plant explosion, then immediately return to work or school or play. Virtually all of them depend upon a massive inventory of automobiles, trucks, busses, planes, and an assortment of utility vehicles from golf carts to boats.

And every one of these modes of transportation depends upon explosions.

237

One hurts and the other helps. One kills and the other expedites. What makes the difference? That cute golf cart or that massive airplane–both are moved by an engine which controls explosions. When the explosions are controlled in a system and can be ignited or extinguished by a driver or a pilot, they provide controlled movement at 20 or 600 miles per hour. When they are not controlled, they can destroy property, injure, or even kill.

All of us have explosions. We deal with grief in the loss of a loved one, or anguish about sickness or conflict or financial shortfall, or depression about real or imagined problems. Left uncontrolled, any of these can lead to despondency or rage or even suicide. But if we allow GOD to provide the divine system, we discover that even these explosions can mature and sweeten us. Turn your explosions over to Him, and take off!

And we know that all things work together for good to them that love GOD, to them who are called according to His purpose. Romans 8:28

August 12, 2001

August 23

Nobody Knows

You know what nobody else knows about you. (At least, you hope nobody else knows.) Your shortcomings, your weaknesses, your flaws make you certain that you are unworthy. You know the truth—the ugly truth.

You can go either way. You can lie to yourself and tell yourself you are wonderful and all you do is magnificent. Or you can wallow in self-pity and claim to be worthless. Neither way is the right way to handle what you know about yourself.

Instead, remember that GOD sent His Son into our world to pay with His own life the penalty for the sins of uncounted billions of us. And then recall that GOD raised His Son from the dead, thus giving everlasting life to everybody who would invest faith in Him.

Do you realize that in those unbelievable stories is the answer to your dilemma? Yes, we are too thoughtless, even cruel sometimes. Yes, we are too materialistic—downright greedy. Yes, GOD could very well chew us out because of our bad attitudes and unpublishable actions.

But He doesn't.

He laid all our sins on Somebody else, and He calls us His precious children!

For He hath made Him to be sin for us, Who knew no sin; that we might be made the righteousness of GOD in Him. II Corinthians 5:21

April 27, 2003

August 24

It Comes Back

It comes back. You may think it never does. But it does. You try to a clean, upright life. You do good things for people, even people you don't even know. You don't hurt anybody. You don't even say negative things about people. And what do you get for it? You get passed by while somebody far less deserving gets the job or the contract or the opportunity. You get kicked in the face by people who know very well you do not deserve the kick. You try to put out sugar, and it seems you only reap horseradish. Where is GOD's justice when you are bruised and broken?

Before you swallow the cyanide pill, look around—you've got company. You've seen a good Mama or Grandmama give love and get abuse. The most saintly folk you know seem to suffer the same fate as you. Have you noticed? And who was more deserving of good things than Jesus? Who got hung on a cross for all His good words and deeds? You are not alone.

Jesus gave us a rule we now call "golden." Gold is precious, but it is extremely durable. The rule is that we should treat others, not as they treat us, but as we would like for them to treat us (Matthew 7:12). And the wisdom of Ecclesiastes tells us that GOD rewards us for doing right: "Cast thy bread upon the waters: for thou shalt find it after many days." (Ecclesiastes 11:1) Remember the blessing you did not expect? That is how Divine Payback works. Hang in there!

239

Say ye to the righteous, that it shall be well with him; for they shall eat the fruit of their doings. Isaiah 3:10

June 1, 2003

August 25

Think, Do, Be

Little verbs—but powerful.

You look with envy at somebody who seems to get all the breaks. Do they succeed because they are connected to people in power? Are they given an extra boost because of their family, or because they are pushy, or because of their race? Why can you not be so favored?

By all means, look at such external factors. But we might also want to look inside ourselves. We don't need to envy somebody else or fear constant failure. We are well-connected, too. We are children of the Most High GOD, Who can do all things. So don't paint yourself as a loser, as a person who never gets the good stuff. Say, "I am GOD's child. I am somebody. With my Father's help, I can make it." And if you tell yourself you are a winner, you are.

So if we think we are somebody, we are. And if we are somebody, we will do bold things. And when we do bold things, we will be a proud and able child of GOD. Don't whine because John or Mary has done well. Look inside yourself and look up. Lean on your GOD, and do better!

240

For as he thinketh in his heart, so is he. Proverbs 23:7a

June 8, 2003

August 26

How Can I Get Rich?

Deep inside each of us (or by far most of us) is a paradox. We are acquisitive, and yet we admire unselfish people.

We want as much as we can get. If we are selling, we seek the highest bidder for our merchandise or service. If we are job-hunting, we will take the job that offers the highest pay, not the job that may be most rewarding. We react quickly to being short-changed. We are acquisitive.

And yet, if we reflect on who are the people who have had the greatest impact on our lives, we paint a totally different image. They are not the rich and powerful and famous. In fact, the people we admire most and consider memorable are often people without much money or renown. That mama or teacher or scout leader or coach holds a special place in our memories not because they acquired much, but because they gave much.

What a paradox! But it says that there is a little spark of GOD within us, even while we are scratching and pushing to maximize our profit. Something good inside us tells us that it is more blessed to give than to receive (Acts 20:35). We ought to stir up that spark and find ways to give to others, to help others. It is in giving that we are ourselves enriched. An old Chinese proverb seems apropos here:

If you want happiness for an hour—take a nap.

If you want happiness for a day—go fishing.

If you want happiness for a month—get married.

If you want happiness for a year—inherit a fortune.

If you want happiness for a lifetime—help someone else.

I have shewed you all things, how that so labouring ye ought to support the weak, and to remember the words of the LORD Jesus, how he said, It is more blessed to give than to receive. Acts 20:35

September 15, 2002

August 27

What Shall I Render?

That's the beginning of the question raised by the psalmist in Psalm 116:12. As we count blessings (and you must do that occasionally) and realize that whatever wholeness of body, whatever sharpness of mind, whatever achievements or possessions or inventory of family or friends we have, all came from GOD. And the universal religious response of worshippers of all faiths is to give something to GOD in gratitude and submission.

Tithing? Giving GOD the first one-tenth of every paycheck, plus an offering (a kind of celestial "tip") is one way. Prayer? Especially prayers more often per day and prayers for somebody else beside yourself and your own circle of loved ones. Witness? Telling somebody else about GOD and His blessings to you is a powerful way of rendering to GOD your love for Him. Finding a cause that demands of you a sacrificial gift of your time or skills and staying consistently faithful to that cause tells GOD you are grateful that He sent His Son to save you even when you neither requested it nor expressed appreciation for it.

When you and I accept the notion that worship is not attendance to public services, but a genuine surrender of our best to GOD, we will find countless ways to render unto the LORD in response to His benefits toward us.

What shall I render unto the LORD for all His benefits toward me?
Psalm 116:12

242

March 6, 1994

August 28

You Can't Touch That

I had gone because it was polite to go. The elementary school science exhibit was crowded, noisy, and hot. The chatter of hundreds of children, the squeals of doting mothers exploded from a dozen directions at once, and we were continually stepping over tiny pre-school siblings who only wanted to get to the refreshments stand. I muttered to my teacher-escort, "It's getting a bit late," which should have been her signal to show me to the exit from this chaos.

Then I saw it. A fifth-grader had created a display with a neat maze of wires surrounding a plastic tile about a foot square attached to a little generator of some sort. He was a classic nerd with slicked-down hair and a dark suit (hate kids who look like me!), and he was pouring water over the tile. Miraculously, some invisible force-field diverted the liquid to either side of the place where it should have fallen onto the tile and pushed it mysteriously over the side of the tile and into a bucket below. The tile remained totally dry! What an exhibit! I forgot the pandemonium of the exhibit hall.

243

That is what the Spirit of GOD does for us. He provides us with insulation against whatever pain or grief or failure life tries to pour on us. If you are trying to ward off difficulties without the Teflon Presence of GOD, you are in trouble, and you will get hit from all sides. Suffering is the common lot of the human animal.

But if you give your life to Jesus Christ and lean on His invincible power to protect you, you will find an incredible fact: You will lose a loved one, but be protected from grief; you will endure illness, but have joy on the sick-bed; you will face defeat, but be at peace in an inner victory. If GOD is with you, you need not fear any evil. If He is not...

Yea, though I walk, through the valley of the shadow of death, I will fear no evil: for Thou art with me; Thy rod and Thy staff they comfort me. Psalm 23:4

April 10, 1994

August 29

The Real Boss

We are on the threshold of the campaign season, candidates for mayor, or for city council, or for a vacancy on the School Board position themselves to be seen and heard. Will voters endorse candidates with strong law-and-order platforms or ones who promise to work to preserve and upgrade deteriorating neighborhoods? Will they fill vacancies with individuals who have been intimately connected to the system or put in office gutsy outsiders with no strings attached?

It does not matter who gets to be the Mayor, or whether we have fourteen or four hundred council members, or even whether the current president succeeds himself or is shockingly overturned by some dark horse. The real boss is none of the above.

Who really decides our destiny, controls the flow of history, overthrows the tyrant and liberates the oppressed? It is not anybody we elect to public office or who gets hired to be the CEO. The real boss is not the one who does all the talking. Can you guess Who He is?

Let every soul be subject unto the higher powers. For there is no power but of GOD: the powers that be are ordained of GOD. Romans 13:1

August 11, 1991

August 30

Oh, Say, Can You See

Those five words are a national stimulus that calls for an automatic, even unconscious response: We stand up. It reminds us of the greatness of a nation and of the necessity to respect it. If we listen to any of the words at all (and we seldom do—we stand and think about the game or try to remember if we set the alarm before we left home), we also hear the theme of victory coming out of a struggle we might have lost. "Our flag is still there."

Life is a struggle, with its share of near-defeats. In fact, some setbacks seem to be defeats. We label them as defeats. We have done our best, but got betrayed anyhow. We prayed fervently and sincerely, but lost our loved one in spite of our prayers. We have tried to live Christian lives, but success comes to rascals with no ethics and no standards. Surely, we have lost the battle. So why waste more time praying, believing?

Because the final determination is not a matter of happenstance; "good" or "bad" luck does not control our destiny.

If we could see with the eyes of GOD, beyond our own hurt, further than our own timespan, we might understand that despite the glare of rockets and the bursting of bombs (the immediate hurts and setbacks), GOD is still on the throne, in total control, with victory over death, the grave, and "bad luck" for those who trust Him.

Times were when we were in a mess and thought maybe suicide was not such a dumb idea. Then we laughed at ourselves for not being so depressed when GOD worked things out for us or lifted our soul with healing we knew did not come from medications or counselors. We remember some former victory we saw with our own eyes. Then we should trust Him when the skies are dark and the shells are flying and we cannot find friends and stay on the battlefield. The banner of Jesus is still there!

Delight thyself also in the LORD; and He shall give thee the deserves of thine heart. Psalm 37:4

August 27, 1989

August 31

Look Again

If you have the kind of job that requires a secretary, an aide, or an administrative assistant, you know the challenge. People to apply for such jobs are plenteous. People who can handle such jobs are few. If you have to have such support, you are truly blessed if you have a worker who is reliable, self- starting, warm and friendly toward your clients or customers, and can learn the needs of your operation. An effective secretary or aide is exceedingly valuable (always worth more than the salary you pay him or her).

In the old TV series "M*A*S*H," there was a corporal assigned to the Commanding Officer of the military hospital. He was called "Radar," perhaps partly because he was responsible for radio communications with the front and with headquarters; but also because he seemed able to anticipate the needs of the CO. The CO would begin to order Radar to get something or contact somebody, and the corporal had already begun to do it, often to the embarrassment of the CO, who was supposed to be in charge. In one episode, the CO was about to take an R&R (rest and recreation) break to Seoul. He was already aboard the helicopter that was to take him there when he remembered his razor. He yelled at the corporal to rush back to his quarters to get it, and Radar responded with characteristic omniscience, "It's already in the side pouch of your bag, Sir!"

You have a GOD Who really is omniscient. He knows your needs before you know them, and provides for you before you realize you need provision. There are cloudy days when you are depressed, or afraid, or confused; when you have been given bad news about an illness, or have been crushed by grief; when you have experienced failure, or just a real bad hair day. On such days you need a dose of strength. You don't have to scream in panic to GOD. He has already provided strength for you. It is in a side pouch called "faith." Praise GOD for having always been there for you and tell Him you trust Him to give you a boost right now—it was provided before you knew you would need it! Take another look into your faith-pouch—JEHOVAH-JIREH has done it again.

A double minded man is unstable in all his ways. James 1:8

February 6, 2000

September 1

Said I Wouldn't Tell Nobody

The old spiritual does not use the best grammar. But it packs the punch of a powerful spiritual truth: You cannot bottle up the explosive dynamic of the Holy Spirit. If He fills you, you just can't "keep it to yourself." The prophet Jeremiah 20:7-9 says the LORD had gotten on his last nerve. He was sick and tired of the LORD. And he would quit preaching and get a job on a construction site. (That is a somewhat free translation.) But GOD's word was in his heart as "a burning fire shut up in my bones, and I was weary with forbearing, and I could not stay."

"Praise ye the LORD." It is more than a proper response to His majesty, His transcendence, His grace, His redeeming love—it is something you cannot contain even as much as you can contain a sneeze. Praise is combustible; it ignites a fire you cannot suppress or ignore. But like the smoke rising from a pleasing sacrifice to GOD, it moves GOD to respond to you. GOD is not aloof, implacable, inscrutable, without feeling. GOD is sensitive to praise. He inhabits the praise of His people (Psalm 22:3), and hears the cry of those who appeal to Him for mercy.

247

When you feel a little prayer-wheel turning, and you know a little fire is burning, don't lock the door of your heart and mumble, "I will not make mention of Him, nor speak any more in His name." Don't throw a blanket over your Hallelujahs, or sit on your "Thank you, Jesus." Holding your breath is hazardous to your health; suppressing your praise is deadly to your faith.

Throughout this month we will be urging you to let your family, your neighbor, the world know that you love GOD, and you don't care who knows it. Want blessings to come down? The master key: Let the praises go up!

Open to me the gates of righteousness: I will go unto them, and I will praise the LORD. Psalm 118:19

August 2, 1998

September 2

Sin-Proofing

We have developed protections against many hazards. The watch on our wrist is waterproof. The batteries in our electronic toys are leak-proof. The vest worn beneath the police officer's uniform is bullet-proof. But can anything protect us against our natural inclination to violate the principles of GOD?

David says the word of GOD can. "Thy word have I hid in mine heart," he says, "that I might not sin against thee" (Psalm 119:11). Did you know that as devout and pious as we are, who sacrifice Sunday morning to go to church to praise GOD, well over half of us—about 65%—have not read all of the New Testament? That is the portion of the Bible which details our redemption and salvation!

Americans spend an average of 45 minutes a day in cars, and most of our cars have tape players, or we have access to electronic devices with earphones. What better way to pour GOD's word into our minds?

248

And once we have been mesmerized by the four gospel stories, blown away by the power of the Holy Ghost in Acts, raised to heavenly heights by the letters of Paul, James, Peter, John, Jude, and the writer of Hebrews, and driven to shouting by the Revelation, we will find it easy to forgive offenses, to turn away from greed, to say no to impure passions, and to praise GOD anywhere, any time, in front of anybody. The best sin-proofing is at your finger (press "Play").

Thy word have I hid in mine heart, that I might not sin against thee.
Psalm 119:11

June 13, 1999

September 3

I Am in Charge

It is still good for a laugh. Over twenty years ago, then-President Ronald Reagan was shot by a deranged man, and the nation was stunned. Was there to be another presidential assassination? In the chaos surrounding the shooting in a Detroit street, the question was raised, "Who takes over while the President is down?" Secretary of Defense Al Haig, clearly out of place, replied, "I am in charge!" Well, the Vice President and the Speaker of the House quickly corrected him and shuffled him out of his self-appointed leadership.

But you and I are in charge, assigned by GOD Himself to subdue and have dominion over His creation. Yes, we have made more a mess out of our world than Haig could have made out of executive government, because we are corrupted by sin. But despite all that, Jesus has told us that we are responsible for the spread of the gospel, and He has not set up a backup plan in case we are lazy or clumsy or preoccupied or all of the above. So we are continually reminded that we are missionaries, witnesses, the only messengers of Divine truth He has.

249

Why would GOD place incompetents in such a place of authority and responsibility?

Well, He didn't exactly ask "F" students to do rocket science.

Remember when your parents, or your teacher, or your coach gave you a big job, maybe too big for you to accomplish successfully with your still-undeveloped skills? They did not leave you alone—they watched you carefully, and were there to catch your bike when it wobbled, right?

That's what GOD does. He pushes us out there and sends the Holy Spirit behind us to be sure we can handle the job. So get out there, and tell the world about Jesus—you are not really left to do it all alone. He's got your back!

And, lo, I am with you alway, even unto the end of the world. Amen.
Matthew 28:20b

August 29, 1999

September 4

Steer Me Right

I am rushing through the airport, ignoring most of the bustling traffic, the garish signs with spectacular photos of juicy steaks or brilliant diamonds or the best casino-hotel in Las Vegas, even the necktie shop where I always pause to drool. But suddenly I am stopped by a remarkable scene. A young girl is walking down the corridor, eyes straight ahead. She is obviously blind, being led by a gorgeous snow-white German shepherd. The magnificent animal is what catches my eye. Somebody else, rushing like me, whizzes past him. A child pats his massive back before a frustrated mother can pull the youngster away. Voices blare from loudspeakers all around him, announcing flights or warning people to keep their luggage with them. The aromas of pizza and barbecue and hamburgers waft around his sensitive nose. But he never responds to any of them. He is trained to do one thing—lead his young follower to the proper departure gate. And she needs no cane, nor shows any uneasiness about all this chaos. She trusts the animal who leads her to American Airlines flight 1404.

Ever get upset because things don't go the way you want them to go? You know you are qualified, but you don't get the job. You are certain she is the perfect woman for you, but she keeps saying, "No." The death of your mother, just when she seemed to be doing so much better, devastates you. Life is not fair!

Or is it life?

The psalmist ends Psalm 139 with a plea to GOD: "Lead me in the way everlasting." Powerful prayer—but dangerous. David is asking GOD to direct him to where he ought to go, to steer him away from where he ought not to go. And if you know that all things work together for good for GOD-lovers, you can understand how some disappointments and trials are for your strengthening, not because GOD wants to hurt you. Even grief can be a door to greater maturity. Follow where He leads—He will not steer you wrong

Search me, O GOD, and know my heart: try me, and know my thoughts. Psalm 139:23

August 13, 2000

September 5

He'll Make It All Right

The classic story told by Jesus about GOD's love for us is in Luke 15, and even people who know little of the Gospel story know this one—the Prodigal Son. He is proclaiming Heaven's joy when a sinner repents. During this month when we focus on prayer, its power and its value, we are reminded that Jesus told us to approach GOD in prayer as "Father," which is not a religious title. And a fragment from that parable may help us to understand why the term "Father" is the title of choice for Jesus when He teaches us to pray.

Luke 15:17-21 describes a turnaround in the attitude of the son. He had demanded more than he deserved. He had arrogantly forsaken his father and his brother and gone into "a far country" to squander the inheritance. When his foolish extravagance and his greedy friends had drained him, and he was getting the punishment he deserved, he repented. (Anything familiar about that?) And he realized that he still had some place to go. He understood that he had forfeited any right to be accepted by the family, but he was determined to go home.

That says much.

He knew he had lost any right to son-ship, but he knew the nature of his father and felt that even if he could only be a hired servant, he would be treated better than he was being treated in the swine- fields in the far country. He did not expect privilege; but he knew he could expect compassion.

The rest of the story says he got both.

When you pray, remember you are not just addressing an omnipotent GOD; you are talking to a Father. As the old song says, "Tell Him what you want."

251

Blessed is he that shall eat bread in the kingdom of GOD. Luke 14:15b

October 15, 2000

September 6

Don't Choose Door Three

Pick a card. Choose a number. Which door? Is the answer A, B, C, or D? Part of the excitement of modern games, whether on television or at the casino, is the matter of choice. And "your final answer" may determine whether you win a large amount of money or the trip to the Fiji Islands or the sports utility vehicle. The choice is ours. And the praise of family and friends or the boos of audience or spectators depends on that choice.

The most important choices in this life ought not to be left to our skilled guessing. David says that he cannot escape GOD's pursuing love and guidance. GOD's guidance is available to you for the asking. Some of our dumbest choices are the result of not asking for that guidance before we make the choices.

252

He will not always direct us as we would expect Him to. But if we ask Him to open doors for us, we should be sure to also ask Him to close doors. We want Him to open those doors we should go through, but to close (even to slam in your face) those doors through which we ought not go. Haven't we seen Him allow some effort we have made fail, and we have been frustrated by the failure? And then some opportunity or some new relationship we had not expected emerges, far better than whatever had not worked out?

We don't want to go through life trying to guess which is the right path to take. Jesus sets the example for us by constantly appealing to His Father in prayer. Whom should He choose as disciples? What should He say to the crowds? How should He handle a needed miracle? When He approached a storm at sea or a demon-possessed child, He knew precisely what to say and do—because He had asked His Father which door He should enter. Don't guess; we have a Divine life-line. Ask the One Who knows!

Even there shall Thy hand lead me, and Thy right hand shall hold me. Psalm 139:10

October 22, 2000

September 7

Still There

When you come to the end of an episode—you leave a job, you complete a major task, you pack up to move to another town, you graduate—when you face the challenges of the new and unknown, tomorrow can be frightening.

Yes, the new job may not be all pluses. And how much at home can you feel among strangers in Denver after the warm embrace of Bryan? You were popular in high school, but will you get trampled by the crowds in the university? Tomorrow can be—is—more than a bit frightening.

But when we look back, we have seen the Hand of One Who guided us through the hazards and provided for us when we had no clue how we would make it through. Yes, we have the scars of past struggles. Yes, we have run into blank walls. Yes, we have yelled at Heaven when we thought GOD had forgotten us while He was blessing millionaires. But as we reflect on our yesterdays, we can see that "one set of footprints." We know GOD has been there with us in our fiery furnaces.

253

Take a pregnant pause to remember how good He has always been to you. Then when you have made a mental list of His blessings to you, face your tomorrow with the certainty that since He brought you out of Egypt, and led you across the hazards of the wilderness, and has the blood running warm in your veins today, He is still there with you. Trust the GOD of yesterday to remain the GOD of tomorrow.

LORD, thou hast been our dwelling place in all generations.
Psalm 90:1

August 25, 2002

September 8

When All the Witnesses Agree

The most famous trial in history is playing on television sets all over the world. Perhaps if there is television on the Russian satellite, it features that trial, too. That trial is constituted of the same ingredients as the most inconsequential hearing in the smallest community—the testimony of somebody who claims to know something about the circumstances or the parties to the dispute. You cannot come to a clear verdict without witnesses. And since in this high-profile trial there has not been revealed a murder weapon, the testimony of witnesses becomes absolutely critical.

So you are sick and have not been given much hope of recovery. So your heart is broken because you have lost a loved one, and you are not sure you want to keep living yourself. So your back is against the wall and you do not see your way out of the mess you are in. Is this "throw-in-the-towel-and- pass-me-the-cyanide" time? You bet your horoscope book it is not!

254

One of the major features of any worship service is testimonies. People who were not ordained ministers and who do not normally speak in front of a congregation, tell us what blessings GOD had given them. Some speak of fortunate developments; some even report miracles. When one person says such things, we can always dismiss it as a fluke or as a misinterpretation of events. But when witness after witness says, "I was hopeless, and GOD pulled me out of the pit," maybe we ought to listen. Since GOD did it for all of them, He will surely do it for you. Hear them and trust Him!

Offer the sacrifices of righteousness, and put your trust in the LORD.
Psalm 4:5

March 26, 1995

September 9

You Can't Miss It

These words keep echoing in your head while you search diligently for the street or the store or the house. Somebody gave you directions, and the tag line was, "You can't miss it." But you have, and you are thinking decreasingly Christian thoughts about the giver of directions.

Auto manufacturers have worked on that problem. Now, I am told, if you can afford them, there are luxury vehicles with built-in computers that ask only your point of origin and your intended destination, and they literally talk you through the correct route: "Turn left at the traffic light—go straight ahead two and a half miles—"

GOD provided such a luxury for His people long before IBM and General Motors. These directives unfold the path to peace and joy. On one occasion, Dr Jeremiah Wright of Chicago's Trinity United Church of Christ came to Wheeler bearing white-hot messages direct from the heart of GOD. He leaves behind the vibrations of the Holy Spirit giving clear and precise directions. "Bow down and worship." "Close eyes, shut out world, and pray." "Open Bible and find fresh truths for today." "Tell family member, neighbor, co-worker about how good GOD is to you." "Go straight through your storm trusting Him."

255

The Holy Spirit is not the private property of preachers, gospel singers, and saints who are "holier than thou"; He indwells our world, and will fill you, directing you from inside and telling you exactly what to do, where to go, how to best glorify Jesus Christ. You don't have to depend upon somebody telling you how to live day to day. He is your Guide and Teacher. And you don't even have to be wealthy—just faithful!

For the LORD GOD is a sun and shield: the LORD will give grace and glory. Psalm 84:11a

January 14, 2001

September 10

Souvenirs & Prayers

The body of Mother Teresa was laid in the ground from whence it came. The world-wide coverage of her burial included some expected speculation that her burial site will become a shrine. Pilgrims from many nations will travel to that spot, expecting a miracle. For a Christian in a Hindu state, she made quite an impact; enough to have a state funeral, although she held no office of state.

Funny, how easily Christians forget the First Commandment: "Thou shalt have no other GODs before me." Last month it was Graceland, where thousands came twenty years after the death of Elvis Presley. Last week, it was Kensington Palace, the home of Princess Diana. Surely the little Albanian nun from Yugoslavia would be horrified that her burial ground would become a shrine, a place where people would bring their loved ones to be miraculously healed. If neither Elvis nor Diana understood, Mother Teresa did—there is only one GOD we ought to worship; we ought not impute sacredness to earthly places and things.

256

Aren't you glad you do not?

So can you be as devoted to Jesus as you are to that shiny new car? Can GOD be as precious to you as that bonus? Is it possible that you can be as excited about the LORD as you are about that child or grandchild? If you and I can focus upon the Kingdom of GOD and His righteousness, all that you need will be supplied.

But seek ye first the kingdom of GOD, and his righteousness; and all these things shall be added unto you. Matthew 6:33

September 14, 1997

September 11

There Shall Be Wars

It has been decades since the last military base was closed down in Vietnam. The same people who enjoyed the luxury of peace (however shaky) are now part of nations at war. We heard celebration because Operation Desert Storm was such a devastating first strike against our Iraqi opponents, and because our side sustained so few casualties. But on the night the war began, some of us gathered to pray, and we included prayer for our enemies.

It is the nature of human society to spawn conflict, and whether we throw spears or hurl Cruise Missiles, scripture has promised us that there shall be "wars and rumors of wars" (Matthew 24:6). But it is not the nature of the children of GOD to celebrate wars. We take the strange course of loving enemies, of doing good to them who hate us, of praying for those who despitefully use us and persecute us.

Our children mimic what they see in us. If we overeat, they learn to be gluttons. If we lie continually, they learn to take the truth lightly. And if we act as though violence is the answer to human differences, they will grow up depending on force and weapons to support their wants and views.

257

We are at war; that is an ugly necessity—one of the fruits of sin. But we can set an example before the children and young people who watch our every move. If we pray for the people of Iraq while we pray for our own forces; if we speak only positively about Saddam Hussein, while others portray him as the worst monster since Nero; if we support our service people but oppose war as a way of solving international differences, we will be acting as a peacemaker. And peacemakers shall be called the children of GOD.

And ye shall hear of wars and rumors of wars: see that ye be not troubled. Matthew 24:6

January 20, 1991

September 12

How Do You Deal with Grief?

The phone rings, and something inside you turns to ice, although you don't know who the caller or what the message is. Then comes the crushing blow—your loved one has died. You try to suppress hysteria, but the ice inside melts, then boils, then erupts in a geyser of anguish. You scream at GOD; you curse every doctor; you wish you could die yourself.

Or the news hurts deeply, but something inside you softens the blow with a cushion of faith and acceptance. And you begin an efficient process of adjustment, thanking GOD that your loved one was such a blessing to you.

What is the difference between these two reactions?

A continuing relationship with GOD that strengthened you long ago for this awful moment and becomes a reservoir of strength for those around you who have been flattened by the loss.

258

A powerful performance follows long practice or rehearsal or preparation. A masterpiece emerges after years of not-so-masterful attempts. The ability to bounce back when adversity strikes comes only when you have spent much time in reflection on GOD's word, in prayer, in fasting. It is not an instantaneous response; you run hard before you break a long-jump record.

Don't wait until the bad news hits you. Exercise your spiritual muscles now; read, pray, praise, comfort others. Then when that fateful call comes, your soul will be tough enough to absorb the blow.

While we look not at the things which are seen, but at the things which are not seen: for the things which are seen are temporal, but the things which are not seen are eternal. II Corinthians 4:18

August 10, 1997

September 13

Smelling Roses

There are days when you wake up depressed. Money is short. Husband or wife or children or family are not acting right. Friends have let you down. The folks you must work with are messy, and if you could find another good job you would leave this one in a heart-beat. On top of that, the old body is accumulating problems—cardiac or pulmonary, renal or circulatory, muscular or rheumatoid, dental, ophthalmic, dermatological, or tumorous—whatever can go wrong has gone or is going wrong. Some days just ought to be erased from the calendar.

But then, in the middle of your pity-party, you learn of somebody who has lost everything in a fire or a storm. Word comes to you that somebody has been told he or she has only weeks to live. You hear of somebody who has had to endure a series of deaths close to him or her, in just a few months. Or you learn of a once-vital and active person who has had a single stroke and become little more than a vegetable.

No matter how bad it is for you, somebody else is carrying a heavier burden than yours. While this may not be your best day, it is a day that the LORD has made, and you have reason to rejoice and be glad in it. Do a little survey of things you are glad you have, and you will realize that you have much for which somebody in Somalia or Pakistan or Haiti or Houston would give a right arm. You are blessed in a multitude of ways.

So quit gazing at your problems and count your blessings. Praise the LORD for what you can think of, and while you are praising Him, you will think of more and more. Tell Him you are glad He loves and cares for you, and that you love Him with all your heart.

And check out how bright and beautiful a day this is!

Rejoice in the LORD, O ye righteous: for praise is comely for the upright. Psalm 33:1

January 27, 2002

September 14

We Are Family

Sometimes the modern church tries to imitate the corporate world. At other times she attempts to mimic secular government. The church has even made efforts to replicate education systems (we do want to appear intelligent!).

All of these are the wrong model.

We are not judged on business acumen, or parliamentary propriety, or doctrinal brilliance. Jesus judges us on the basis of our love. Neither business, government, nor education is held together by love.

We are family. Our primary function is to rear generations who love GOD and each other.

What a challenge, in an age when even our children have learned cold violence and narcissistic self- centeredness, but not compassion or respect or reverence! We have taught them computers and finance, but not how to be family.

260

We ought to be business-like. We ought to exemplify democracy. And we ought to learn GOD's word and its principles.

But most of all, we ought to teach our children that GOD is their Father and that all humans are brothers and sisters. It is better that they become family than that they become rich.

If GOD be glorified in Him, GOD shall also glorify Him in Himself and shall straightway glorify Him. John 13:32

February 13, 1994

September 15

Do It—Or Else

John tells the story of a man born blind who was healed by Jesus (John 9:1-7). That story carries a powerful message, far beyond the healing of a blind man. It says that if we obey GOD, nothing is impossible to us.

The story of those seven verses is that Jesus and His disciples found a man born blind. (congenital, incurable, beyond the reach of ophthalmology.) There is a dialogue between Jesus, His disciples, and the townspeople that is alone worth considering—but that dialogue is not our focus here. A simple act is. Jesus spat on the ground, mixed His saliva and the dirt into a muddy salve, and smeared it on the man's eyes. (UGH!) Then Jesus commanded the blind man to go to the Pool of Siloam and wash.

That command is the key to the man's healing.

261

Verse 7 says the man obeyed Jesus, and when he washed his face, he was able to see for the first time in his life! Without embellishing these seven verses, suffice it to say that we miss some miracles simply because we do not obey Jesus' commands. We don't have to understand them. We cannot modify them. Somebody could have provided a basin of water closer than the Pool of Siloam. The miracles GOD wants to work for us demand that we obey His commands.

Believe in the LORD Jesus Christ. Love one another as He has loved us. Forgive one another. Give a cup of cold water in His Name.

If the blind man had not washed in the Pool of Siloam, he might have missed receiving his sight. Are you missing some miracle because you will not obey?

Rest in the LORD and wait patiently for Him. Psalm 37:7a

October 21, 2001

September 16

It Hurts If You Hold It

I grew up in the city and sometimes feel a bit envious of those who have fond memories of the country. I was well into my teens before I knew that not all cattle were "cows." But I was fascinated by visits to the rural areas, by the simple, work-oriented life-style, by the warm network of families. One lesson I learned had to do with "chores," which, apparently, every member of farm families had.

A young friend of mine had to milk three cows before breakfast every morning. I remember him getting scolded by his father for being late to take care of that responsibility. He and I rushed out to the barn where the animals were, and I could hear the cows making more than the usual "moo-ing" sound. They were almost screaming. My friend explained to me what the problem was, and then I understood why his father was so upset. If you don't relieve the animals of the milk buildup in their udders, it is painful to them. GOD made them to dispense milk, not to hold it.

262

Now, decades after that experience, I look back on it, and see myself in it. GOD intended for me to dispense my testimony, to tell my story, to be a witness for Him. I was not built to be a spiritual introvert, to keep to myself the truth about Jesus Christ and His love. In fact, if I don't witness for Him, I hurt myself, and you may hear the screams of pain—proper punishment for somebody who won't tell the story!

The LORD is my rock, and my fortress and my deliverer; my GOD, my strength, in whom I will trust; my buckler and the horn of my salvation, and my high tower. Psalm 18:2

April 30, 1995

September 17

The Best Marketing

In many churches, the fifth Sunday is traditionally days for missions. They are the time when we stress the primary reason for the existence of the church: that all people might be told about salvation through Jesus Christ.

The church of Jesus Christ is really a massive sales operation.

We are being besieged by sales pitches virtually every waking hour. Long before you see them in stores and places of business, they are on signs on buildings and vehicles and billboards. They are throughout whatever paper or magazine we read. They scream at us whenever we listen to radio or watch television. They are part of what stuffs our mail boxes. We cannot escape being pitched by somebody.

But the most effective sales are the glowing reports by somebody we trust. Our parents or relatives or friends tell us how fabulous the new restaurant is or what a batch of bargains they found in the resale shop, or how effective for their allergy was a medication they bought across the counter, or what an incredible movie is at the fourteen-screen cinema. We are most likely to try that product or place or event. There is no salesperson like the one who touches us one on one.

263

When Jesus called His first followers, the foundation of the church He was to build, He made them one-on-one salesmen. He intended for us to be "fishers of men." Let's go fishing!

And Jesus said unto them, Come ye after me, and I will make you to become fishers of men. Mark 1:17

July 31, 1994

September 18

Is Your Eye on the Ball?

I marvel at the skill and coordination of athletes. I am not always sure that my marveling is admiration. Maybe some of it is pure jealousy. I remember trying to play basketball in high school, and realizing that I could not do "razzle-dazzle" ball handling. The Harlem Globetrotters were my heroes, because they could handle a basketball with incredible dexterity.

Later, I learned that my problem was not that I was stupid. I was not concentrating enough on the movement of the ball.

Life deals with us that way. GOD allows life to throw at us some people who need to be loved or counseled or just listened to. Unless we are attentive, they will bounce away from us before we realize GOD had sent them into our lives.

Or He sends to us opportunities to do something special for ourselves, our families, our communities. There may be only a brief window during which we can seize those opportunities. And if we grab the ones that will help ourselves, but reject those that would help the community, we may forfeit the first!

What is GOD pitching at you with lightning speed? Is it a chance to help somebody who may not be lovable, or whose need comes at an inconvenient time? Don't miss that ball—your own blessings may be a part of it! Is it an opportunity to use your influence to improve the neighborhood, or the city? Who knows but that if you accept the throw, dozens or hundreds or thousands of people would benefit? And who knows but that if you miss the ball (or refuse to catch it), there is no backup person to perform the service you were ordained to perform?

When GOD throws, be watching. Your task and your joys are attached. You accept or reject them together. Stay alert!

The righteousness of the perfect shall direct his way: but the wicked shall fall by his own wickedness. Proverbs 11:5

March 20, 1994

September 19

We Learn Best from the Mean Ones

No elementary school pupil would say such a thing. Probably, few secondary school students would say it. But at some point in our maturing, we learn that the very teachers we hated were the ones who drove us to excellence in grammar or problem-solving or musical or athletic performance. There is a paradox in life: What is comfortable or fun seldom helps us to be the best.

A young couple's baby died after only a few months of life. Why would GOD allow such a thing to happen? Is He really that sadistic?

Paul tells us He begged GOD to rid him of some physical ailment but GOD left him with it. Surely Paul was disappointed in GOD, Who is fully capable of healing, or even of raising the dead, but Who deliberately refused to heal him. But Paul says he learned out of his disappointment to "glory in infirmities," because he discovered that he was strong when he was weak (2 Corinthians 12:7).

It is normal to complain when GOD does not erase some painful burden, or rescue us from grief or failure or sickness. It is not normal to be grateful for infirmities, for hardships. But in wiser moments, we will remember that pain helps us to mature, and that adversity is one of the ways in which GOD toughens us, sweetens us, teaches us compassion, makes us wiser.

265

And God is able to make all grace abound toward you; that ye, always having all sufficiency in all things, may abound to every good work.
II Corinthians 9:8

November 6, 1994

September 20

GOD Does Not Need Our Equipment

When you go to Sunday School you will find that GOD performed a military miracle with a rag-tag army led by a man named Gideon. He was no Joshua, no David with royal trappings. The lesson, from Judges 7, does not report the conversation between Gideon and GOD in Judges 6, where he protests that because he is from the wrong side of the tracks, he could not lead his nation (6:15). But it does reflect GOD's side of the conversation: It carries Judges 7:7, which makes the same promise as does GOD in Judges 6:16: "You don't need many troops or much equipment; I will take what you have and win the battle for you."

Just a Sunday School lesson, to be slammed shut when we tuck the Sunday School book under our arm?

No! It is a resounding, echoing promise that if we surrender our weakness to GOD, He will transform that weakness into strength. So you are sick. Or your heart is broken. Or your bills have inundated you. Or the relationship you had so hoped would be beautiful has turned ugly.

266

Common sense will tell you to give up. It is hopeless. You are not pure enough to deserve Divine help, anyway. But GOD does not operate on our common sense. He finds us poorly-equipped and unworthy, and fights our battles for us—and WINS! Trust Him.

And the LORD said unto him, surely I will be with thee, and thou shall smite the Midianites as one man. Judges 6:16

October 9, 1994

September 21

Practice Makes Perfect

It is easy—very easy—to find something wrong. That hip, or ankle, or wrist is hurting right now. You are still mad at your husband, or wife, or child, or friend, because of what he/she did. That usher directed you to this seat, when you wanted to sit in that one. And that alto in the choir is looking at you funny—what is the matter with her?

If you find things wrong easily, it is because you practice too much. Want life to be sweeter? Then begin a new discipline. It will be a little awkward at first, but like most skills, it gets easier with continued practice. Try thinking of what is right in your life.

Before you realize it, you will be able to enjoy rainy days and to make the best of good conversation when the flight is late and to be glad that even with some pain, you can dress yourself and go out of the house. Life is so full of little blessings that you really don't have time to complain to GOD, because of the multitude of praises you have to send up. You can cancel your protest about a lazy City Council or an inept State Legislature, and praise GOD that you live in a land where the people have some voice in government. You can delete that complaint about the hurting hip, or ankle, or wrist. Just stand up, and praise GOD that you are not a quadriplegic. See how practice improves your game?

267

Praise the LORD. Praise the LORD, O my soul. Psalm 146:11

March 3, 2002

September 22

When Your Religion Itches

This is the first day of autumn. The air—even in Houston—is a bit more brisk, and homeowners can change their lawn chores from cutting grass to raking leaves. In school, the children begin to use more red, yellow and orange crayons. And the caterers adorn their head tables with golds and browns.

All of these changes reflect an annual phenomenon that everybody sees but nobody understands—the time when Nature gives up her fruits. But even though harvest-time is beyond our powers to explain, it ought to teach selfish man a lesson or two.

A tree that does not drop its fruit dies. Refusal to yield its ripened ears kills the stalk. And we are reminded every year that we must give if we are to continue to grow. When GOD prospers us, we must either share it or be destroyed by it.

268

Many areas of sharing exist. Every day presents an opportunity to listen to GOD's plea to be heard. When GOD speaks, we need to respond to Him. And we cannot say that we do not have the time or the money to share. We must admit that GOD has given us all we have, and He gave it to us partly for ourselves and partly for our neighbors.

So if we feel an itch on this autumn day, it is just a little reminder that it is time to drop some fruit!

Every branch in me that beareth not fruit He taketh away: and every branch that beareth fruit, He purgeth it, that it may bring forth more fruit. John 15:2

September 25, 1977

September 23

When Autumn Leaves Start to Fall

The cascading violins of a Mantovani arrangement, the tumbling declensions of the Roger Williams piano down-scaling, the elegant browns and tans of the cashmeres and worsteds in the TV commercials for fall men's wear, the colorful decorations on ten thousand school bulletin boards—these all proclaim that summer is over, and it is time to celebrate the quiet glory of autumn. Today is the first day of autumn.

When individuals reached "the big Four-0" and there is no longer any device by which they can define themselves as "young," they may struggle against the reality of the autumn years by lying about their age (or simply cleverly taking the Fifth) or by resorting to youth-extending tricks like hair color or obsessive belly-flattening or even highly secret, cosmetic surgery. Or they can celebrate that maturity by setting off the gray of their hair with coordinating garments and by offering to mentor those who are following in their footsteps.

Sneaking and hiding and lying through autumn is not an option.

When we shall look back on our autumn, will we see adults who were guided through the hazards of growing up by the hand of strong experience with GOD and circumstance? Or will we find only discarded tubes of hair-coloring and overly-garish clothes?

269

The days of our years are threescore years and ten; and if by reason of strength they be fourscore years, yet is their strength labour and sorrow; for it is soon cut off, and we fly away. Psalm 90:10

September 27, 1992

September 24

Lookin' Good!

"I know I look better in dark suits. (In light clothes, I am ugly—so, of course, in dark clothing I am gorgeous, right?) That great suit bought in St. Louis would be the one. The shirt must have shrunk; I have a bit of a tug-of-war with the collar. But I can hide the pull-lines behind the necktie. Have the pants shrunk, too? Got to find a better cleaner; they're ruining my clothes! Looks like the belt is a bit smaller than I remember it. That's impossible—I have always been thin. Who switched belts on me? Well, I'll go on and wear the light suit, but I won't be gorgeous!" How many times has this monologue been recited?

We know the problem. Years and good food. And we know the answer. Dieting and exercise.

GOD has poured blessings on us, and we have gorged ourselves on His goodness. We don't need to pray when everything is going so well. We really do not have much time to read GOD's word when we are healthy, prosperous, and busy. How can you spend valuable hours with the sick or the hurting or the unsaved when we have so many meetings and social functions to handle and so many people clamoring for our attention?

One day when we need firm spiritual muscle and good spiritual shape, we discover we have grown flabby.

We must not wait until we are ugly before GOD. We can cut back on psychological junk-food, and go on an Opti-fast of spiritual self-indulgence. We can set up a good regimen of prayer, Bible study, and comfort for the sick and the hurt. When the merciless lens of adversity takes aim we must be spiritually in shape—and gorgeous inside!

Create in me a clean heart, O GOD; and renew a right spirit within me. Psalm 51:10

April 5, 1992

September 25

How Would You Like It?

She sits sobbing quietly at her lunch table. She has worked hard, but is still unappreciated. He comes home long-faced, and tells his wife nothing is wrong. Of course she knows he is lying. He has trained a subordinate, and the subordinate has been promoted over him. You lie in the hall of the emergency ward in pain, while workers laugh and talk and ignore you. It hurts to be mistreated. So how do you treat people?

Want to know how to treat people? Ask yourself how you would like to be treated, and you have a full manual. Jesus' Sermon on the Mount has little "shouting material" in it, and yet it is timeless in its profundity and spiritual depth. It contains that full manual. "Therefore all things whatsoever ye would that men should do to you, do ye even so to them: for this is the law and the prophets" (Matthew 7:12). The "Golden Rule" is not just Jesus talk—it is the heart of all scripture! You can praise GOD in thousands of decibels, but if you do not treat properly your brother or sister, your praise falls on deaf ears.

So what would GOD like to see you and me doing for Him?

If "the law and the prophets" are summed up in the Golden Rule, He would like to see us telling that sad young lady at the lunch table she has done a good job. He would like to see us being fair and just in our treatment of employees and subordinates. He would like to see us sensitive to people's needs, whether somebody with a flat tire in the rain, or a sick person who is seldom visited, or a child who needs to he encouraged because he or she is not as smart or as pretty or as popular as his or her peers. We are grateful when somebody goes out of his or her way to be kind to us.

Well, if we like it, that's our cue when our turn comes!

If a man say, I love GOD, and hateth his brother, he is a liar: for he that loveth not his brother whom he hath seen, how can he love GOD whom he hath not seen? I John 4:20

April 22, 2001

September 26

Just Do It

The crowd is loud and boisterous, waiting for their team to come onto the floor. Many of them wear the colors of the team—some have painted their faces or colored their hair to highlight their team. They are true fans (i.e., "fanatics") of their team, win or lose. When the stadium is darkened and the spotlight pours its massive white circle on the floor, the team members run out into the beam of light. And the fans go wild. The noise is ear-splitting. The hometown crowd is truly behind its team.

That should be enough fan support.

But not yet. Cheering girls in bright team colors and the team mascot with his curious costume run out onto the floor to demand even more fan support. The deep bass-baritone of the announcer instructs the crowd. The mascot is going to throw into the air a towel in the team colors; and while the towel is in the air, the crowd is to shout at the tops of their thousands of lungs. When the towel lands on the floor, everybody is to be stone silent. The towel goes up, the cheering girls begin to jump and shout and urge the people to do likewise, and the very walls rattle with the thunderous cheering. The cloth touches the floor, and you can hear a pin drop. And they do it again to make sure that no fan fails to yell for the team.

272

There is a message in this strange ritual: You do not cheer because the team is winning; you cheer because the team deserves the support of its home town.

To a more significant way, praise GOD for sending His Son to die for us. We don't praise Him in gratitude for His blessings last week. We don't praise Him to appeal for blessings this week. We don't even praise Him because we feel great today.

Praise is intentional, deliberate, given simply because He is worthy of praise. So don't wait until you feel like praising GOD; just do it!

Bless the LORD, O my soul: and all that is within me, bless His holy name. Psalm 103:1

August 5, 2001

September 27

Sailboats & Steamships

Children may never have heard it. But adults surely heard it when they were children. Some Sunday School teacher or youth worker would talk about sailboats, which have to be driven by the wind, and steamships, which have engines inside themselves and are not dependent on the wind. And the motivator would urge individuals to be driven from inside by values rather than to be pushed from outside by peers and popular trends.

Mission Sundays remind us that the church of Jesus Christ has a mandate—a commission—orders from the LORD. We are to be missionaries. But if the only time we witness is when we feel the push of duty, then we are useless to Christ. Jesus followed orders, too. But He was not driven by cold duty. He obeyed His Father and redeemed us because He was "moved with compassion." He loves us.

If we love a sinner, we want to rescue him or her from damnation, and so we witness to him or her. (A friend will not let a drunk friend drive. Surely, a friend will not let an unsaved friend go to Hell.) If we love Jesus, we will be a missionary eagerly, gladly. We will not have to be pushed by mandate or commandment.

273

So how are you doing with your "missionary engine"? Does it fire you up to pray for people who are not family or friends? Does it rev you up to learn the Bible so you can pass its riches on to somebody who needs to know about a loving GOD and a redeeming Savior? Does it drive you to join witnessing teams so that others can extend their witness beyond the church walls? Does it make you suddenly pick up the phone to call someone who needs a consoling word or a listening ear?

If you are a missionary driven from the inside, you are Jesus' kind of missionary!

...He that exhorteth, on exhortation: he that giveth, let him do it with simplicity; he that ruleth, with diligence; he that showeth mercy, with cheerfulness. Romans 12:8

April 30, 1989

September 28

Better Than a Horn of Plenty

So you're amazed that there is always new stuff in your old Bible? You've been listening to the New Testament on tape and familiar scriptures keep pouring out new meaning? Well...

Divine stuff is like that.

Ever seen a cornucopia? Yes, you have. It is the familiar "horn of plenty," continually overflowing with fruits, vegetables, and flowers. Story is, it is the horn of a goat named Amalthaea. No, this was no ordinary goat. Seems that the GOD Cronus, king of the Titans, feared that one of his children would dethrone him, and so he swallowed them as soon as they were born. But his mate Rhea saved the infant Zeus by substituting a stone wrapped in swaddling clothes and hiding him in a cave in Crete. There he was suckled by the nymph-goat Amalthaea, and survived until he could overthrow his cruel father and become the chief Greek GOD. At the death of the goat who had mothered him, he blessed one of her horns with endless plenty. (Haven't you been dying to know all that?)

274

Well, Zeus and all those other beings are mythology. But GOD really has blessed His word with endless treasure. No matter how often you look at the story of creation or the struggles of the Hebrews in Egypt or the Ten Commandments or the wealth of the Psalms or the narratives of the Gospels or the power of the Epistles or the magnificence of the Revelation (deep breath here), you will find some new insight, some fresh perspective, some unseen side of some character or some teaching you had not seen before.

Psalm 1 describes the righteous man as meditating on GOD's law day and night, and becoming a fruitful tree by the waters. The real cornucopia is not the horn of a goat—it is the ever-abundant word of GOD. Bon Appetit!

I will delight myself in Thy statutes: I will not forget Thy word.
Psalm 119:16

July 25, 1999

September 29

With Everything

There are times when a dainty hors d'oeuvre is a proper tidbit. You are elegantly attired in your formal best, at the exclusive function in a sophisticated setting. And you delicately balance your Bohemian crystal and your creamed salmon (one pinkie carefully extended) and smile about nothing in particular.

Then there are those sloppy T-shirt and ripped jeans times when you want a big, messy hamburger; not a neat White Castle, but one from a greasy little shack in the 'hood. It should be big and juicy, and loaded with lettuce, tomato, mayonnaise, ketchup, and onions. In other words, you want a chin- dripper "with everything."

Jesus says we should love the LORD our GOD completely. In other words, we must love GOD with everything. Your sloppy sandwich is not complete without ripe tomato squirting its juice onto your T-shirt. Our love for GOD is not complete unless we do it with wide open throttles.

We love Him with our time (and at least 17 hours a week are given to His service without expecting pay). We love Him with our abilities (and the best of those skills are made available for Him without compensation). We love Him with our personalities (and we will be civil, even sweet, whether the other person is right or wrong, because we must reflect His Spirit). We love Him with our money (and we do not quibble about giving Him the first tenth, plus an offering, or wonder if He will forget to bless us in return). And we study and pray and fast and witness to Him constantly—not because it is Christian duty, but because we love Him so much. It is not a dainty, elegant, proper love. It is juicy, even sloppy!

And thou shalt love the LORD thy GOD with all thy heart, and with all thy soul, and with all thy mind, and with all thy strength: this is the first commandment. Mark 12:30

September 27, 1998

September 30

How Did Mama Know?

It seems such a contradiction. We work to make it possible for our children to get the best possible education. We glorify scholarship, putting high-achieving students on an "honor roll." We reward those who make the highest grades with grants of money so that they may continue to develop their acumen. Our vernacular sparkles with admiration for high intellect: We may dub a brilliant person an "Einstein," after the great mathematics and physics genius; we urge support of scholarship funds with the warning, "A mind is a terrible thing to waste"; a giant computer corporation uses a single word as its global theme—"Think." We are sold on brain-power.

And yet each of us knows somebody who puts to shame brilliant thinkers with what we call "mother-wit." The very term hints that mothers, even without much education, sense what scholars might miss entirely and can work out ways to shepherd their children even when they do not have an abundance of resources. What gives mother some strange advantage over the Rhodes scholar?

She appreciates education, but she relies on GOD.

"She" refers not only to mother, but to anyone who knows that there is a Power beyond reason that can achieve the impossible, reverse the irreversible, perceive the invisible. And that divine Power will convey to His faithful servants that sixth sense that guides us through hazards, over hurdles, and around obstacles. The finest adults you know were most often reared in homes without spectacular intellect. The sweetest, most giving, most servant-like spirits may have been "C" students. They may not be able to give a profound lecture, but they can get a prayer through when Phi Beta Kappas have hit the proverbial stone wall.

Learn all you can from books; but pray for the "mother-wit" of the Holy Spirit!

Thou hast hid these things from the wise and prudent, and hast revealed them unto babes. Luke 10- 21

July 22, 2001

276

October 1

If You Cannot Sing Like Angels...

Have you ever considered the primary job description of angels? Yes, they punish bad guys (Genesis 19), they deliver messages (Judges 6, Luke 1), and they even release folks from jail (Acts 4, 16).

But their primary mission is none of the above. Isaiah gave us the best picture of what they do 24/7 (if you dare use that imagery for Heavenly beings). He said they sing praises to GOD (Isaiah 6:2, Revelation 4:8) without even taking pit stops. Far more than dealing with us here on earth, they focus on GOD, and praise Him unceasingly. So the old spirituals notwithstanding, angels are not primarily singers. And despite the best-written scripts for movies and television, they do not primarily follow you and me around, trying to get us to live good lives.

Now, if these eternal beings, creatures of GOD with supernatural powers beyond anything we know on this earth, praise GOD endlessly, how about you and me? The biggest favor GOD has done for them is to create them. For you and me He sent His Son to die to redeem us from our sins—and we were fully guilty as charged! Why should angels praise Him so continually, and you and I, who have been redeemed by the blood of His Son, find it hard to have the time or the inclination to praise Him?

Be an angel—you don't need a great voice, nor wings to get to the other side of the world—just praise Him because He is worthy of praise!

277

Bless thou the LORD, O my soul. Praise ye the LORD. Psalm 104:35b

September 26, 1999

October 2

Patch It In

Clearly I come from the wrong generation. "Crack" was what you didn't step on on the sidewalk, "rap" was what the teacher did to your knuckles when you shot a spitball; a "chip" was junk food that came in a bag; "patch" meant to put a piece of cloth on a tear or glue a rubber square on a leaking inner tube (a leaking what?). None of them referred to drugs or music or computers or audio-video. A few weeks ago, I gave my bride a Christmas present—a big-screen TV and some components with a cluster of speakers which promise to provide "surround-sound." Since she came from the same generation I did, she was not overly impressed. But, determined to provide her with big, clear pictures and incredible sound, I asked three of our members who know everything there is to know about entertainment centers to install all of this stuff for us. They did. But she was not interested in "surround-sound" and suggested that we could scatter the speakers around the house so that music could be conveyed to other rooms. So I have called one of them back to place them and activate them as she wants. He came over last week and told me what he has to do. He must get some extra wire, reaching into the dining and living rooms, and then "patch" the speakers into the amplifier. (No, I don't know what all that means; but I expect it to make music emerge in rooms other than the den.)

278

That is what GOD requires of us. His grace has made salvation available to us. Now, He commissions us to tell those we live with, those we work with, those we have fun with, about what things the LORD has done for us and can do for them. That is witnessing. It is Heaven's strategy for "patching" the power of the Holy Spirit into folks like you and me, so that the joy of salvation can be broadcast through earthen vessels. Are you patched in?

For the LORD GOD is a sun and shield: the LORD will give grace and glory: no good thing will he withhold from them that walk uprightly. Psalm 84:11

January 25, 1998

October 3

LORD, Make Me an Instrument

We have a mission under GOD, a reason for living. We are designed to be witnesses to GOD's love. He has sent His Son to show us how to live, to die in our stead to redeem us from our sins, and to assign the Holy Spirit to direct us in our witness for Him. We do not live to develop skills to acquire income to enjoy maximum luxury. We live to exalt His Name, to surrender to His will, to tell all we can about His glory. St. Francis of Assisi prayed to be "an instrument of His peace."

That has major implications.

It means, of course, that we ought to preach Jesus to everybody we can reach. But being an instrument of His peace means more than evangelizing.

It means that our lives ought to brighten the world in which we live. Our homes ought to be places of love and closeness. Our co-workers ought to consider it a joy to work with us. Friends ought to look forward to having contact with us, because we bring such warmth to those contacts. Even strangers ought to find something about us that makes them feel comfortable, even welcome, around us.

279

Our witness is not so much our words as our behavior.

The best way for me to convince you that you ought to come to, or draw closer to, Jesus, is for you to see the spirit of Jesus in me. The best salesperson for a product or service, they say, is a satisfied customer, oozing enthusiasm for that product or service.

Neither yield ye your members as instruments of righteousness unto sin: but yield yourselves unto

GOD, as those that are alive from the dead, and your members as instruments of righteousness unto GOD. Romans 6:13

October 31, 1999

October 4

W<small>HY</small>   P<small>RAISE</small>
~~How~~ Do I ~~Love~~ Thee?

I PRAISE YOU FOR WHO YOU ARE AND FOR WHAT YOU DO.

I praise You for Who You are.
     You are the Almighty, All-knowing, All-present GOD.
     You are maker and sustainer of the universe.
     You are the source of all blessings, and of all judgment;
       your justice indicts, and your mercy redeems.
     You are ruler of the natural and the supernatural;
       neither angel, demon, nor creature can exist without you.
     Your will is absolute; you govern without assistance, counsel, or
     advice.
     You are all power, all righteousness, and all love.
     There is none beside you. You alone are GOD—all by Yourself.

I praise You for what You do.

280

     You made me as a wondrous machine, superior to any device
     humans can make.
     You created a universe especially as an environment for me.
     You exalted me to have dominion over all you had made.
     You made me innocent of sin and exempt from sickness or death.
     After I sinned and was sentenced to eternal condemnation, you
     sent your Son to take my punishment, to redeem me from my
     damnation.
     You sent your Holy Spirit to help me to get back to You, and to
     learn to do Your will.
     You woke me up this morning, and yesterday morning, and the
     day before, etc., etc.
     You pour out on me mercies totally undeserved, because of Your
     Son.
I praise You because I have to! HALLELUJAH!

*The heavens declare the glory of GOD and the firmament showeth
his handiwork. Psalm 19:1*

August 23, 1998

October 5

My LORD Is Watching All the Time

Don't know how or when it happened But somewhere in our history we turned Jesus into a Teddy bear. He became willing to accept any behavior, any attitude, and reply with a pre-recorded, "Father, forgive them." Somehow we re-cast Him as One Who is totally unaware of what we do in private, as One Who assumes that our hand-clapping, shouting, and holy dances is a real manifestation of our stewardship to Him. Coming before the church in tears makes up for all our failure to share our time and talents, to spend so much on ourselves that nothing is left to bring to His altar. We have portrayed our Jesus as a good and kind shepherd, but not as LORD, Master, and King.

Have we forgotten that He is both?

Yes, He forgives our iniquities and accepts us despite our foibles. But He is neither blind nor gullible (certainly not stupid). When He kept a steady gaze on the treasury as people brought their offering to the Temple, He knew the Pharisees gave nice-sized offerings; but He praised only one—the widow with her mite (Luke 21:1-4). When He narrated parables about a Samaritan, servants with gold talents, or a rich man who refused to give bread to a beggar, He was making a very strong point: You must account to GOD for the way you handle the blessings He gives to you. And when He spoke of the righteous and the unrighteous on His right and left hands, going to punishment or reward depending on how well they had treated the poor and the oppressed, you could not miss His message—Jesus is watching your stewardship more than your public praise.

281

He takes to His own bosom the suffering. But the same "gentle Jesus" is the sharp-eyed Judge Who sees all you do and hears all you say. How are we doing with the time, talent, and treasure He has given to us?

For the LORD is our judge, the LORD is our lawgiver, the LORD is our King; He will save us. Isaiah 33:22

March 5, 2000

October 6

Laugh at the Funny Clown

A visitor to our town is fascinated by a comic figure in TV commercials. A man yells breathlessly about couches and dining room furniture and mattresses. He jerks and jumps and seems wildly frenetic as he babbles at top volume about quick delivery and a huge inventory that has everything we could possibly want in a furniture store. Then he snatches a dollar bill out of his hip pocket, holds it up like a victor's trophy and virtually screams that his furniture store will save you MONEY! The performance has our visitor in stitches. "Who is this clown? I have never seen a commercial like that!" (Uncontrollable waves of laughter.)

How could our visitor know? This "clown" is a multimillionaire who has built his furniture business into an empire, and has given millions to charities and non-profits. This "clown" has run dozens of other furniture stores out of business. This "clown" is a super-salesman and is passionate about his merchandise.

282

That's what the church is supposed to be.

If we really took the Great Commission seriously, we would be super-salespersons of the glorious gospel of Jesus Christ. If we were at all passionate about our own salvation, we would be beating the drum at every opportunity to witness to others who need salvation, too. And if we did more fervent "clowning" for the LORD, perhaps we could take away from Satan a whole lot more of his clients!

Hearing of thy love and faith, which thou hast toward the LORD Jesus and toward all saints; That the communication of thy faith may become effectual by the acknowledging of every good thing which is in you in Christ Jesus. Philemon 5-6

March 30, 2003

October 7

Yes, You (He) Can

There is a difference between fact and Truth. The fact is no one can change the ways of an old sinner. The Truth is, no matter how long a person has been a reprobate or how low he has lived, direct contact with Christ can totally reverse his direction and completely change that person's lifestyle. The fact is if three competent doctors diagnose someone's case as terminal, the person will die. The Truth is the touch of the Master Physician cannot only extend one's life, but can totally erase all symptoms of his "terminal case."

It is not that fact is not reliable; it is that Truth transcends fact. And Truth (with a capital "T") is not subject to the same conditions as fact, because it proceeds from the mind of GOD.

That is why no child of GOD should ever give up or feel that his situation is hopeless. Even when the facts push you into the proverbial corner, you ought simply to climb over them on to the ladder of Faith. Jesus was inclined to challenge people to overcome the impossible with faith. "According to your faith be it unto you," he said to the two blind men in Matthew 9:20—never regarding the "fact" that there was no cure for blindness. The Truth was He—GOD—is the Light of the World!

283

So check out your list of impossible odds, your catalog of guaranteed defeats. Fold that list up with a firm belief that with GOD nothing is impossible. Then confidently lay it at the feet of the Master, believing that He Who loves you will not ignore your need—if you trust Him. After that surrender your will to His, knowing full well that His will must be done; but also be assured that He can handle your impossibilities. When you have done all this, lift your chin, put on your smile, and go out and cheer up somebody else. Our own "facts of life" have been absorbed into the eternal Truth that GOD is in complete control.

But Jesus beheld them, and said unto them, With men this is impossible; but with GOD all things are possible. Matthew 19:26

November 13, 1988

October 8

What's under the Hood?

There is a renewed interest in a sport that had died down a few years ago—"hot rodding." This is a racing sport based on older cars modified so that they are faster and stronger than older cars should be. Hot rodders will take a 1939 Ford or a 1942 Studebaker, remove its existing engine, transmission, and suspension system, and "hot rod" it. You may be looking at an old body, its rattles welded tight, its finish glassy bright, and think it is just a restored antique. In fact, it may have a 1996 truck motor under its slightly enlarged hood and the re-sized chassis and springs of a Land Rover. Its quaint outward appearance may belie the leonine roar and the burst of speed that leaves smoking tire-marks behind it.

That is what a Spirit-powered Christian is like.

You have confessed that you are a sinner. You have accepted Jesus Christ as your LORD and Savior. You have received the empowering, indwelling presence of the Holy Spirit. And you have committed your life to witnessing for your LORD.

284

People looking at you in the office simply see a quiet, friendly, consistent worker. People who know you as friend or neighbor assume you have had good home training, because you are gentle, helpful, considerate. Many will credit your parents with your good character, your honesty, your reliability. What a good job they did!

But you know what really drives you. You are not just a "nice, old-fashioned lady or gentleman." The power of Heaven itself gives you incalculable resources, and neither sin nor sickness can keep up with you when the Holy Spirit revs up your soul. Go! Go! Go!

I will love thee, O LORD my strength. Psalm 18:1

November 3, 1996

October 9

Just Try

Diehard football fans know the name. The old story about Roy Regal and his "wrong-way" run is enlightening. The details are not important, but Regal caught the ball and ran with it in the wrong direction, almost making a touchdown for the opposing team before his own teammates tackled him. He was sure he would be expelled from school or at least kicked off the team. But his coach issued the famous words, "Boy, the game is just half over. Go back in there and win!"

That is how GOD does with us. We ought to have been condemned for our sins, but He sent His Son to die for us and then through His resurrection to win the game for us. And He does not ask that we make up for our sins, only that we do our best.

Much of the world demands success. GOD only asks effort. You receive awards for superlative performance. GOD blesses us just for trying

Good intentions do not go far in this cynical and callous world. If you cannot produce excellence, you can be quickly eliminated. Only with GOD is it enough that you tried, that you wanted to do well, that you struggled.

We who are called by His name ought to accept one another as he does—not because we achieved well, but because we tried.

Jesus never preached, "Blessed are the righteous, for they shall be filled." His sermon was much different and more hopeful. We may not attain righteousness, but we ought to be working on it. If we are, promises Jesus, we shall be filled.

Blessed are they which do hunger and thirst after righteousness: for they shall be filled. Matthew 5:6

April 6, 1997

October 10

When Do We Say the Prayer?

When you were a child (fifty years ago, last year, or right now), somebody told you that you should pray on at least two occasions: when you sit down to eat and before you lie down to sleep. Three or four times a day is a pretty good pattern for saying prayers.

It is woefully insufficient as a pattern for praying.

"Saying prayers" is what we have all learned to do—some with considerable expertise. "Praying" does not require expertise or eloquence. It is the outpouring of the soul from the deepest levels. It is the reach upward toward GOD. It does not begin with a salutation nor end with an "Amen." Whether or not you have ever learned a prayer, there is an almost instinctive raising of the spirit toward Heaven when you know you need GOD. Be confronted with a major crisis, and if you do not consider suicide, you will pray.

So when, or how often, or under what circumstances, should we pray?

Jesus is our model for prayer. He obviously did not limit His conversation with His Father to meals and bedtime, nor squeeze them between a salutation and an Amen. When Paul admonished us to pray, he was underscoring Jesus' counsel that we "ought always to pray and not to faint" (Luke 18:1). So how long did Jesus spend in prayer? Luke 6:12 tells us that it was all night sometimes!

We ought to talk to GOD all day and all night—that's how continually He blesses you!

Pray without ceasing. I Thessalonians 5:17

July 27, 1997

October 11

Honor Them Anyhow

So much has changed since the first time. I am in Africa today, in Ghana, the first nation in sub- Sahara Africa to win independence, the home of DuBois' Pan-African initiatives, of Marcus Garvey's Black Star, and of Kente cloth, universally recognized as the cloth of Africa. When I first visited this continent, I giggled at the undeveloped economy, at the still-primitive technology. I looked down on the old villages with their thatched roofs and their simple tribal sociology. And I was clearly superior to them in my theology—I knew about one GOD Who sent a Redeemer; they still put out food for bush GODs, who never ate it. I was above Africa.

That was over forty years ago.

I still see an economy that cannot match Wall Street, and there are still little villages with elders and naked children and chickens and goats. But today, I do not giggle. In the passing decades, I have seen the wisdom of the Fifth Commandment: "Honour thy father and thy mother" (Exodus 20:12). As an older man, I know how much I owe to the parents and grandparents and great-grandparents from whom I am descended. My parents did not have much education or money, but their sacrifices made it possible that I could go to college. My grandfather had to bend to Jim Crow laws all his life, but he taught his grandson never to consider himself inferior. I owe so much to my forebears.

287

So today, I see the naked children, but I also see how loved they are in this strong family environment. I see the symbols of other religions, but I see how reverent they are to their faiths—and I am ashamed of how we take for granted our GOD, Who sent His Son to redeem us from our sins. The pride we have came from a proud people who knew they were worthy. The brightness of our children goes back to pre-historic times and civilizations of broad-nosed people. And our tendency to have faith in GOD comes very naturally from Africa, where there are many religions but no atheists at all!

Look not every man on his own things, but every man also on the things of others. Philippians 2:4

May 28, 2000

October 12

Thanks for the Bruises

The sixteenth chapter of Matthew is a remarkable chapter. It holds up a mirror to us who promise to be faithful to GOD. It shows the high courage and keen insight of Jesus' first followers. Jesus asks His disciples who they think He really is. Peter, often the spokesman for the other followers, proclaims that Jesus is the promised Christ, the Son of GOD. Jesus praises Him. Then Jesus tells His disciples that being the Christ means He must suffer and be killed. Peter, again speaking for the other eleven, boldly rejects such a pessimistic projection. And Jesus, Who had just recognized the Divine source of his first statement, now brands the same speaker as a dummy whose ventriloquist is Satan! (Matthew 16:13-23).

This dialogue represents not only Jesus and His disciples, A.D. 28, but Jesus and His disciples today. We sing the right songs and pray the right prayers, even quote the right scriptures when we preach or teach or witness. But with all our outward piety, we have a tough time dealing with principles of Matthew 16:24-26. Did you really think that following Jesus would be a guarantee of easy living or blessings in return for your faithful work?

288

Jesus promises only that He will be with us and He will; but not only in Paradise. He will be with us when we are rejected, when we are unjustly treated, when no one thanks us for our labors. Jesus tells us in Matthew 5:11 and 12 that we are in great company! Rejoice about it!

Then said Jesus unto His disciples, if any man will come after me, let him deny himself, and take up his cross, and follow Me. Matthew 16:24

October 7, 2001

Houston Public Library
Check Out Summary

Title: Laughter, tears, silence : expressive med
itations
Call number: 204.35 D743
Item ID: 33477475354891
Date due: 11/3/2017,23:59

Title: Mother & son : the respect effect
Call number: 248.8431 E29
Item ID: 33477485420468
Date due: 11/3/2017,23:59

Title: 15 invitations from Jesus to-- come close
r : a ca
Call number: 248.4 R896
Item ID: 33477454154012
Date due: 11/3/2017,23:59

Title: Lawson's leaves of love : daily meditatio
ns
Call number: 248.84 L425
Item ID: 33477000684508
Date due: 11/3/2017,23:59

October 13

Elegy to Ordinary Saints

How did it happen? You worship on Sunday mornings. Millions are asleep, or fishing, or on the golf course, or just reading the papers. This is a day set aside by most businesses for employees to be off from work. Hotels feature great brunches. Theatres expect larger crowds. But you get dressed and come to church.

Was it because somewhere in your childhood or your young adulthood you heard a dynamic sermon that persuaded you that GOD must have priority in your life? Was it because an incredible choir or a dynamite singer or singing group blew you away ten or twenty years ago?

Probably not.

Most of us who follow Jesus have established patterns of worship and study. We attend worship services, go to Bible studies in churches or even on the job, try to live according to His principles, and praise Him for blessings rather than credit ourselves for them. We can trace those patterns back to some time in the dim past. But very seldom did those patterns begin with a great sermon or series of sermons. Almost never did they get started with a dynamic song or song service or concert.

289

Some simple saint in our background was the catalyst.

Mama or Big Mama made us go to church and Sunday School. A teacher without theological training or a youth leader who loved us or a Christian neighbor who cared got us started. Effective witnesses do not have to be dynamic or brilliant or famous. Christians who "turn the world upside down" are ordinary people who love the LORD. Let's turn our world upside down for Jesus!

For I am not ashamed of the gospel of Christ: for it is the power of GOD unto salvation to every one that believeth; to the Jew first, and also to the Greek. Romans 1:16

August 26, 2001

October 14

What Is Man?

If GOD created the entire universe with all its galaxies, and sustains every microbe and the molecules that constitute living beings and inanimate structures—how can He care what happens to you and me? That is the question raised by the Psalmist in Psalm 8. But in response to his own question, he praises GOD for not only caring, but elevating humans to a high position of stewardship for all of that universe.

That blows up a popular stereotype.

Christians often bifurcate GOD into an Old Testament deity of power and law and a New Testament deity of compassion and mercy. Wrong! Our New Testament declares that GOD loved us so much that He sent His Son to redeem all people. And Psalm 8 declares that the same GOD, against Whom we rebelled shortly after He created us, made us managers of His universe. He is a GOD of power; He is a GOD of law. But at the same time He is a GOD whose compassion and mercy allows us to survive when our sinfulness should annihilate us, Whose grace, despite our stubbornness, puts us in charge of the microbes and the molecules!

290

Don't you dare give up when life is rough with you! GOD sees you, cares about you, and carries you in His bosom. He is your Shepherd.

The LORD is my shepherd; I shall not want. Psalm 23:1

October 8, 1995

October 15

I'll Make Me A Man

The poet who gave us the Black National Anthem also gave us a whimsical view of the beginnings of humankind in a poem, loosely modeled after a slave-sermon, called "The Creation." He depicts GOD as a kind of divine artisan Who sat down on a hill by the side of a deep, wide river where He could think;

And He thought and He thought

Till He thought:

I'll make me a man!

That portrait of GOD was primitive, "toiling over a lump of clay," but it catches the reality of what you and I must do. We have to take black boys, rough-hewn and unformed, and toil over them "like a mammy bending over her baby," until GOD can breathe into them His own image. From the slums and the parent-absent suburbs, from surroundings of violence and drugs, from schools staffed by teachers who don't care, in neighborhoods with locked doors, we must take these little lumps of clay and mold them and shape them into something that looks like GOD.

291

Your pre-occupation cannot be with horsepower or 8% or a condo in Nottingham Forest. You have to care about the boys wearing black skin who grow up to be drug-addicts or pediatricians, killers or attorneys at law, illiterate drunks or teachers who produce merit scholars—all depending on whether you bent over a boy, helping him to become a strong black Christian man. You have to!

And the LORD GOD formed man of the dust of the ground and breathed into his nostrils the breath of life; and man became a living soul. Genesis 2:7

February 19, 1995

October 16

I'm O.K.

Attitudes go through cycles. After decades of aggressive feminist rhetoric, a march of men in Washington draws praises from women. (Another all-male march is being planned as you read.) We watched a whole generation in a quest for pleasure—and now we are quite strict regarding smoking, alcohol, drug use, multi-partner sex. We talked racial harmony for a while—now we have to do another study on the racial divisions we admitted in 1968.

Attitudes change with new experiences, new lessons.

When you embrace GOD, your self-image changes. David asked, "Who am I, LORD, and what is my family?" (2 Samuel 7:18). Abraham described himself as "nothing but dust and ashes" (Genesis 18:27). Gideon wailed, My clan is the weakest in Manasseh, and I am the least in my family (Judges 6:15). Even the eminent Isaiah once put himself down as "a man of unclean lips," living among a people of unclean lips.

But GOD made an immeasurable difference in them all.

So you think something is wrong with an unmarried adult? You have your theories about singles as socially maladjusted, unhealthily tied to parents, overly finicky about partner-choice, gay or lesbian? And you would like to project your stereotypes on them, so they will cry "I am a worm and not human."

As long as singles (or anybody else) remain separated from GOD, a sense of inferiority is a normal attitude. But once they become new creatures in Christ, happy seekers after the will of GOD, they cannot wallow in self-pity, nor can they allow you and me to paste labels of our own making on them. Whether Abraham or Gideon or David or Isaiah or whoever—when you are with Jesus, you are somebody! Rejoice in who you are—a child of the King!

Then went King David in, and sat before the LORD and he said, Who am I, O LORD GOD? and what is my house, that thou hast brought me hitherto? IISamuel 7:18

October 22, 1995

October 17

Where Are the Nine?

The Gospel writer Luke records an incident in the ministry of Jesus in which ten men, all afflicted with the dreadful disease leprosy, begged the LORD to heal them. He did, One of the men returned to thank Jesus, and He raised the burning question: Were there not ten cleansed? but where are the nine? (Luke 17:17).

That story is not a parable. It is an incident from the actual ministry of Jesus. And it is a reflection of reality, harsh and constant. We are not by nature thankful animals—as says the song from "South Pacific" about prejudice, "we must be carefully taught." As we approach the formal holiday of Thanksgiving, we are reminded again of our blessings. But how easily we can get side-tracked and overlook those blessings, and the vessels through whom they come!

Have you thanked your parents/mate/children/siblings for any value they may have to you? What a great time to send a note or to phone some teacher, some mentor, some supervisor, some friend wise in counsel! GOD has made available to you more than good things— He has sent some hardships to toughen and sweeten you. Can you thank Him for adversities that are helping you to mature? It is so easy to be one of the nine, busy about many things—be the one who stops long enough to thank GOD, and the people He has sent into your life.

293

O give thanks unto the LORD; call upon His name: make known His deeds among the people. Psalm 105:1

November 19, 1995

October 18

The Shape of a Christian

Should you ask the average person on the street, "Are you a Christian?," except for some few who are clearly adherents of other faiths or who enjoy philosophical jousting, most Americans would answer, "Yes." This would confirm the Gallup poll that says that 93% of Americans believe in GOD, and most of those who believe in GOD accept Jesus Christ as His manifestation. "Yes, I am a Christian," then, would express their belief.

But Jesus says belief is not the proof of the pudding.

It is not enough to accept teachings about Jesus—you demonstrate your faith in Him by what you do for Him. Prayer and Bible study and worship attendance is insufficient discipleship, unless you include acts of mercy and righteousness.

GOD is laying at your feet a man beaten and left for dead. You cannot pass by on your way to the Temple. Your faith requires that you stop and prove that you really love Jesus!

294

If ye love Me, keep My commandments. John 14:15

January 26, 1997

October 19

How Much Do You Love Me?

Those of us with a bit of gray on top (showing, dyed, or bald) remember some lyrics from a song popular long ago that ask, "How much do I love you?" And the answer is a question: "How deep is the ocean? How high is the sky?" The clear meaning is that his/her love is unlimited. You will remember the familiar squib about somebody asking Jesus how much He loves them, and He answers, "This much," as He stretches out His arms and dies.

Love is not something you say; it is something you do. And you demonstrate it over and over again, not just on a special occasion.

If you love Jesus, you will not put limits on your demonstration of that love. You will worship Him continually. You will live according to the highest moral and ethical standards possible. You will give freely of your time, your skills, your money to carry out the witness He commissioned us to carry out.

When the father who is told by the court he must support his children and their mother pushes his lawyer to try to get the minimum he must pay, he is saying, "I don't love them." Ignore his rhetoric; watch his actions. When the tired school teacher says, "Don't ask me to work in Sunday School or Children's Church; I have paid my dues for the 183 days I had to put into those kids in the District," he/she is saying, "I like the pay-check, but I do not love the children." Ignore the rhetoric. Check out the reality.

295

Now, really, how much do you love Jesus? No, don't tell us—show us!

And be ye kind to one another, tenderhearted, forgiving one another even as GOD for Christ's sake hath forgiven you. Ephesians 4:32

June 8, 1997

October 20

What Difference Do I Make?

Actors desire Oscars or Tonys. Musicians covet Grammys. Athletes push hard for championships. It is normal to want to be recognized as the best in your field. All of us would like financial windfalls, whether through a salary that may be more than we deserve or an unexpected inheritance—or winning a lottery. It is normal to want money above and beyond our basic needs.

But the best achievement of all is to make a positive impact on people's lives.

I remember two individuals of this distinction. They are/were followers of Jesus Christ who have had a powerful influence on young people. They both can boast of being successful, productive adults who are doing well in their fields and among their peers because of the imprint these two teachers made on them in teen or pre-teen years. Both of them are/were driven by their sense of responsibility to GOD; and both therefore drove others—students, co-workers, family, friends— to do their best for Him (and for themselves). Both have stacks of plaques and trophies with no market value at all. Neither left behind a fortune or national or international celebrity. But both will be remembered long after whoever won the super lottery or who was captain of the NBA Championship team of ten years ago.

Because they made a difference.

It matters little what we are champion of or that we can buy a half-million dollar house cash. It matters much whose life we have elevated.

If any man serve Me, let him follow Me; and where I am, there shall also My servant be: if any man serve Me, him will My Father honour.
John 12:26

May 20, 2001

October 21

In & Out

What we think about most commonly is determined by what we feed our minds most commonly. What we can talk about most easily is determined by what we have heard and read and viewed most easily. What comes out is what has gone in.

The clothes horse can talk glibly about fashion and designers and what is "in" and what you should not be caught dead in. The sports nut can amaze you with statistics about players and teams and trivia about historic passes or catches or speeds. Couch potatoes and movie lovers are encyclopedic about actors and movie titles and TV shows and Oscars and Emmys. They communicate whatever they have spent the most time enjoying. What comes out is what has gone in.

Similarly, if we intentionally establish a regimen of daily prayer, what seems stiff and artificial at first becomes natural and easy, and we are praising GOD for good stuff or leaning on Him for stuff we need on a regular, almost subconscious basis. If we put down the sports pages and the cheap novel to read through the book of Romans or Psalms (to be followed by Ephesians or Isaiah), we will find ourselves spouting rich phrases from Paul or David without thinking about it.

What is even better, we will wake up anticipating new blessings each day and will find it easy to encourage or comfort somebody with insights we have been digesting. When GOD's word is a regular part of our spiritual diet and prayer is as common as aiming the remote, more common than aiming an expletive at a thoughtless driver, our words will be inspirational because our thoughts will be above common thoughts. What comes out is what has gone in.

As the living Father hath sent Me, and I live by the Father: so he that eateth Me, even he shall live by Me. John 6:57

September 17, 2000

October 22

GOD's Zoo

We joked about it while we were dealing with crises on the church grounds. We had spent days working with the grandmother whose van sank in the river, killing five, and we had given generously for the burial of her son, among the five. We were struggling with a deluge of people who had descended on our Missions and Mercy office, storm victims swelling the normal number. And we were simultaneously working on proposals for funds to support a ministry to prison releasees and their families and black boys who needed help with basic educational skills. We realized that Wheeler Avenue Baptist Church is a zoo.

So it broke the tension when somebody cracked, "Do you think we can persuade GOD to let this be just a Sunday church?" (Nervous laughter at a question on the border between joke and blasphemy.) And a quick repartee from another: "If we can persuade the Devil to just work Sundays!" (More nervous laughter, while we searched the skies for possible lightning bolts.)

298

Yes, the church is a zoo, loud with the cacophony of cries of the hurting. And no, neither GOD nor Satan will take a six-day vacation between Sundays.

But that is exactly as it should be.

We exalt a GOD Whose love includes church members and unchurched people, people who worship Him and people who worship nobody, the deserving and the undeserving. We exalt a "Missionary GOD," Whose Son has assigned us a world-wide territory.

So if we understand even partially Matthew 28:19, 20; or Luke 4:18, 19; or Acts 1:8, we know that we must deal with our zoo, and it is no joke !

But ye shall receive power, after that the Holy Ghost is come upon you: and ye shall be witnesses unto Me both in Jerusalem, and in all Judea, and in Samaris, and unto the uttermost part of the earth. Acts 1:8

July 29, 2001

October 23

LORD, What Wilt Thou Have Me To Do?

When Saul of Tarsus met Jesus face to face on the Damascus Road this was the second question he asked the LORD. (The first was, "Who art thou, LORD?" Acts 9:5-6.) The lesson is clear: When we meet Jesus face to face, we are willing to take assignment from Him.

We can dodge, but we cannot keep from being hit with some challenge or assignment.

What will thou have us to do about the material comforts and the excess trinkets, gadgets, and garments accumulated?

What will thou have us to do about my attitudes regarding people who may share our faith but who do not share our color and our politics?

What will thou have me to do about empty pews in our church where there could be a wino or a prostitute or a homeless person?

What will thou have me to do about the tough times we try to get through without prayer?

A revival always brings inspiration, and it gives us a needed lift. But if the only thing we get is an inspirational lift, then our intake valve is stuck.

The important question always, "LORD, what will thou have me to do?"

299

LORD, what wilt thou have me do? And the LORD said unto him, Arise, and go…and it shall be told thee what thou must do. Acts 9:6

October 15, 1989

October 24

Ask Not...

Over a generation ago, a young President challenged this nation in an innocent age before the assassinations of political and moral leaders, before the nightmare of Vietnam, and before we sank into a sick narcissism that plunged us into the age of AIDS and drugs. His challenge was, "Ask not what your country can do for you; ask what you can do for your country."

Still, we echo that challenge on much higher grounds than national purpose. Jesus has not called us to "enjoy" or to "be inspired," but to serve, to minister without the certainty of compensation or even appreciation, to die carrying out a commission for people who may not even know we died. Our LORD has not called us to be an audience, but fellow-servants with Him. We have been given a mission.

When we gather to enjoy, we may gather unequipped, without any other preparation than our casual clothes and our credit card. But if we gather to work, we must bring tools and skills and commitment.

300

We are challenged to be part of the larger mission in the community. We must know our Bible better than the average Sunday School student. We must allocate some time when we will be available to the sick, the unsaved, the hurt. It is not enough to minister "when we have to." And we must develop our skills of prayer, of counseling, of expressing love. So we have to accumulate tools, sharpen skills, affirm and back up commitment.

GOD's love for us was not a casual emotion, expressed when it was convenient for Him. It was a deep, gut-wrenching outpouring of the best He had—the giving of His only begotten Son for persons who could not have cared less. That is what He calls us to do: to ask what we can do for our LORD.

Seek Me daily, and delight to know My ways. Isaiah 58:2

July 30, 1989

October 25

Take Good Care of It

New mothers marvel at it, when they see their newborn for the first time. There is not a physician, novice or veteran, who has not been amazed at it, when they see its built-in powers of self-healing, or when all their examinations cannot reveal all its complexities. It is the human body, an unparalleled miracle of organs and muscle, hung on a skeleton, skillfully wrapped in skin and decorated with hair, and controlled by the most sensitive computer ever devised. It is a gift from GOD, with which He elevated us above all of His creation.

And we take it for granted.

Among us are those who deal with the damaged human body. Whether they must struggle with the ravages of cancer or HIV-AIDS or are recuperating from surgery or being rehabilitated from heart attack or stroke, they recognize how precious is health. If they are able to remember, they can recall when they could jump out of bed feeling great, or could work all day, party half the night, grab a short sleep, and be ready to go again at sunrise. They may long for the days when they could walk briskly, or raise their arm above their shoulder, or eat anything on the menu. They do not take for granted the body GOD gave them. Nor should we.

301

We have been told that we must be stewards of all that GOD has given us—we talk about bringing to Him the first fruits of time, talent, and treasure. We ought to be good stewards of this incredible machine we live in. If we still have good health, we ought to eat right, avoid addictive substances, exercise, rest properly, get regular medical, dental, optical checkups. If we have lost some of our health, we ought to do the best we can with what is left.

Taking care of GOD's gift to us is not just good hygiene. It is good and faithful stewardship.

What? Know ye not that your body is the temple of the Holy Ghost which is in you, which ye have of GOD, and ye are not your own? I Corinthians 6:19

April 30, 2000

October 26

Jump—He'll Catch You

It is a bit fuzzy as I look back over sixty-four years to remember, but it gently comes into focus when I strain a bit. We had a shed behind our house in St. Louis. It was not a garage. It was not a storage building. It was a shed. An old rickety frame structure about nine or ten feet high. We did all sorts of unauthorized things around that shed. We shot illegal marbles behind it (illegal marbles were "for keeps," and were a juvenile form of gambling). And we encouraged the smaller children to climb up onto its roof and jump off into the arms of bigger boys. I got more than a few whippings about that shed.

When I was about eight years old, I jumped off the roof. A twelve-year-old was to catch me, but at the last second he stepped back and I fell flat on my belly. OUCH! It was a great joke to him, but my fifteen-year-old uncle slapped him so hard he fell, while I tried to get enough breath to cry. After the twelve-year-old ran screaming home, my uncle told me I could not retreat into the house and drown in tears. I had to go back up onto the roof of the shed and jump again, or I would be scared of heights for the rest of my life. (Now as I reflect on this incident, I ask myself, What do fifteen-year- olds know about acrophobia?) I vaguely remember being virtually pushed back up the ladder to the top of the shed by sympathetic neighborhood boys, and Uncle Cleo standing tall and strong in the grass in front of the shed, his outstretched arms welcoming me to jump.

The image is fuzzy, but the symbolism is strong.

This story from my personal memories carries a strong message. When we experience tragedy, we must push ourselves to praise GOD anyhow, remembering that He is our refuge. Among Moses' last words to Israel just before he went up into Mount Pisgah was to trust GOD. Life is frightening, but GOD is ready to catch us.

302

The eternal GOD is thy refuge, and underneath are the everlasting arm. Deuteronomy 33:27a

June 25, 2000

October 27

You'll Never Walk Alone

GOD's intent for the universe has never been fulfilled. He intended a perfectly balanced, unified, and harmonious universe with all creatures living according to His will. But because our ancestors rebelled against Him and every descendant including you and me are continuing to rebel against Him, He has to deal with a corrupted universe that suffers imbalance, disunity, and disharmony. Part of His design involved a creature divided into two sexes, the male and female of which would engender families. But since the two initial creatures rebelled against His will, all of the families bear the taint of corruption. GOD's work ever since that rebellion has been to redeem His universe, and to reconcile His corrupt creatures to Himself. This is where we come in.

His intent did not include people living single because neither human conflict or rejection, divorce or death were designed by GOD. He intended that men and women would come together and "multiply and replenish the earth." But the fact is that we do have people living single. Shall we blame them for having suffered whatever traumas in our corrupt social system have left them alone?

303

That is where Jesus comes in.

Today, we look at the harsh reality of a bruised and broken society, and rather than bemoan its scars, we join Jesus in helping to put Humpty Dumpty together again. He never married. The Holy Spirit appointed Paul to begin the ministry to the larger world beyond the Jews; and Paul was a single man. As we celebrate a ministry to singles, we do not have to give them lists of eligibles or put on parties to help them meet partners. What we will do is to tell them that if they cling to Jesus Christ, they are not alone. They are in the best relationship human beings can have.

He that believeth in the Son hath everlasting life: and he that believeth not the Son shall not see life; but the wrath of GOD abideth on him.
John 3:36

October 27, 1996

October 28

We Can Fly

Birds are everywhere. They congregate in lines on the power lines running behind our homes. They form choirs and use our neighbor's live oak as their choir-stand. They always know when we have just washed our car—does Satan guide their instinct? But the most majestic birds we know are celebrated in scripture: "But they that wait upon the LORD shall renew their strength; they shall mount up with wings as eagles; they shall run, and not be weary; and they shall walk, and not faint" (Isaiah 40:31).

Once when my wife Audrey and I were experiencing an Alaskan cruise, we encountered these incredible birds. Among the most remarkable sights we saw in Glacier Bay were the eagles, floating above the blue-white mountains of ice, then suddenly nose-diving to the frigid surface of the water to snatch in milliseconds a 20-inch salmon from the waves. I thought of pigeons flapping noisily as cars approach their feeding spot near the remains of an animal. There is no comparison between these familiar creatures of urban Houston and the regal birds Isaiah likens to those who are strengthened by their faith in GOD. They do not flap wildly nor stop at every mouse-corpse. They soar. And they shift from gliding to swooping in an instant; and there is no one who can challenge their possession of their catch. Our birds blend into the scenery of every day and are easily ignored.

304

The prophet says that if we are plugged into GOD's power we do not tire or faint, but are continually made new. And he chooses these magnificent creatures to symbolize GOD's continual energizing of His children.

Before you throw up your hands, lean on GOD about your situation and discover the difference between frantic flapping and victorious soaring.

As birds flying, so will the LORD of hosts defend Jerusalem; defending also He will deliver it; and passing over He will preserve it. Isaiah 31:5

August 11, 2002

October 29

Ever Heard a Stone Shout?

GOD does not need us. He is self-sufficient. He can work without our talents. Nothing we can buy is anything He needs. Our compliments do not exalt Him, nor do our insults injure Him. We can take our ball and go home, and His work is not affected one whit. GOD does not need us.

He asks for our help. He wants us to be His messengers, stewards of His gifts, His servants to carry out His work in the world.

We have to say something to salve our self-image when we face the harsh reality that GOD can function quite well if we did not even exist.

The truth is He does not want to do it alone. He really does want us to bring our gifts to His altar, however rough and unpolished we may think they are. Uneducated? Burdened with bad habits or bad attitudes? Do not know the Bible well and do not pray enough? We should bring our two fishes and five barley loaves to Jesus anyway and watch Him transform them into the ingredients of a major miracle.

305

He says if His followers do not help Him, the rocks will cry out. He can do it alone, but He will not. And if we will not help Him, He will find somebody who will. (And it will not be an arch-angel; it will be something or somebody rough and unpolished.)

I tell you that, if these should hold their peace, the stones would immediately cry out. Luke 19:40

August 22, 1993

October 30

A Time for Children

Halloween is traditionally the beginning of the "children's season." Costumes and treats may be enjoyed by adults, but they are designed to delight children. Thanksgiving is a family time, when often entire families re-unite around a big dinner table. Children are definitely included, and grandchildren are a main feature. But before the Halloween candy is on the table in the entry, Christmas decorations are going up in the major stores, with a special eye on the children's market. They know we are going to buy a scarf for Aunt Tillie, but the merchants are banking on newer and more expensive toys for the children. It is indeed a period for an emphasis on kids.

But aside from what we provide to entertain or feed lads, what are we teaching them?

That you can extort "treats" out of adults by threatening to play cruel "tricks" on them? (Most of our little ones have no idea what the phrase "trick or treat" means—how early do they learn?) That you express thanks by gorging yourself on a huge meal while millions go to bed hungry? That the most important gift is really the most expensive—or at least the most current?

On the threshold of the Christmas frenzy, let's find the time to teach our children the real principles of these holidays. Halloween (All Hallows' Eve) really teaches that GOD has overcome death, and that the grave has no victory. Thanksgiving ought to tell them how important it is to recognize GOD as the source of blessings Who is worthy of our praise. Christmas is intended to remind us of GOD's gift of His own Son to redeem us from our sins and from certain damnation. We ought to use these weeks to re-focus the minds of our children from selfish impulses to impulses of praise. Share with them a book or a movie that emphasizes the true spirit of Christmas. If we did not know what to tell them about Halloween or Thanksgiving, we should know some good things to share with them on Jesus' birthday.

As arrows are in the hand of a mighty man; so are children of the youth. Psalms 127:4

November 26, 2000

October 31

There Are No Goblins

Was there ever a time when you did not want to sleep with the closet door open or when you were certain that the creak outside your door was something coming to get you? By the time you reach a "cool" age, you begin denying that dark rooms scared you—and if you deny long enough and loudly enough, you may come to believe you never had such fears at all.

Everybody is frightened by something. But the antidote for fear is a sense of security. Maybe the lights provided some of that sense; surely Mama or Daddy did. And every child needs the sense of security that insulates us against fear.

So do adults.

It isn't shapes in dark closets or noises outside the door any more that scare us. Maybe it is uncertainty about our ability to perform well or to be accepted by our peers or about income or health or cracks in relationships. And we need a sense of security that tells us we're going to be O.K. The best source of that sense of security is not lights or parents, but GOD, Who protects us even in the midst of adversity.

Come out from under that cover! The LORD is in the room!

The Psalmist sings words of truth:

The LORD is my light and my salvation; whom shall I fear? The LORD is the strength of my life; of whom shall I be afraid?" Psalms 27:1

April 27, 1997

November 1

He Won—For Us

Christians of the world rejoice because Jesus rose from the dead. Jairus, or the widow of Nain, or Mary and Martha, can all agree that this is ample reason to rejoice. All of them rejoiced when Jesus raised their loved ones from the dead. But our joy is much greater than theirs. Jesus conquered death for their particular families, and that was magnificent. But the daughter of Jairus, the son of the widow of Nain, and Lazarus, brother of Mary and Martha, were only raised to continue mortal life. They would all have to die again.

We have infinitely more reason to praise, to shout, to rejoice. When Jesus emerged from that tomb on the first day of the week following Passover, He conquered death for all who believe in Him. For you and me, "death" is no longer the end of life—it is no more than a transition from mortality to immortality. We now can pass gently and swiftly from a body that ages, and gets sick, and is injured to an incorruptible body that is totally impervious to the circumstances of this world. We are not limited to succeeding in this life. If we are not celebrities, if we do not control wealth, if we do not wield great power, that's O.K. We are real somebodies in the eternal Kingdom Jesus has prepared for us. He recognizes us all as great, because we have been bought at a price beyond calculation and will wear crowns like royalty—we are preferred guests at the table of the LORD.

You have a sick or ailing body? You have discord with your mate or with members of your family? You are struggling to make ends meet? You are miserable on your job and have no known options? You are painfully lonely and feel you will never find somebody who will love you for yourself? Then do what Jairus did, what that widowed mother from Nain did, what the sisters from Bethany did—take your situation to One Who is no longer in a tomb, but Who rose for your needs and mine, and who sits right now at the right hand of His Father. Tell Jesus your needs, and He will pass on the word to the Father, and the One Who conquered death for us can surely shine the light of joy into your life!

And she shall bring forth a son, and thou shalt call His name Jesus: for He shall save His people from their sins. Matthew 1:21

308

November 2

Raise Your Right Hand

You have been asked to appear in court on behalf of your friend or co-worker. He/she has been sued or accused and needs somebody to testify to his/her good character. You gave the usual excuses about your work schedule or your discomfort in courtroom situations, but he/she and his/her attorney assured you that it would not take up much of your time and that you did not need to have a lawyer's familiarity with either the case or court procedures.

Your real reason for reluctance you may never have expressed. You were not certain of the innocence of your friend or co-worker. But his/her lawyer knew already that was in the back of your mind, and so the final arm-twist was "You don't have to testify to the innocence or guilt of_____; all you have to do is to tell the court that you have known him/her to be a good citizen. You are not an expert on his/her behavior; but you can testify to what you have known about him/her. Surely you can do that. Right?"

So you said, "All right." And now you are sitting outside the courtroom waiting to be called to be a "character witness."

That is what you must do for Jesus.

If you raise your right hand and swear to tell the truth, the whole truth, and nothing but the truth about Jesus, you have agreed to tell only what you have experienced with Him.

You don't have to know Hebrew history. You don't have to know the Ten Commandments by heart nor the themes of the sixteen writers of prophecy. You do not need to be articulate about Pauline theology nor be able to quote chapter and verse about Christian eschatology. You don't need to know the profound truths about the essence and attributes of the Messiah.

All you need to say about Him is what you have experienced.

You can tell somebody you have been down, and He lifted you. You can testify that you have been without direction, and that He has shown you the way. You can proclaim that you have been miserable, and that He has filled your life with joy. You can say that you were blind and now you see.

And you know what? The most persuasive argument you can give for Jesus is the argument that comes from your personal experience with Him. Somebody will try Jesus if you just tell them what you know about him. So tell the whole truth!

> *That in every thing ye are enriched by Him, in all utterance and in all knowledge; even as the testimony of Christ was confirmed in you.*
> *I Corinthians 1:5-6*

November 15, 1992

310

November 3

He Opens Doors

We don't need a sainted grandmother to tell us that. In our own lives we have seen GOD provide at times when you were certain there was no hope—even if you did not give Him credit for doing it.

But the same GOD Who opens doors for us sometimes deliberately closes them before we can enter them.

We become disappointed when we don't get the job or the appointment we wanted? After we cried and pouted and fussed at GOD, something far better came along; and we realized that GOD provided a "ram in the bushes" that was better than what we had wanted. The Apostle Paul tells us in Acts 16 that he tried diligently to set up a missionary route to the East, but the Holy Spirit kept closing doors in his face. Then finally there came the vision of the man from Macedonia, and he realized that GOD wanted the church of Jesus Christ to expand to Europe first before it could expand to Asia. History has proven GOD right again—and even the stubborn Paul understood why GOD prevented him from going East.

311

Should we pull down our Thesaurus of Profanity to find new cuss-words to throw at Heaven? No. When GOD is in the door-closing mode, we should remember Job's words and trust GOD with our life. His agenda is always the best!

The LORD gave, and the LORD hath taken away; blessed be the name of the LORD. Job 1:21b

September 29, 1991

GOD Wears No Rolex

We may not admit it, because it would be impertinent—but we often have a problem with GOD. He simply will not conform to our schedules. Of course, we would not tell Him that. But when we need a blessing, we need it by Thursday at 3:00 p.m. And all too often our deadline passes without His having respected it. How can we file our complaint with Him without risking bodily harm?

We have gone to Him with our needs, detailed them, copied them in triplicate, and backed them up on CD. He could not possibly miss what we need and when we need it. Yes, He has a few hundred million other folks listing their needs at the same time as we; but He is fully able to handle all of our petitions simultaneously. After all, He is omniscient! So why does He allow our problem to gather dust when with a snap of His cosmic finger He could make us instantly healthy, wealthy, and wise?

312

Because He operates outside our piddling clocks, our miserable calendars, our petty schedules.

Remember when the doctors had informed the family to assemble because Big Mama would probably not last the night; and we were a little miffed at GOD because we had been praying for her for weeks while she got progressively weaker; and all night we alternated between praying for her and fussing at GOD; and at 6:00 in the morning she opened her eyes, sat up in bed, and asked for bacon and eggs? Remember? And remember that she is still around, complaining about Deacon White's long prayers?

Don't forget that when you are chiding GOD about not respecting your deadline! Praise GOD—there is no time-piece on His wrist!

But as for me, my prayer is unto Thee, O LORD, in an acceptable time: O GOD, in the multitude of Thy mercy, hear me, in the truth of Thy salvation. Psalm 69:13

September 24, 2000

November 5

The Final Word

The rhetoric was at highest pitch. The administration of the largest and most powerful nation on earth was screaming that Saddam Hussein must be stopped now! The nations who taught us our culture and our technology, France and Germany, were telling us we were too hasty, and they would not support a sudden military strike. Peace protesters had filled the streets around the Capitol in Washington and U.N. headquarters in New York to yell their points of view to both sides. Newscasters were at peak volume reporting crowds rushing to Target and Wal-Mart and Home Depot to stock up on plastic sheeting and duct tape because of the dangers of deadly chemicals in the subways or a truck loaded with explosives—we were under "orange alert."

And while we were hyperventilating, GOD shut us all up.

Over 27 inches of snow fell on 15 states, and Washington, New York, and the entire Eastern seaboard was shut down. Children rejoiced that schools were closed, and the newscasters stopped talking about an orange alert to marvel that with all our 21st century weather technology, we were helpless. GOD's quiet whiteness had paralyzed 80 million people; and our most sophisticated, top- secret planes were anchored to the snowy ground. The last word did not belong to either Washington or Baghdad. It belonged to the One Who supervises the universe.

GOD can help us overcome whatever obstacles we face, or can stop in an instant whatever schemes we devise. The President is powerful, and Saddam is super-tough. But GOD is awesome—and totally in charge!

The earth is the LORD's and the fullness thereof; the world, and they that dwell therein. Psalm 24:1

February 23, 2003

November 6

Where Your Mouth Is

...that's where, according to the popular adage, we are supposed to put our money.

During campaign season, the media is saturated with political rhetoric. To a stranger just dropped on earth from the planet Ogbu, it would seem that election sites full of leaders who care deeply about their followers—their employment, their housing, their education, their safety from crime. But to those of us who listen to campaign claims year after year, it is just talk, designed especially for campaign season and intended to be discarded like used crepe paper after the candidate wins or loses.

That may be all right for political candidates. It is not all right for servants of Jesus Christ.

314

We produce our share of talk, too. Our Bible studies and sermons and workshops and special programs all tend to grind out one commodity in abundant measure: talk. We discuss, interpret, testify, argue and proclaim with all the fervor of gadget pitchmen on the shopping channels. And it is very easy to discard most of what we have said after the sermon or class or program is over.

Living in these times presents a challenge. How many preachers/teachers/leaders/talkers will commit themselves to adopt a specific task as Christians and be dependable in the fulfillment of that task? Who wants to take up the cross of drugs or tutoring or ministering to the homeless or the incarcerated?

Jesus measures our love for Him by our willingness to feed His sheep, not by our eloquence, not our skills in argument in Sunday School classes. Today and always, we need to put our money where our mouth is.

That ye might walk worthy of the LORD unto all pleasing, being fruitful in every good work, and increasing in the knowledge of GOD. Colossians 1:10

October 8, 1989

November 7

You Scratch My Back...

Long before a student attends college and takes his first course in physics, he learns the difference between a live ball and a dead one. (The live ball bounces.) And he has giggled as he releases the inflated balloon and it flies into the air with an awful "blaat." So when his physics professor drones out the axiom, "For every action there is a corresponding reaction," he perks up and says to himself, "I know what that means!"

A reciprocity exists between the Creator and His creatures, too. If you trust GOD and keep His commandments, His blessings are poured out on you. But if we reject GOD and disobey His mandates, we pay some ugly consequences. The miracle is that even though all of us know that GOD reacts with mercy or wrath depending on our own behavior, we still ignore His leadership and try to capitalize on our own poor understanding. And we seem surprised when our sins bear bitter fruits!

GOD has required that He be put first in our lives.

If we bring to Him the best that we have—the first fruits of our skills, our time, our resources—He reacts by filling our cups to overflowing. But if we put ourselves at the top of our list of priorities and cater to our own profit and pleasure (pitching to GOD any leftovers we may have), His reaction is to leave us with our own self-exaltation, and we plunge downward.

Christians/Believers proclaim the message of stewardship of time, of talent, and of income, and act with faithfulness. Then we can watch Him react with surplus blessings.

315

Bring ye all the tithes into the storehouse, that there may be meat in mine house, and prove now herewith, saith the LORD of hosts, if I will not open to you the windows of heaven, and pour you out a blessing, that there shall not be room enough to receive it. Malachi 3:10

October 6, 1991

November 8

Hallelujah Anyhow!

We have no right to set the tone of our praise according to the joys or problems of the day. Praise is not climactic—it is intentional. It is not measured by good or bad days. The words of David in Psalm 34 are like a baseball to the head and hit us: "I will bless the LORD at all times: His praise shall continually be in my mouth."

GOD's blessings to us are not based on how we treat Him. Sunshine and rain are sent to the just and the unjust (Matthew 5:45). He protects us even when we ignore Him. He rescues us from calamity despite our disobedience. His love is not driven by our attitudes or our behavior, but is the essence of His being—GOD is love.

So when you have just been promoted, or when you have been told your job has been terminated; when you are in the pink of health, or when your doctor breaks to you the news that your condition is chronic; when mate or children or friends treat you royally, or like garbage—whatever your condition, wake up and praise Him. During the day, pause at your desk or on your job to praise Him. In the evening, turn off the sitcom or the quiz show to tell Him He is worthy of praise.

316

I will sing of the mercies of the LORD for ever: with my mouth will I make known Thy faithfulness to all generations. Psalm 89:1

September 9, 2001

November 9

When You Need It

One of the marvels of modern medicine is the development of "time-release" capsules. I do not know how they work. But inside the capsule is a multitude of tiny pellets of medicine, somehow designed to break down at differing rates. Some of the medicine is released almost as soon as it reaches the stomach; some is released later; and some is not released until hours after the first medicine enters the system. This is a poor medical description, but the system keeps releasing new medicine as the body needs it.

But while it is a poor narrative for a doctor or nurse or pharmacist, it is a pretty good analogy for what GOD does for us.

I have consoled hundreds of families who have lost loved ones, and who have dealt with dozens of deaths. Death is not an unfamiliar experience for a pastor (or a physician, or a funeral director, etc.). But when the cold visitor comes to our house, he stabs us with a pain for which we have no glib words of consolation. Whatever we have said in an effort to comfort others must be tested in our own time of grief. And that is the time we discover what GOD does for us who grieve.

He sends strength to adjust to the pain of the moment of death. He sends more to adjust to the hurt we share with loved ones as they come to learn of the death. He sends additional strength to buoy us up for a wake and/or funeral service, and for the awful moment at graveside when pallbearers deposit the remains of our loved one on the straps over the grave. And He keeps sending little doses of strength as relatives and friends leave to return to business as usual and we find ourselves alone with our memories. He sends what we need when we need it.

Praise GOD for "time-release" love!

The LORD is my strength and my shield; my heart trusted in Him, and I am helped: therefore my heart greatly rejoiceth; and with my song will I praise Him. Psalm 28:7

July 23, 2000

November 10

Celebrating Through Tears

This has traditionally been the time for consumer fever. It begins with Halloween and the rush for costumes, decorations, parties. It ignores Thanksgiving altogether and plunges into an orgy of advertisements about things to buy and events to attend, with a loose reference to the birth of Christ (seldom mentioned), its brakes not fully applied until New Year's Eve. This has been the season of credit card insanity.

But something has stunned us.

We stumbled nervously through Halloween, most children not allowed the usual joys of free "trick- or-treating." As mega-corporations lay off employees in the thousands, who knows how much we can risk with American Express or MasterCard this year? Meantime, the often-ignored Jesus Christ has been shown more respect in the past 54 days as people have sought out churches—and surely synagogues, mosques, and temples have likewise seen increases in attendance.

318

Remember what our parents tried to tell us when we were young and foolish? "Just live long enough, and you'll understand." Well, tragedy brings pain, but it also brings some maturation, some seasoning to its victims. Nobody wants suffering, but while suffering is a cruel companion, she is an effective teacher. Enjoy the holiday season, but remember to thank GOD for all His mercies! We come into this season a bit more sober, a little more aware of our dependence upon GOD.

O give thanks unto the LORD; for He is good; for His mercy endureth for ever. I Chronicles 16:34

November 4, 2001

November 11

Honor Them for the Risk

On May 30, the nation paused to honor the veterans of our wars, from World War I to the peace-keeping operation in Bosnia. Many of us will fail to salute them, and that holiday may be just another break from work, another opportunity to shop or fish or play golf or just "chill." That is tragic, because it accuses us of ingratitude. Many people who went into the armed forces died for our country. Many more were permanently impaired. But even those who came back without a scratch risked their lives for the rest of us. We surely ought to express appreciation for that risk.

We have survived because of other people's risks for us. Our parents risked their happiness to sacrifice for us. Teachers risked their time and effort that we might learn the basic skills of life. Perhaps some employer risked a great deal to give us a chance to work in some company or agency or institution. We ought to express in some way our gratitude for their risks.

But the greatest risk of all was the risk taken by GOD when He sent His Son into a hostile world to die for our sins. Do we dare take for granted such a massive risk? We ought to praise Him without ceasing for making the ultimate sacrifice on our behalf.

If we develop the habit of saying "thanks" to some of the people who have taken risks for us, and especially if we can elevate that gratitude for earthly risks to praise and thanksgiving for the risk GOD took, then we can more easily and more naturally say "thanks" to our veterans, (even if we are pacifist or disagree with our foreign policy in some conflict).

Believe me that I am in the Father, and the Father in me: or else believe me for the very works' sake. John 14:11

May 26, 1996

November 12

Learning from the Dogs

The 1904 Nobel Prize in medicine went to a man who explained why we get hungry at lunch time. Ivan Petrovich Pavlov experimented with dogs to determine that by repeated association, an artificial stimulus (such as a bell) could be substituted for a natural stimulus (such as food) to cause a physiological reaction (salivation). He called this reaction a "conditioned reflex" and taught us that most acquired habits depend on chains of conditioned responses.

Modern movie thrillers use this technique regularly. If a sudden loud noise frightens viewers, then why not employ sudden bursts of loud sound in connection with the attack of a dinosaur or a murderer to create a shock response? They would not be nearly so likely to be startled by the silent video of the moment of horror as by the combination of the image plus the explosion of sound.

Similarly, persons who complain every time something goes wrong become conditioned to finding something wrong. The time will come when they complain when nothing serious is wrong, simply because they have conditioned themselves to complain.

So why not deliberately say, "Thank you, Jesus!" every time we think of something we are thankful for—a fair degree of health; family or loved ones or good friends; relative comfort, even if we do not have luxury; the absence of grief in our own household, at least for the past year or few months; a job, even if it is not the highest-paying job in the company or institution?

Yes, we can condition ourselves to feel grateful for more and more things. And the first thing we know, we are more likely to say, "Thank you, Jesus!" than to whine, "Why me, LORD?"

Thank you, Dr. Pavlov! And thank you, Jesus!

In every thing give thanks: for this is the will of GOD in Christ Jesus concerning you. I Thessalonians 5:18

September 12, 1993

November 13

Making Ourselves Sin-Proof

They were so busy they did not notice they were being watched. A chubby little boy in the blue and yellow uniform of the Cub Scouts and an eleven-year-old in Boy Scout khaki were standing in a light rain outside the bus that would take them to camp. Both were printing their names on plastic lunch bags with felt-tip markers.

A pitiful little whine went up from the Cub: "How come mine gets rained off and yours doesn't?" His older co-camper leaned over the youngster's baggage, rain dripping from his cap, and said quietly, "Your marker doesn't have the right kind of stuff in it. You can use mine." So the little fellow took the marker with "the right kind of stuff," scrawled his name big enough to be seen from the street, and proudly placed it near the luggage bay of the bus.

Some denominations define "holiness" and living free and above sin. Other denominations argue with that definition, assuming that no mortal can rise above sin. Some correctness exists on both sides. As long as we are on this side of the Jordan, we will do things that are not in line with the will of GOD. But that is no excuse to let normal impulses, passions, ambitions, reactions wash away our commitment to Jesus Christ. If we have really surrendered our lives to Him, He has changed us from the weakness which allows good intentions to be washed away and has given us a new spiritual indelibility that resists the Devil and stronger with each new attacks on us. No, we do not escape Satan's attacks, nor are we invulnerable to making mistakes. But with the Holy Spirit leading us into greater and greater faithfulness to Jesus Christ, we are more and more impervious to the temptations and wiles of our Enemy.

We may still stumble, but we will live above sin if deep in our heart we have "the right stuff."

Nay, in all things we are more than conquerors, through Him that loved us. Romans 8:37

April 16, 1989

November 14

Jesus (?) Comes In

It looks like Jesus. It makes sounds like Jesus. The prophets promised us Jesus would come—so this must be Jesus. Right?

"It ain't necessarily so."

Much religious talk goes on. Celebrities and heads of state openly profess their belief in GOD and show up in churches and religious meetings. Two preachers ran for President in the 1988 election; and in many political campaigns nowadays, it is common to hear candidates affirm that they feel it is "GOD's will" that they run, and win. Religious music, especially gospel music, is universally popular now. Gone from the music store shelves are the categories "sacred," and "secular" music because the distinctions are no longer clear.

Does all this mean Jesus has really become our first love?

It all depends on what people really want to commit to Jesus. It is not enough to have a warm feeling about GOD and His mercies. It is not sufficient to accept the joy and peace that comes with religious sensibilities or in the fellowship of the religious community.

322

We have to admit that we are sinners and we have to face the cross of Christ and all that it means for the saint as well as the sinner, and we have to build our hopes on nothing less than Jesus' blood and righteousness. We cannot enjoy gospel music and exciting preaching but continue to live a worldly lifestyle. Jesus requires that we take up our cross and follow Him every day. That means being excited about Him when there is nothing colorful or inspiring going on around us— indeed, even when circumstances are painful or disappointing.

We must be careful, for The Anti-Christ looks very much like Jesus. But the one component he cannot imitate is the cross—Jesus' and mine. The commercial says, "Look for the union label." The Spirit says, "Look for the cross."

...Whosoever will come after me, let him deny himself, and take up his cross, and follow me. Mark 8:34

December 10, 1989

November 15

What Can We Do for GOD?

It is a feature in many old stories. The king or the emperor wants to know what kind of subjects he has. So he disguises himself with old peasant's clothes and goes out among his people. Most often, he is disappointed with the way the majority of his subjects treat him while they think he is only a common peasant; however, always he finds some noble and heroic person whose kindness and compassion justify his experiment.

GOD sees many reactions to Him as He walks among us.

He sees the priests and Levites, intent on their Bible study or their prayer time, passing by robbery victims on the Jericho Road. He observes the fickle crowds, hands raised in praise, singing their Hosannas to Him as He moves closer and closer to His cross. (They are absent when He is tried by a kangaroo court and sentenced to die without due process.) What is GOD looking for from us?

Jesus made it crystal clear.

323

He wants us to be poor in spirit, meek, merciful, pure in heart, peacemakers; He wants us to hunger and thirst after righteousness, and to rejoice when we are persecuted for His sake. He wants us to show our discipleship by our love for one another. He wants us to use the power of the Holy Spirit to witness to all of His teachings.

That may not be withdrawing to read scripture twelve hours a day. That may not be rushing to the prayer meeting or shouting more loudly than ten other persons. It may not be being present in the sanctuary five days a week or singing in three choirs.

It is treating every human being as though he or she were Jesus visiting us. It is reflecting the gentle compassion of Jesus even when the person needing our compassion is guilty and worthy of punishment rather than compassion. In a word, His "new commandment" is not ritual or public praise. It is that we love as He loved us.

This is my commandment, that ye love one another, as I have loved you. John 15:12

September 20, 1987

November 16

The Bush Burned with Fire

The fire of the burning bush did not attract the attention of the shepherd Moses, but the fact that the leaves on the bush remained bright green and alive did. What kind of fire was this?

In many ways, the LORD ignites us and sets us aflame, but not to destroy us. The fire of Heaven makes us much more alive than any earthly pleasure or achievement or possession ever could.

Some of us commit more of our time and talent to GOD than we would have before, because we have been burned. Others of us will be sweeter-spirited and less critical than we would have before because we have been burned. Many of us will spend more time in prayer and meditation on GOD's word than we might have otherwise, because that fire has got into us.

324

We find that bringing our best to the altar of GOD does not diminish us. We can work for Him to the point of exhaustion—and feel exhilarated rather than worn out. We can give Him more than we could logically afford and rejoice as He sends back to us more than we had sacrificed for Him. We can love somebody unlovely or undeserving and be surprised when somebody we thought did not know us from a hole in the ground becomes a blessing to us.

Everybody burns out. We begin to wear out the moment we are born and move steadily toward our last gasp. Burning out is a common fate for us all...unless we are set on fire by GOD's Spirit. Then we do not get older; we get better!

But the manifestation of the Spirit is given to every man to profit withal. I Corinthians 12:7

April 29, 1990

November 17

A Good Bounce

Children learn it early. How high the ball bounces depends on how hard you throw it against the floor or the wall. A good pitcher knows better than to throw his fast ball at a home run hitter—that's the time for his best slow curve because a hard throw may end up over the fence. The principle of bouncing balls is the principle of blessings. You want major blessings? Then throw out major praises, major compassion, major sacrifices. As we enter into the Thanksgiving/Christmas seasons, we have once again the opportunity to observe the bounce of blessings. Even at an earthly level, if you receive an expensive gift, you feel obligated to respond with something you did not get at the Fire Sale. How much more will GOD keep His promise that if you give sacrificially of your time, your skills, your money, He will pour out unmeasured blessings upon you?

On earth it is "tit for tat," quid pro quo, you scratch my back, etc., etc. In Heaven, GOD has a much stronger bounce-back. You give a tenth. He pours out more blessings than you can contain. You show faith no bigger than a mustard seed. He makes mountains move for you. You surrender to Him a life worth less than an old car that no longer runs, he pours out on you a redemption that makes your life everlasting. With GOD, there is no simple formula for reciprocity; there is an inscrutable principle that when our weak praises go up, we are buried under avalanches of blessings coming down.

325

This season, we ought to do more to express thanksgiving than to recite a cold and mechanical prayer over a big, indigestible meal. We ought to find ways and times to praise GOD loudly and repeatedly; we ought to scour our environment and find people who need our help, and offer that help; we ought to use our contacts to witness to people how good GOD has been to us, and how good He wants to be to them; we ought to restructure our Christmas giving so that it is not simply conveying merchandise to family and friends (and people we want to impress), but acts of compassion to people who have no reason to expect that we care about them. Throw a hard ball of praise and expect a strong bounce of blessings!

The blessing of the LORD, it maketh rich, and He addeth no sorrow with it. Proverbs 10:22

November 7, 1999

November 18

Why Did GOD Do It ~~to~~ for Me?

She was at the right place at the right time.

She had just gotten off her night shift job and groaned wearily as she unlocked the door, with visions of hot bath and soft bed in the next very few minutes. The telephone shattered the silence, and she groaned again, but put on her cheery voice with a bright "Hello." The woman on the line hardly introduced herself before she began to pour out her story of violence and abuse by a boyfriend. Now the tearful woman was on the street and had been told to call her. She put down her purse and erased the visions of hot bath and soft bed and began to counsel the woman at the pay phone. She told her to stay there. She went back to her car, found the wretched woman at the service station near the telephone, invited her into her own car, took her back home, and spent the next four hours offering her motherly advice, hot coffee, and a warm bed for the night. Why did GOD place this miserable woman in her life?

326

Because she had been that woman.

She had spent many years addicted to alcohol, and somebody had helped her to get rehabilitation. Now she proudly wore a thirteen-year 'chip' which marked her as clean and sober. Her round smiling face had become a familiar encouragement to dozens of other people who needed to know that GOD redeems us from all kinds of addictions and gives us joy that can (and must) be shared with others still struggling with life's pains. She was at the right place at the right time for a wretched soul who had seriously considered suicide.

What pain have you borne which equipped you to comfort somebody else? Who has shown compassion for you, at least partly because they know from bitter experience what you are going through? Never assume that adversity is a curse from GOD. It may very well be equipment for a blessing you must deliver tomorrow. "All things work together for good to them that love GOD, to them that are called according to His purpose."

If there be therefore any consolation in Christ, if any comfort of love, if any fellowship of the Spirit, if any bowels and mercies, fulfill ye my joy, that ye be likeminded. Philippians 2:1-2a

September 10, 2000

November 19

Get Away from Those Phonies!

A very sincere acquaintance of mine has quit going to church. He is very sincere. And he says he simply cannot stand the number of hypocrites in church.

I don't blame him a bit. Hypocrites are a pain in the derriere.

That's why I have quit going to football and basketball games, and all other athletic events. There is so much show and razzle-dazzle—phony! I have also quit going to movies and looking at television. Those are not true stories; just actors selling fiction. Even the news is slanted. And I don't go to stores any more. Yes, they smile and say, "Good afternoon," but those hypocrites don't really care about me. All they want is my money. So I don't eat at restaurants, or take airlines, or drive a car (you have to endure sales and service people). There is not much left for me but family. And just the other day I realized that family is full of hypocrisy, too. My granddaughter drew a picture. She showed it to the family. And would you believe those insincere rascals raved and bragged about that little scratchy mess as though it were something beautiful? So I am just resigning from family because we have hypocrites like that in the family!

If you miss me, I will have gone into the desert to find a cave where I don't have to deal with hypocrites.

I won't be alone, though. I'm going to ask the guy who quit the church because of the hypocrites there.

He answered them and said unto them, Well hath Esaias prophesied of you hypocrites, as it is written, This people honoreth me with their lips, but their heart is far from me. Mark 7:6

April 28, 1996

November 20

When All Else Fails...

In this age of "gadget explosion," new trinkets appear on the market endlessly. When we buy the absolute last word in computer technology, a new device appears that makes it obsolete in weeks. Once a telephone was just a telephone. But now there is a multitude of types, styles, and capacities for what was an ordinary household or standard business item—and a whole catalogue of companies who make and service them. The sound and video world is overwhelming. Available is a host of audio devices, a plethora of sizes and prices of TV sets (with or without radio components, with or without VCR's, etc., etc.), a salmagundi of lighting appliances, a potpourri of calculating gadgets.

And for all of these (plus whatever goes into the kitchen, the den, the boudoir, the bathroom, the garage) there are little booklets—sometimes in four or five languages.

It is frustrating that we cannot buy a cheap watch and set it and wear it. We have to take a six-week course in watch-setting to be sure the stop-watch function and the multi-time-zone function and the date function are all properly set, too.

328

Well, if we need instructions on how to add five figures on our super-duper, absolutely-the-latest- developments calculator when we are buying bagels, cream cheese, and orange juice at the supermarket, how much more do we need instruction on how to live through the hazards of life in the twenty-first century?

Obviously, the book of instructions for living would be much more complex than the book of instructions for a hair dryer. And it is much more critical that we read the one that tells how to find personal joy and peace and direction than that we know how to program our VCR.

Of course, we know what that instructions book is! We can carry the instructions with our camcorder case so we will not miss shots we want to catch. But if we carry this special instructions book in our heart, we will not sin against GOD (Psalm119:11). The Hitachi manual will not help us with our Sony. But the Great Instructions Manual is good for all situations "for doctrine, for reproof, for correction, for instruction in righteousness"—and whether you are Japanese-made, or German-crafted, or made in the USA, this book will help you to be "perfect, and thoroughly furnished unto all good works" (II Timothy 3:16-17). When all else fails, be sure to read it!

Thy word is a lamp unto my feet, and a light unto my path. Psalm 119:105

November 8, 1992

November 21

Too Sweet

"When life hands you a lemon, make lemonade." That is such a snappy little squib. It puts a pleasantly positive spin on trials and tribulations. We could leave those eight words alone as self- contained wisdom.

But there are some implications that deserve a bit closer look.

Lemonade is water and sugar, with lemon juice as a third ingredient. The above squib does not suggest discarding the lemon. It tells us to include, to incorporate, to embrace the sour fruit. It must be part of the mix. A drink consisting of only water and sugar would be sickeningly sweet, but would miss the unique tang or piquancy that gives lemonade its character.

Bottom line: Don't trash the lemon. You need it.

Israel went through four centuries of slavery in Egypt and cursed generations of pharaohs. But the time came when they quit cursing the pharaohs and cried unto the LORD. The lemon they dealt with then gave them the strength of character they have today. Paul went to the LORD, asking that He would remove a worrisome thorn in his flesh. GOD told him, "Keep the lemon, my son—my grace is sufficient for you."

329

Yes, something you must deal with is painful. And your prayers that GOD will make it vanish seem to all on deaf ears. But life at its best is not all sweetness. There is a necessary tang that comes only from hardship and struggle—the young can be pretty, but only those who know suffering can be wise.

Think positive, and make lemonade of your lemons. But don't whine about the lemons. Thank GOD for the sour elements that make you appreciate His grace.

And he said unto me, My grace is sufficient for thee: for my strength is made perfect in weakness. II Corinthians 12:9a

October 10, 1999

November 22

The Cumulative Nature of Thanks

Funny thing about thanking GOD—while you are thanking Him for one thing, another comes to mind.

At this season, we are forced by tradition to try to remember things for which to thank GOD. If you have a pattern of thanking GOD regularly, blessings come easily to mind—you can roll them out in cascades. If you seldom give GOD credit for good things, it seems more difficult to think of what He has done for you, as over against what you have done for yourself. Have you ever tried to pray a prayer of thanksgiving without asking GOD for anything for yourself or for somebody else? Saying thanks to GOD takes some effort because you and I are essentially selfish animals, and we often ascribe to our own efforts and ingenuity what are really blessings from Him.

But if you make the effort, it becomes easier with each try.

330

While I am thanking Him for food in a world of hunger, I am reminded of many ways in which my predicament is good. I have a family, nuclear and extended. I live in an age beyond those who suffered slavery. Even the racism that stings me is nothing like the suppression my parents and grandparents knew. While I am thanking Him for what progress we have made in equal opportunity, I am reminded that only in America could we have the political situation we have all laughed at. Nobody questions how leaders are named in China, or Nigeria. You wouldn't hear of "re-counts" to determine the will of the voters in Haiti. So while I thank GOD for food and clothes and shelter and family and loved ones and better conditions for living, I must also recognize that these things did not happen because we are smarter or more efficient—but because GOD is so good.

I just thought of six or seven more blessings. I'd love to tell you about them, but I have run out of space. So I'll just say, "Thank you, LORD!"

Make a joyful noise unto GOD, all ye lands. Psalm 66:1

November 19, 2000

November 23

Let's Do Thanksgiving

Language always flows into little crevices of custom where unique vernacular develops. That just means that each region of each nation is capable of producing its own peculiar phrasing or word usage. "Come see us, y'all heah?" is not a Bostonian phrase. "Like totally awesome, man," may be Ninja turtle talk, but with a definite California flavor. And people from West Texas do not normally pronounce "can't" as "cahn't" the way the Kennedys do. Funny how these little turns of phrase can mark an identifiable region in the United States.

In certain areas of the country, the term "making groceries" is a description for grocery shopping. But it is an interesting commentary on a region that has long been frontier agricultural/livestock country. It is an active term and reflects an active style of life.

Thanksgiving ought to be an active term.

An expression of thanks can be limited to words, but words do not convey true gratitude. Even prayers made up of words, however fervent or eloquent, do not prove the sincerity of gratitude.

331

A grateful friend remains quietly loyal when everybody else retreats. He or she can demonstrate that loyalty wordlessly. Even a pet shows gratitude without being able to say anything. Thanks is an action item, not a matter of rhetoric.

Those thankful to GOD for all the blessings He has bestowed on them "make thanks" or "do thanks" rather than just "say thanks."

Enter into His gates with thanksgiving and into His courts with praise: be thankful unto Him, and bless His name. Psalm 100:4

November 24, 1991

November 24

Everybody Loves Givers

You don't want to go, but you will. You will get a fresh hairdo or haircut, lay out your better clothes, and set your VCR to tape your favorite medical show. You have to attend an awards dinner, grin at people whose names you do not remember, struggle to swallow rubbery chicken breast, and try not to yawn during long speeches bragging on the honorees. Everybody has to endure at least a few such affairs.

The person or persons being honored are local celebrities. They are rich or powerful or well- connected or all three. You never award a faithful school teacher or a rain-snow-or-sleet mailperson. (They could not help the non-profit to raise money.) And so you groan as the program goes on and on about the CEO or the Governor or the multimillionaire owner of ten automobile dealerships. Why did you have to be obligated to this dullness?

332

But wait a minute. The honorees are not just any rich persons, not just any CEO's. They are very carefully culled out of all the rich and powerful moguls in town. The non-profit cannot give awards to people, however well-connected, who are known to be corrupt or ruthless. If they are going to get good press out of their dull dinner, they must select as honorees people who are admired and respected, not simply loaded.

So even when you are going after the powerful to give crystal to, you diligently search for people who have given time and money for the improvement of the community. (Even if they are ruthless, they must seem generous.) If flawed humans elevate those who are givers, how much more does GOD? You want a reward more enduring than crystal or brass on an oak block? Then be generous with your time, with your talent, with your money; and GOD will abundantly reward you.

...good measure, pressed down, and shaken together, and running over, shall men give into your bosom. Luke 6:38

September 22, 2002

November 25

Somebody's Knockin' at Yo' Door

An earthquake topples a freeway—at rush hour.

A tornado rips through a busy aerospace community—at rush hour.

A freak thunderstorm blows a cafeteria wall down—at lunchtime.

The dead and injured are not worse sinners than the survivors. But Jesus' words sound an ominous warning to those of us not yet struck by these calamities: "Repent!"

Few scandals occur without warning.

When we are ticketed for speeding, the time we get the ticket was not the first time we exceeded the speed limit. We just kept risking getting caught until we finally did. Nobody dies with cirrhosis of the liver because of one drink, or with lung cancer after sneaking one cigarette. We just keep defying the odds until they catch up with us.

News commentators do not claim that these strings of tragedies constitute a pattern. Certainly, they do not see in them a cosmic warning. And if we add to the tragedies the rise of crime, of drug abuse, of child and wife abuse, of massive famine and starvation, etc., we still have only an unexplained necklace of tragic news stories.

333

But shouldn't GOD's people be able to see in such a necklace "signs of the times"? How much coughing must we do to realize our habits are dangerous to us? How many warnings before we know we must pay a penalty for our violations? When do we stop looking at these things as unrelated "accidents" and start hearing "Somebody knockin' at our door"?

Behold, I stand at the door, and knock: if any man hear my voice, and open the door, I will come in to him, and will sup with him, and he with Me. Revelation 3:20

November 19, 1989

November 26

The Lightning Draw

Any child over five (and a few under five) knows what that means. It has nothing to do with electrical storms or art. It refers to a person who can pull a gun quickly. Anyone into Westerns, cops- and-robbers, violent revenge, or futuristic stories about laser weapons understands a fascinating element is always the swift and accurate handling of a deadly weapon.

Would it not be great if we could be as quick with good things?

What if we could stage a high-noon contest to see which child of GOD could pour out compliments and blessings before anybody could spit out insults and indictments.

What if we could practice generating forgiveness as fast as, or even faster than, an enemy could offend us? Can we imagine how you could wound Satan?

Think what it would mean to you if you could take Jesus seriously. Suppose that even before we made a moderate, or even minor decision—much less a major one—we could whip out a prayer for guidance; or before our feet hit the floor in the morning, the words we think hit the air, or our head hits the pillow at night, we could fire off a communication to Heaven. Just suppose! Can we imagine how many blunders we could knock off, or how many failures we could blow away?

What if we practice the lightning draw in spiritual warfare—and take deadly aim against the Prince of Darkness. BANG! BANG!

334

...Men ought always to pray, and not faint. Luke 18:1

October 27, 1991

November 27

It Was Not the Alarm Clock

Most Christians are familiar with this statement. It is a testimony of the sustaining power of GOD. Old saints used to say, "He watched over me while I slept and slumbered. And then He touched me with His finger of love, and woke me to see a day I never saw before, and bade my golden moments to roll on sweetly." Neither Shakespeare, Dostoevsky, nor Baldwin can top that for majesty of rhetoric. Younger Christians simply affirm, "He woke me up this morning, and started me on my way."

The bottom line is GOD wakes His children up.

When GOD's Holy Spirit moves among His people, they are always motivated to do something. When Jesus touched the men He chose to be His apostles, He used an imperative verb: "Follow me." When He challenged Peter to prove his love for Him, He confronted him with an imperative: "Feed my sheep." His promise was that He would send the Holy Spirit after He ascended into Heavens, but He also promised that when the Holy Spirit descended upon His followers, they would be witnesses unto Him unto the uttermost part of the earth. Remember the jailer who had flogged and bound Paul and Silas in the Philippian prison? When he was faced with the power of their GOD, he stopped brutalizing them and washed the very scars his whips had put on their backs! (Acts 16:27- 33).

If a revival brings new members into the church, fine. If the preaching of an evangelist sends us home refreshed and invigorated with new insights, great. But the real task of any revival is to wake us up, to make us active for Jesus, to drive us out into the vineyard to work. It is one of GOD's alarm clocks.

Having therefore obtained help of God, I continue unto this day, witnessing both to small and great... Acts 26:22

January 10, 1993

November 28

Say, "Thank You"

In the ancient days of radio without television, and good cooking without microwave, kind greetings in the streets, and boys taking off hats inside, and girls who aspired to be mothers (with legitimate mates), there was a universal practice among those who reared children. Children were taught how to express gratitude. Even if they did not want the white cotton stockings Aunt Edna brought, they had to smile sweetly and say, "Thank you, Aunt Edna."

Whatever happened to that?

Did it disappear when photo-electric eyes opened doors for us and there was nobody to thank? Did if vanish when we were prospering during the seventies and thought we were responsible for our own prosperity? Or is it just that we are so busy we do not have time to think about blessings and the Source of blessings?

If you are not in the last stages of a chronic illness, bearing twenty-four hour pain and beyond medical help, you ought to say, "Thank you." If you have any idea where you will sleep tonight—or have only to make a hotel reservation to work it out, we have reason to say, "Thank you." Since this page is not in Braille, you obviously can see (and have learned to read). Surely, that is worth a monosyllabic "Thanks."

There have even been some white stockings from Aunt Edna that you did not like. Perhaps, a job fizzled out and opened the door for a far better one. Maybe a painful separation led you to a partner much more compatible. Thank GOD for the adversity with the silver lining. Look back at the white stockings and say, "Thank GOD for heartaches that precede joys."

Practice thanking GOD, and your whole outlook will be more positive. You will see sunshine you had not noticed before!

Giving thanks always for all things unto GOD and the Father in the name of LORD Jesus Christ. Ephesians 5:20

October 28, 1990

336

November 29

A Penny for Your Thoughts

We become what we think about. Wise parents fill the environments of their children with what they want them to think about. Books, ideas, success, good music and good art, an orderly, well-organized house, clear aspirations—all these things good parents try to include among the influences on their children. (We didn't mention faith because many "good" parents do not count it as essential, although nice.) But if, despite the best efforts of good parents, the kids gravitate toward low ideals, loose discipline, bad gambles, the sloppy child becomes a sloppy adult. You become what you think about.

Does your mind wander away from the good and positive and productive to that which is profitable or power-generating or sensual or addictive? Then slap your mind and push it toward high things. We know that faith is essential, not just "nice." You have to make yourself pray, or focus on GOD's word, or see opportunities for witness or helpfulness in everyday experiences. Make yourself think about GOD, about what He is doing for you every day, what opportunities you have to witness for Him, to serve Him, to boost the joy of others with what He can do for them. And as you concentrate on such thought-directions, trivial or mean or dirty things get squeezed out. You find yourself acting more kindly, treating others better, liking yourself better.

During this season you will be pushed to think "Buy!" "Enjoy!" "Expect!" This has become the time to focus on materials and indulgence and extravagance. Don't be pushed. Control your own thoughts. If you can center your thoughts on the love that sent GOD's Son into our world and can be driven by the motives He taught, you will have less appetite to be greedy and grasping and pleasure-drawn and power-driven. You will look and act more like Jesus. Exercise your mind till it hurts. You become what you think about.

For I say, through the grace given unto me, to every man that is among you, not to think of himself more highly than he ought to think; but to think soberly, according as GOD hath dealt to every man the measure of faith. Romans 12:3

December 10, 2000

November 30

Gimme Your Money

This is a mercenary world. Everything comes with a price. It is a rare joy to see people volunteer, because human services also come with a price. Small wonder that the words of Paul to Timothy, "For the love of money is the root of all evil" are so easily shortened to "Money is the root of all evil" (cf. I Timothy 6:10). From the hustling car or furniture dealer to the oily-smooth funeral director to the worrisome telemarketers who always call at suppertime, we have become wary of anything or anybody seeking our money.

So who is surprised when we cringe when the church pushes tithing? Because He made you in His image—and He is not a miser; He is a giver. He gives His best, and He requires that if you and I are to be called by His Name, we must give our best, too. But notice. He is not seeking profit. He asks that we give a fraction, and reap overwhelming abundance. Any tither can tell you that his or her bottom line swells inexplicably on a regular basis. No accountant on earth can explain why tithers prosper as they do. But imitate GOD, and you share His unlimited wealth!

338

Be ye therefore followers of GOD, as dear children; And walk in love, as Christ also hath loved us, and hath given Himself for us an offering and a sacrifice to GOD, for a sweet smelling savour. Ephesians 5:1-2

March 17, 2002

December 1

He
Whoop! There It Is!

We borrow for the introduction to this season a popular vernacular interjection: "Whoop! There He is!" to mark the season called Advent. It is the prelude to Christmas and represents with its colorful circle of candles the four comings of Christ: As an infant-Savior in Bethlehem: As a martyr-Savior at Calvary, As a Redeemer-Savior at Resurrection, As Judge (not Savior) at Judgment.

Baptists do not universally celebrate Advent. But it is a powerful reminder that Jesus Christ keeps entering our lives.

Jesus comes after long and elaborate predictions by many prophets and signs. But He comes without warning. We had been told that a virgin would bear a Child Who would save us; that He would die an ignominious death; that He would overcome death and rise again; and that He would extract His church from this world and then destroy the world. But each of these comings was a shock to many. Shepherds and cynics, people who lived on prayer and people who lived for profit, lovers of GOD, haters of GOD, and people ignorant of GOD—all looked up, and there He was!

339

He appears when we were most in trouble. He grieves when we do or say something we ought not. Have we given Him credit for our achievements or appealed to Him when we faced closed doors?

We do not "find Christ"; just open the eyes of our soul, and there He is again!

For unto us is born this day in the city of David a Saviour, which is Christ the LORD. Luke 2:11

November 28, 1993

December 2

It Wasn't Supposed to Work That Way

The second candle in the Advent wreath represents when Jesus comes as an executed criminal bearing our sins—one of the four ways that He comes.

This coming is a bittersweet celebration because none of this would have been necessary had we not sinned. When GOD created us, He created us innocent of sin, with no need of a Redeemer. But when we rebelled against GOD, we opened the Pandora's Box that unleashed all the ugliness of sin, and made it necessary that GOD would have to become a frail human being and live in the filth of our sin. The most tragic of these four "advents" is the cross of Calvary, where we killed Him. (Yes, we were there when they crucified my LORD.)

Given Jesus' matchless love for sinful humankind, we ought to repent with many tears for our own sins, the sins of our children and our elders, the sins of the world—and we ought to commit to Him that we will praise Him for salvation and work to witness to the entire world that Jesus, Who comes repeatedly into our world, saves to the uttermost.

340

Had we obeyed GOD's will in Eden, none of this would have happened—no thorns and thistles, no sickness or death, no cruelty or injustice, no poverty or natural calamity. But since we disobeyed, there had to be Bethlehem, and Calvary, and the garden tomb, and Judgment Day. He could/should have annihilated us. But "O, how he loves you and me!"

Behold the Lamb of GOD, which taketh away the sin of the world.
John 1:29

December 6, 1998

December 3

It's a Bird! It's a Plane! It's Jesus!!

They were looking intently up into the sky as He was going, when suddenly two men dressed in white stood beside them.

Many arguments among believers about the "rapture," the return of Christ for His church—surprisingly little information in scripture. But the best information we have comes from a half dozen verses in Paul's letter to the church at Thessalonica (I Thessalonians 4:13-18). Verses 16 and 17 describe an awesome opening of the Heavens and the cataclysmic descent from Heaven of Jesus, Who will instantly resurrect all the righteous dead since Adam and just as instantly transfigure all the righteous who are still alive from mortal to immortal, then lift the entire mass of righteous humans to Heaven, leaving only the unrighteous on earth.

Since there is absolutely no indication of when this will take place (Matthew 24:36ff), the message of this third Sunday in Advent is simple—Take out your insurance now!

This same Jesus, which is taken up from you into heaven, shall so come in like manner as ye have seen Him go into heaven. Acts 1:11

December 14, 1997

December 4

As a Thief in the Night

Jesus tells us He will come back. On this fourth Sunday in Advent before the celebration of His birth, we think about that style of arrivals—a thief in the night.

It reminds us that if we did not receive Jesus when He came as a Baby to identify with us, or as a martyr on a cross to redeem us, or do not when He comes in glory to retrieve His church from the world—if we rejected Him in all those "advents" into our world, we must deal with Him when He comes as judge, to punish us. And we will have no warning. He comes silently, suddenly, unannounced (Matthew 24:42).

On the 25th, we celebrate the birth of Jesus. (We know He was not born then, but does it really matter what the calendar date was?) Prophets had predicted His birth, even specifying the town in which He would be born. The entire worship system GOD conveyed through Moses is stuffed with types that point to the Judaea. His coming was a

342

total surprise. From innkeeper to Him, The words of John express a tragic indictment against us: "He was in the world, and the world was made by Him, and the world knew Him not. He came unto His own and His own received Him not" (John 1:10, 11).

Beware lest the merchants and the promoters of entertainment blind and deafen us to the Baby Who is born among us. Beware lest the Zeitgeist of an unbelieving age blind and deafen us to the coming of the Judge of all the earth. Accept the Baby, the Martyr, the returning LORD, and you will not have to face the Judge!

I charge thee therefore before GOD, and the LORD Jesus Christ, Who shall judge the quick and the dead at His appearing and His kingdom. II Timothy 4:1

December 21, 1997

December 5

GOD Follows Orders?

That is absurd! What kind of heresy—no, blasphemy—would lead any idiot to even suggest such a thing? Nobody tells our GOD what to do! He is absolutely independent of any rules and regulations! GOD is completely sovereign! Orders? HAH!

No question about His sovereignty, His self-sufficiency, His absolute control. But He does follow orders—His own.

He created a universe of order. He established a system of laws to govern first His universe, and then the people He placed in charge of it. Nothing GOD does is without system. And He follows it, to the letter. He decreed that if we sinned, we would face dire consequences. When we did, however much it hurt Him, He imposed upon us expulsion from Himself, the weakening of the once-flawless body so that it would be vulnerable to sickness and to death, the cursing of the universe so that natural catastrophe would be a normal part of its routine, and the complete subjection of the human species to sin and therefore to damnation. He was not happy to propose such penalties— but He had to, because His own essence is justice. He ordered Himself to punish us and wept over it.

343

Just as much as His essence is justice, so His essence is love. His love required Him to redeem us, although He knows, and we know, we do not deserve redemption. He had to impose a death sentence on us, because we violated His divine purpose for creation. But He also had to work out some method for rescuing us from the very punishment He Himself had decreed! (Don't try to understand it—if your essence were both justice and love, you would—but who can understand the Mind of GOD?)

We commemorate the unbelievable love-act of GOD, Who reduced Himself to human flesh and permitted Himself to die like a sinner— for sinners! Why would He tolerate such an insult? Why would He permit you and me to crucify Him? Because GOD had to follow orders: His own orders, to punish us, but to redeem us with His own blood!

Now therefore ye are no more strangers and foreigners, but fellowcitizens with the saints, and of the household of GOD. Ephesians 2:19

April 1, 2001

December 6

Remember Your Birthday?

Of course, you do. It is one of those anniversaries everybody remembers. It can be used as your entry code for your computer, as the combination for your lock, as the date for the renewal of your driver's license because it is one set of numbers everybody remembers. Of course, you remember your birthday.

Of course, you do not.

You were there on your birth day, but while you have an elephantine memory that goes back to three years old, or even two, you cannot remember what happened on that most important day that began your life. You are totally dependent on what other people tell you about it. Does that mean anybody can question whether you were born?

Of course, no one will. There is no question about whether you were born. You are; therefore, you came to be. Your existence is proof positive of your birth even though you cannot prove your existence by a verbal argument. You cannot remember it, but it happened because you are here!

344

Some Christians are intimidated by their more demonstrative brothers and sisters because they can shout out the day, the hour, and the exact location of their conversion. If you cannot tie down your faith to a specific moment of spiritual trauma, you may feel insecure about your status in Christ.

Do not.

Your memory of your re-birth is not important. You have the promise of Jesus. So you don't need to remember the moment of your birthday. Celebrate it anyhow!

Him that cometh to me, I will in no wise cast out. John 6:37b

June 28, 1992

December 7

"Anyhow" Love

He was a totally indefinable animal—a homogenization of a dozen breeds, bearing little resemblance to any. A mutt. A mongrel. Canine stew. Wet, cold, and trembling, he waited faithfully outside the cheap bar for a master who was getting drunker by the gulp. He was forgotten in the icy rain. He must have known that he would be abused again when his master staggered out, disgusted with himself and angry at the world, having only the shivering dog as an available victim.

Why don't dogs run away from such mistreatment?

When we look at ourselves with sober and honest eyes, when we strip away the habitual lies we welcome from friends and repeat to ourselves, we see an ugly copy of the drunken, abusive master of that pitiful animal. Our public actions may mask innermost attitudes. But two people know us at our worst.

We each know our hypocrisies, our hostilities, our neglect of duty, our leaks of cruelty, our selective compassion.

And GOD knows the inner ugliness we struggle to hide.

345

So why doesn't GOD turn His back on me and condemn me to eternal punishment?

The second Sunday in Advent tells us Jesus came as Savior to Calvary to die for us. The cross outside corrupt Jerusalem, the mutt outside the bar; they illustrate "anyhow" love.

Jesus loves us anyhow.

We flame of the second candle, the candle of the cross. We learn to love somebody at least as much as that un-pedigreed dog? Can we press toward the mark of loving as Christ loves us?

A new commandment I give unto you, That ye love one another; as I have loved you, that ye also love one another. John 13:34

December 6, 1992

December 8

How Do We Spell "Holy"?

An apology may be in order to the manufacturers of Rolaids.

They claim that when bad substances attack our digestive system, there is in their product something so good that it neutralizes those bad substances, and we feel better.

So how do we accomplish that in the spiritual realm?

When corruption and violence and unethical practices and promiscuous sex and foul language and substance abuse, etc., etc., etc., fill up our world, how do we keep from being infected by it all? How can we live righteously in this kind of climate?

We can abstain; we can refuse to associate with people who practice sinful things; we can mount campaigns to close down bad places, to defeat bad officials, to punish bad citizens, to censor bad productions/publications, etc., etc., etc. But we will not produce more righteousness, just more prohibitions.

Sin is not something we do; it is who we obey, or resist.

346

Jesus could walk with publicans and sinners and never sin. His associations did not make Him sin; His total obedience to His Father kept Him from sinning. We can bleach our lives of all bad habits, and still be mean-spirited, spiteful, and unlovely. If we want to be holy, we need not give up a list of vices but latch onto Jesus, learn how He clung to His Father's purpose for His life, and observe how He prayed before every action.

We do not have to avoid all contact with sin. Indeed, we were commissioned to plunge deliberately into a sinful world with a message that could redeem it. A strong relationship with Jesus makes it possible for the recovering alcoholic to spend the evening at the bar drinking ginger ale and witnessing.

"Holy" is not the eighty-two things we do not do; it is the one thing we do.

I beseech you therefore, brethren, by the mercies of GOD, that ye present your bodies a living sacrifice, holy, acceptable unto GOD, which is your reasonable service. Romans 12:1

July 25, 1993

December 9

What Is the Best Gift You Ever Got?

GOD comes to us as a suffering Servant.

Your best gift was not the mink coat, nor the sports car, nor the trip to the Cayman Islands. It was a dramatic rescue from total annihilation. You had been brought before the court of GOD, and tried before the councils of Heaven, and found guilty on all counts. And you had been sentenced to eternal destruction in Hell. Nor had you been framed—you really are guilty!

But even while you were lying in your death row cell, Jesus Christ, fully aware that you were guilty as charged, volunteered to be put to death for you so that you could go free! If somebody pulled your name out of a hat, and on that basis gave you a hundred million dollars, tax free, that would be a miserable gift compared to what GOD gave you when He gave His Son for your redemption. Talk about Christmas gifts!

"Greater love hath no man than this, that a man lay down his life for his friends" (John 15:13).

347

Yes, GOD comes to us as a suffering servant to give us the best gift we ever got (or ever will).

A Christmas tree is a symbol of the season. What does a cross say? Far more than "Merry Christmas"; it says, "GOD loves me!"

Every good gift and every perfect gift is from above, and cometh down from the Father of Lights with whom is no variableness, neither shadow of turning. James 1:17

December 4, 1994

December 10

The Greatest Gift Of All

The second Sunday in Advent and the first Sunday in the month both speak of the same event: the coming, or "advent" of Christ as Savior, by giving the ultimate gift. He died and we commemorate that "gift" by lighting a second candle, and by partaking of bread and taking the LORD's supper.

Just out of a season of Thanksgiving, we move inexorably toward the season of Christmas. One expresses gratitude for gifts; one emphasizes the giving of gifts. Both must look Heavenward in praise for this greatest of all gifts. There has been nothing in the total history of humankind that anywhere nearly approaches the immensity of the gift of GOD in the giving of the life of His Son for our redemption. But for that, no material gift, no blessing of health or family, no accomplishment or achievement would be possible for us. But for that, we should have all been annihilated because of our sins.

348

At Christmas-time, we will focus on the birth of Jesus to Mary in Bethlehem (and on the receiving and exchanging of gifts). That is fitting and appropriate. But let us recognize the reason GOD sent that Baby into the manger: so He would be a mortal and could die for us. The birth is made glorious by the mission with which that precious Infant entered our world: to make the gift of His own life the most precious gift of all.

A gift is as a precious stone in the eyes of him that hath it: withersoever it turneth, it prospereth. Proverbs 17:8

December 7, 1997

December 11

Holy Decease

This is the heart of the gospel, that GOD's Son died. It is the primary purpose for which He was born in Bethlehem—not to be educated and become a successful professional and a credit to His family, but to die. His own words were:

Even as the Son of man came not to be ministered unto, but to minister, and to give His life a ransom for many (Matthew 20:28).

So as we commemorate His birth this Advent season, we also memorialize His death. We could scream our anger at Judas Iscariot, who betrayed Him, or at Pontius Pilate, under whose orders He was crucified, or even at Tiberius Caesar, the Roman emperor who approved the orders. But all of these were only tools. He was His own Father Who so orchestrated history that He was legally lynched! There had to be a Lamb slain for us (Revelation 5:6-14) and the Father designated Jesus to be that Lamb.

Only through His death do we live today. Only through His death have we been pardoned for our sins. And He had to be born as a human infant to qualify for human death. Praise GOD! He sent His Son to be born...to die!

349

Now is my soul troubled; and what shall I say? Father, save me from this hour? But for this cause came I unto this hour. John 12:27

December 8, 2002

December 12

I Just Called to Say "I Love You"

Those Stevie Wonder lyrics are the basis of a slick marketing campaign by a long distance telephone service company. They promise they will share the cost of long distance calls to the person called most. Does that mean this company has become excessively generous during this holiday season?

It definitely does not.

It means that they know that there are some people we love so much we will call them repeatedly. If they lower the cost of calling them, we will not save the money. They are gambling that our love will make us call them more, and the company makes money on the volume of calls!

Clearly, human nature does not change much. And, despite the fact that it is a very corrupt imitation of GOD, we are, in fact, in His image. We love imperfectly because He loves perfectly. And love keeps making contact—even when the contact is not appreciated or returned. Love keeps reaching out to the beloved.

Advent reminds us that Jesus Christ, whose first "advent" into our world was at Bethlehem had three others. His second reaching out to us was at Calvary. Most of the people alive today do not appreciate that. But He would not even have considered coming down from the cross because we did not care. If our love does not reach out to Him, still His reaches out to us. He loves us so much that He keeps making contact with us. What a profit that long distance service could make off of Him!

350

Beloved, let us love one another: for love is of GOD; and every one that loveth is born of GOD, and knoweth GOD. I John 4:7

December 5, 1993

December 13

Power Up

This was her first time to be chairperson of the church banquet. She had fretted with dress, hair- style, and nails, and looked lovely. She reviewed in her mind the many details of the program, and now it was time to call the guests to order.

But when she turned the switch on to activate the microphone and blew softly into the mike head, nothing happened. She tapped it, scrutinized the "on-off'" switch to make sure the mike was on, and looked helplessly toward the maitre-de. He quickly disappeared into the kitchen, found the technician, and he rushed over to the podium and turned on the power that activates the amplifier. After an initial squeal, her voice came through loudly and clearly.

Nothing was wrong with the mike. In the language of the technician, "The system had not been powered up."

Life can be like that. Present are all the ingredients of a good life: health, a good mind, family and loved ones around, a decent job, even a promising future. But there is no joy, no brightness. The power that makes life worth living is not a measurable factor like salary or education or social prominence. It is based deep in the soul in a relationship between us on earth and GOD in Heaven. It is the power of the Holy Spirit.

351

When we take inventory of our assets, by all means be grateful for health, loved ones, and prosperity. Thank GOD for a religious up-bringing in a Christian family or for the decision made to become part of the church.

But the fullness of every day demands that we be "powered up" with an intangible Something that helps us override the obstacles and the frustrations of ordinary people and to come forth with a joy that speaks loudly and clearly about Jesus.

After we have tapped the mike, we need to check our amplifiers.

The Holy Ghost shall come upon thee, and the power of the Highest shall overshadow thee: therefore also that holy thing which shall be born of thee shall be called the Son of GOD. Luke 1:35

November 3, 1991

December 14

"Because He First Loved Me"

A popular Christian hymn declares, "Oh, how I love Jesus, because He first loved me." At first glance that makes good sense. Since being loved generates loving, a simple reciprocity would seem the logical pattern for love. As a matter of fact, that is the easiest way to generate love: fly loving.

But when we listen to Jesus' definition of love, we get a much deeper, more complex picture of the dynamics of loving. He does not at all suggest a simple tennis-ball pattern of love. His picture of love is not a bouncing back and forth between the lover and the beloved. On the night when Jesus established our Holy Communion, He re-defined love. At the Passover table, He called for a new picture of love.

He was not defining love as reciprocity, but as conduction! He was saying that the mark of a Christian is not to love Christ because Christ has loved us, but to love other people because we have been loved by Christ! We do not bounce it back; we pass it on. That is indeed a new concept.

Of course, we ought to love Jesus, Who first loved us. But we cannot stop there. We have to love our families because Jesus loved us; we have to love our neighbors because Jesus loved us; we have to love strangers because Jesus loved us; we even have to love enemies because Jesus loved us.

We love him, because he first loved us. I John 4:19

May 2, 1993

352

December 15

Kiss the Frog

A few days until Christmas Day and you are bombarded with ads and decorations and music and tear-jerking TV shows, movies, and plays. But as you have complained year after year, "I just don't have the 'Christmas spirit!'" Since it is obvious that raising the intensity of the marketing or the volume of the music or the proliferation of the decorations will not impart it to you, what will?

I have forgotten which fairy tale or fable featured the incident. But it has become part of the common vernacular. Some beautiful damsel was approached by a frog, and the gross amphibian creature was able to talk. It asked for a kiss. After some persuasion, the lovely heroine overcame her revulsion enough to kiss the slimy animal. And voila! the ugly frog was transformed into a handsome prince. Of course, they were married in an elaborate wedding, and naturally they lived happily ever after.

Think about that silly fable.

Remember that GOD did not come as a handsome prince, but as a Baby born to poor peasants in disgusting surroundings. Who knew that this Infant was GOD?

You want the Christmas spirit? Find a frog to kiss. Do something for somebody who is normally ignored or rejected or just forgotten about. Make Christmas special for a lonely senior or a homeless family with small children or somebody in jail—and guilty. They will not be able to reciprocate with an expensive gift or even send you a classy engraved "thank you." But deep down in your heart you will feel a fresh warmth because you will know that you are acting Jesus-like. He deliberately sought out publicans and sinners, and made it clear that the Spirit had anointed Him to find frogs to kiss (a loose translation of Luke 4:18). So pucker up and let the Christmas spirit in!

Wherefore comfort yourselves together, and edify one another, even as also ye do. I Thessalonians 5:11

December 12, 1999

December 16

I Don't Believe in Santa Claus!

He is still smouldering. Some people, once they have gotten off their chest whatever they are angry about, are relieved enough to go on with their lives with minimal anger. But this brother is not through erupting— maybe again any minute now. He is mad because there is a Christmas tree in the church yard. And as if that were not bad enough, there are evergreen wreaths and Christmas lights inside the nave of the sanctuary. There are even (Gasp!) "Noel" candles behind the choir-stand! How can a Christian church allow all these pagan symbols to be prominently displayed in and around our house of worship?

First, we have to admit he is right—not a one of those things is based on scripture or points to Jesus Christ, the Word made flesh.

But GOD takes all sorts of offerings. If we cannot afford a bullock, He will take a lamb. If we cannot afford a lamb, He will accept turtledoves. If we cannot even afford birds, we can bring Him a gift of fruit or grain. He even blessed a little boy's lunch by making it the basis of a major miracle.

354

The con man is commanded to bring his skills of persuasion, and GOD can turn him into a powerful evangelist. Even if we have spent much of our life fighting, in the streets, GOD can transform us into advocates for the powerless. A prostitute is not excluded either. GOD used a "lady of the evening" to be in the ancestral line of Jesus. Boaz, the great-grandfather of David, was the son of Rahab, the prostitute of Jericho (Matthew 1:5, 6). An intimate understanding of the weakness of men can be used to help identify and weed out hypocrites in the church of Jesus Christ. GOD uses whatever we bring to His altar!

So we need not get bent out of shape because a Christmas tree represents Teutonic paganism. The children like it, and GOD can use its questionable origins to point them to the Holy Baby whose birth signals its appearance every December.

I know, and am persuaded by the LORD Jesus that there is nothing unclean of itself: but to him that esteemeth any thing to be unclean, to him it is unclean. Romans 14:14

December 20, 1992

December 17

Who's at the Top of Your List?

It is that time of year again. It is the shop/groan/pay/groan time when we must buy even for people we do not especially like. It is Christmas-time. (Groan)

Fortunately, though, this season means a bit more than that. It is a time of uncontainable joy that GOD sent into our world His Son to be our Saviour and LORD, and in His Name we share gifts with each other. But if we live in a world where Christmas is shop/groan/pay/groan, a little of it rubs off on us anyhow.

It does not have to.

If you want Christmas to focus on Christ rather than on merchandise, you can take a sacred initiative. You do not have to be programmed by the merchants. If you have not already indebted yourselves for the next five years, you can consider putting the Christ-child at the top of your list. Here is one way to do it: (1) Determine to spend a limited amount for all gifts this year. (2) Make a list of the people to whom you want to give gifts to, and put Jesus' name at the top of that list. (3) Take 10% of the amount you were planning to spend and allocate that to Jesus; then divide the 90% remaining among the rest of the recipients on your list. (4) Prepare a nice note to each of those recipients, explaining that this year you have decided to buy inexpensive gifts and to love all year instead of expensive merchandise once. Send that note with your gift of gloves or scarf or cologne or a Christian book. (5) Contribute the "Jesus gift" money to some cause that Jesus would support (hunger? homelessness? education?), and watch the warm glow of the Christmas spirit fill your heart.

355

You cannot do that by emptying your bank account. And you cannot get that kind of joy at Neiman-Marcus or Saks or Macy's.

And whatsoever ye do in word or deed, do all in the name of the LORD Jesus, giving thanks to GOD and the Father by Him. Colossians 3:17

December 9, 1990

December 18

Gifts in the Garbage

It can make a person feel so ashamed. He has done something very dumb; and he has to try to undo it, and he hopes nobody is watching.

Once a man hid some small gifts in a wastebasket, and forgot they were there. He dumped the usual trash in the basket for the next couple of days, and then on trash pick-up day, he dumped the contents of the wastebasket into the big plastic bag to be taken out to the curb.

Then while he talked on the phone in his office, it hit him like a brick thrown from behind a building: "My gifts!!" The phone conversation was abruptly cut off; he dashed out of the office as though it were on fire, jumped in my truck (if it had not started, he would have had a massive coronary right there), and sped home to rip madly into the trash bag. Fortunately, the solid waste crews had not come, and he did not see any neighbors laughing at him—but he found his gifts in the trash.

356

GOD did deliberately what the man did out of stupidity.

GOD looked sadly down at the mess we had made out of His perfect creation. What had been "very good" when He fashioned it, we had corrupted with our sin. The pristine universe, flawless in its beauty, its unity, its harmony, was now garbage—yielding thorns and thistles, having nature against animals, animals against man, man against his fellow—pure garbage, worthy of Divine incineration.

But into that garbage, GOD sent His perfect, sinless, precious Son. No mistake. No blunder. He did it on purpose. "And the Word was made flesh, and dwelt among us (and we beheld His glory, the glory as of the only begotten of the Father,) full of grace and truth (John 1:14).

Why in the name of cosmic sanity would GOD put such a treasure into the trash of our world? For the same reason He gives us a new commandment to love one another: His love is greater than His disgust. Can we imitate that?

Be kindly affectioned one to another with brotherly love; in honour preferring one another. Romans 12:10

December 17, 1989

December 19

Happy Easter!

No, it is not Easter! But the third Sunday in Advent is a great time to celebrate the Resurrection!

We can think about our mama or daddy or grandparents or other loved ones who have died. We can think about our high blood pressure or bad back or the cancer we have to live with. Or we can think about the miseries of daily existence—family conflicts or job conditions or financial shortfalls—and how often you have wondered if GOD is really fair to us. (It is the losing team that complains about the officials' calls.)

And the good news is that this is not all there is! Thanks be to Father GOD and His Son Jesus Christ, there is a blessed realm beyond this life where all our loved ones are waiting to meet us. There is a divine order to things that promises we will rise above physical frailties and painful circumstances. Because He rose, we also will rise to an incalculable joy and peace and to limitless strength and well-being.

357

That is what the third Sunday in Advent means. The third "advent" of Christ into our lives was at the Resurrection, when He rose from the dead with all power in Heaven and earth in His hands. WOW!

Yes, it is December, but we have the permission of the psalmist to shout anyway. Happy Easter! Because His words climax with thunder in a promise to receive us into the mansions in His Father's house.

Yet a little while, and the world seeth me no more; but ye saw me: because I live, ye shall live also. John 14:19

December 12, 1993

December 20

If You Could Have Anything...

A husband walked into the room just in time to see a handsome African-American man jumping up and down in delirious joy and screaming and babbling before millions on daytime TV. He did not need to ask, but he did. "What did he win? A car?" "Yes," his wife told me; "a $47,000 station wagon." He knew that. The brother would not have gone off like that behind a set of china.

What is most valuable to us?

Ask that same question of the terminal cancer patient or the person who has miraculously escaped death, and he may surprise you. Merchandise is no longer the most precious possession for him. Loved ones have a great deal more value, and the newest and most sophisticated electronic toy falls lower on a list of priorities than another hug for his child or another day with old friends.

358

When we are immature, we can trivialize what is important and get delirious about "stuff." But when we grow up, we learn through many dangers, toils, and snares that the amazing grace of GOD is a Person, not a commodity, and that the fundamental wealth of life cannot be reduced to currency, checks, or credit. The best things in life are people we can love and who love us.

And now abideth faith, hope, charity, these three; but the greatest of these is charity. I Corinthians 13:13

August 2, 1992

December 21

He May Not Come When You Want Him...

Friday the world proclaims that Jesus the Christ is born. Had you and I been living in Palestine in B.C. 6, we would have been surrounded by a negative talk environment. Ordinary people were chafing under oppression by the rich and powerful. The government was corrupt. Crime was rampant. Modern children were not as faithful to older traditions. And people in leadership were commonly involved in scandal. All the nations of the world were dependent upon a single super- power, and it was led by a succession of leaders of questionable integrity—the Caesars. (Does this sound a bit familiar?)

And we would have felt the shrinking of any hope that GOD was going to do anything about it. Centuries ago, the prophets had promised that a Messiah would come to change things. But He had not shown up, and now there were scholars who said the prophets were wrong.

But just as we were giving up, even thinking seriously about suicide, angels told shepherds that a baby was born in Bethlehem. His timing is always exquisite!

359

Behold, a virgin shall be with child, and shall bring forth a son, and they shall call his name Emanuel, which being interpreted is, GOD with us. Matthew 1:23

December 20, 1998

December 22

Myth & Substance

Is there a fat man in red and white fur who comes down the chimney? (He would have considerable problems in Houston!) Was the Barbie in the white dress really made by elves? (Do they have a "Mattel" stamp?) Much of the beauty of Christmas is in its many myths.

But even if you discount the European traditions about St. Nicholas and the North Pole, and are firmly convinced that "Jesus is the reason for the season," you still marvel at the body of myth built up around Him. Was he born in December? Were the magi really kings? Was the star in the east or the west? Was He a pretty blond infant?

Would you believe that most of this does not matter? You can protest against Santa Claus; you can criticize Christians for observing the birth of Jesus at the winter solstice; you can be angry at neighbors with too many Christmas lights. But you cannot deny that beyond all our myth is a solid body of truth with heavy substance.

360

This Baby, born in a stable in a remote village northeast of Africa, has changed history. On Christmas Day there will be little or no violence in war-torn areas. People who are not even followers of Jesus Christ will give gifts, share with the poor, exchange warm greetings with strangers. The concept of public education, of health care for the poor, of government responsibility for the mentally ill or physically disabled all come from the teachings of this Galilean. We have to concede to one undeniable fact: Jesus has had an impact unparalleled in human history.

And the shepherds returned, glorifying and praising GOD for all the things they had heard and seen, as it was told unto them. Luke 2:20

December 24, 1995

December 23

On Christmas

The date is questionable. It probably happened in the spring, not on the fourth day after the Winter Solstice. It certainly did not happen on the zero between "B.C." and "A.D."; more probably about four years before the Romans began their "Anno Domini" calculations. There are even questions about when the Wise Men arrived at the house of Joseph and Mary (today's Sunday School lesson admits that it was as much as a year after the baby was born). Calendars do strange things to great events. (Perhaps the most consistent calendar exception is "Christmas Sunday."

But GOD does not operate according to the Gregorian calendar, or the Jewish calendar, or the Chinese calendar, nor any other calendar man has devised to calibrate the year. Jesus was not born when we thought it proper, but when GOD determined it. "When the fulness of the time was come, GOD sent forth His Son, made of a woman, made under the law" (Galatians 4:4). Winter? Spring? B.C. 4 or 6? Zero between B.C. and A.D.? Weekday? Weekend? Who cares? Joy to the world! The LORD is come!

And they came with haste, and found Mary and Joseph, and the babe lying in a manger. Luke 2:16

December 25, 1994

December 24

Asleep on the Hay

So goes part of the refrain of a carol with one of the saddest opening lines in music: "Away in a manger, no crib for a bed, The little LORD Jesus laid down His sweet head."

It is a clear indictment—but not of the inn-keeper, who had no room in the inn. It is an indictment of all of us who have no room in our busy lives for Jesus. At first, it sounds like a judgment upon us (and, in part, it is). But after a bit of reflection, it turns out to be more a reason to praise our GOD. True, we did not provide a comfortable place for GOD's Son to come into our world; in fact, we seldom give Him first place in our lives. But instead of bringing down mass destruction on His selfish creatures, He humbles Himself to accept the most lowly accommodations possible: a stable among the animals. He Who created all things animate and inanimate stoops to become a mortal among donkeys and cattle. He Who comes to redeem all people is rejected by people, and He meekly bows to the insult of exclusion so that He can save those who excluded Him. While that marks us as reprehensible, it marks Him as absolute Love.

362

It means that our lives are not too filthy for Him to come into it. It means that we are not too insignificant for Him to care about us. It means that He does not love African-Americans and hate Anglo-Americans; He includes us all.

So if the spirit of Christmas means anything, it should mean we ought to work toward including everybody in our love. If we need to forgive somebody, we should remember that we have been forgiven. If there is anybody we automatically reject, we should stop doing it, because the Babe in the trough in the stable behind the inn did not reject us. So we need not convict man, but instead praise GOD; He does not reject us and came that we might have life abundantly.

Thanks be unto GOD for his unspeakable gift. II Corinthians 9:15

December 23, 1990

December 25

A sad note. A pagan date for the holiest birthday on the Christian calendar. Pagan symbols everywhere, and our Jesus hidden behind blinking lights, an avalanche of marketing gimmicks, and hordes of men with pillowed bellies and red suits claiming to represent the meaning of Christmas! What kind of blasphemy is this? GOD ought to strike the nations with a plague more devastating than leprosy, more gruesome than AIDS! Why should Christian people observe such a holiday, whose chief symbol is not a manger, but the evergreen of some unGODly Roman heathenism? Why should anyone allow December to be a month of commemoration or garlands of evergreen to be hung (Ugh!) in a central place of worship? It is the lowest insult to a GOD Who sent His Son into this pagan world to redeem it from that very kind of carnal groveling in iniquity! Is it Jesus using as a birth place the lowly feed-bin or feeding crowds with a boy's lunch? Maybe GOD can use our stuff!

Let everything that hath breath praise the LORD. Praise ye the LORD. Psalm 150:6

December 24, 1989

December 26

Hush! Somebody's Callin' My Name

Something significant is happening at this threshold of the new millennium. We are slipping backward in some areas, but we are emerging as a multinational force at the same time. The miracle of South Africa is still astounding the world, as a black man guides the transformation. The only presidential candidate everybody agreed on is not running—and he is Black.

Some of us can remember when the emphasis on "Negro history" was confined to the single week in February in which the birth date of Abraham Lincoln fell (February 12). Now, not only is an entire month so designated, but the observation is now shared by schools, institutions, and agencies not predominantly black. In the past generation, the national recognition of the birthday of Dr. King and the reflection on the Civil Rights Movement of the 50's and 60's has added more focus on African-Americans. If you have begun to observe the cultural celebration of Kwanzaa (December 26–January 1), then tack on another week. At a time when the nation is leaning heavily to the right, those of us with African ancestry are being urged to celebrate who we are.

But while neither Black History week/month nor Kwanzaa was intended to be religious celebrations, the King emphasis forces us to remember our roots in the church of Jesus Christ and the folkways of a deep-seated faith in GOD. Let us take advantage of these 65 days between the beginning of Kwanzaa and the final day of Black History Month to praise GOD for leading us through the horrors of slavery, the indignities of Jim Crow, and the current frustrations of sophisticated racism. By all means, remember the proud African heritage. But concentrate on Who has helped us survive—not the ancient kings nor the modern civil rights activists, but GOD, Who brought us from ancient Cush and Kemet to the board rooms of the corporate West and the cloakrooms of world government.

364

For whosoever is born of GOD overcometh the world: and this is the victory that overcometh the world, even our faith. I John 5:4

January 21, 1996

December 27

Don't Slam the Door

The writers who produce scripts for comedy have certain devices they use over and over again. The insult is a regular item. Slapstick, especially non-violent slapstick like pies in the face or falling down, is standard comedy fare. Another often used is the one where somebody knocks on the door or rings the bell, and, when the door is answered, the actor slams the door in the face of the unwanted visitor. It is usually good for a chuckle, not a belly laugh.

This down time during the holidays is the slam-the-door time.

Thanksgiving and Christmas are both over. The almost mandatory generosity and good will have been properly saluted. We have given to the hungry, the homeless, people with special illnesses, students in UNCF schools, and the elderly. We have wished everybody "Merry Christmas" and "Happy New Year" and may even have helped to deliver food or other gifts between November 23 and now.

Now, we can slam the door against human need until next November.

Or we may feel that the milk of human kindness is not something that is available only in November and December and that the best way to tell GOD we appreciate His mercies is to make ourselves continually available to pass those mercies on to others.

So even though slamming the door may be good for a chuckle on a television sitcom, it is a grim act of cruelty in real life. GOD did not limit His mercies to months eleven and twelve when we cried out to Him. He heard us in spring, summer, fall, and winter. He heard us during working hours and in the wee hours after midnight. He responded to us when we had been a good and faithful servant and when we were a real monster. He even protected us when we were in the very act of doing something sinful! He is "the GOD of the open door."

So even though it is post-Christmas, we cannot slam the door now. Somebody needs you!

I have given you an example, that you should do as I have done unto you. John 13:15

December 27, 1992

December 28

Manger to Cross

The world marvels at the simple beauty of the story. Even scholarly skeptics who cannot rationalize the concept are mesmerized by its blending of the elemental and the profound. A young virgin becomes pregnant without human intervention, and gives birth to a baby boy in an obscure village in a tiny country in the northeast corner of Africa. And for twenty centuries billions have revered the name of that child. Empires have surrendered their national religions to worship Him, although He never set foot on their territory. What is it about that birth that shapes all human history from that day to this?

Nothing.

Had Jesus just been born in Bethlehem, even by parthenogenesis (virgin birth), and even with the fabled adoration by shepherds from his own country and by Magi from other countries—had that been all, it would have been a quaint but fading memory, lost after a generation or two.

366

But that was not all.

The whole reason GOD allowed Himself to enter human flesh was so that He could succumb to death. In His eternal essence, GOD cannot die. But He had to die, so He became a baby, a boy, a man. The manger was only the front door to the cross, the method by which GOD could be a substitute for all the sinners from creation to judgment. Had the baby not been born, we could not have been pardoned for our sins, and we would all have been condemned to eternal damnation.

Joy to the world! The LORD is come!

And suddenly there was with the angel a multitude of the heavenly host praising GOD, and saying,

Glory to GOD in the highest and on earth peace, good will toward men. Luke 2:13-14

December 10, 1995

December 29

What You See Is What You Get

The wise old man looked like a country hick, whittling his stick in front of the town square. The well-dressed stranger, carrying expensive luggage, walked up to him and demanded: "What kind of town is this, old man?" The old man never stopped whittling as he asked, "What kind of town did you come from?" "It was a cold, mean, stingy town," the stranger exploded, "full of cheap, thoughtless people." The old man looked up and gazed deep into the eyes of the stranger and replied, "Then that's exactly what you will find here." The stranger walked angrily off, and a young man followed him, stopping before the same old man. "Sir," he politely intoned, "I am considering settling in your town. Could you tell me what kind of people live here?" The old man looked up and smiled at the gentle face of the young man. "What kind of people lived in the place you came from?" he asked. "Oh, we had some of the best, most generous, most loving people you ever saw. It is a fine town, and I hate to leave it," said the youth. "Then that is what you will find among the people here," said the old man with a smile.

As you look back over this year forward to the next, you will surely ask yourself, "What kind of year am I going to have?" If you saw only problems and frustrations during the year and reasons to complain and protest, then you can expect problems, frustrations, and things to get on your last nerve in the coming year. But if you saw the grace of GOD providing for you and His love intervening for you in times of outward stress and adversity and if you found more to be thankful for than to whine about, then you can write it in stone: The new year will be a year when JEHOVAH- JIREH will provide everything you need. The thankful will see in the future what they have been grateful for in the past!

That he would grant you, according to the riches of his glory, to be strengthened with might by his Spirit in the inner man. Ephesians 3:16

December 30, 1990

December 30

The Night Cometh

The clock has three hands, and which one you watch depends on whether you are rushing or waiting. Sitting in the doctor's office behind twelve patients at 3:15, needing to be at the airport by 5:30, we gaze at the hour hand. Driving 60 mph in a 30-mile zone to make the appointment for that new job, we throw furtive glances at the minute hand. Sitting still at a red light that has not changed in 55 seconds, before we run the light, we focus on the second hand (and cuss very softly). Time always matters; and whether it drags or flies, time is critical.

Our Master makes it very plain. We are on a short fuse. We have to roll up our sleeves and gird up our loins and do our work for Him "while it is day: the night cometh, when no man can work."

Every day not spent witnessing for the LORD is spent helping Satan build his kingdom. Our time is either holy time or profane time—here is no neutrality about the hours of your day.

We must look over the opportunities we have to be a servant for Jesus. Somebody we know is depressed because they have too little faith. Somebody we know is in need of a helping hand, or just a hug. Some worthy cause that needs supporting has our name on it. Some ministry trying to help too many with too few laborers is struggling until we pitch in.

We should find something we can do—whether with family or with strangers; with the very young or the very old; with the broke or the broken-hearted—and start working right now! As the old folks used to say, "Time's a-wastin'!"

I must work the works of Him that sent me, while it is day; the night cometh, when no man can work. John 9:4

July 30, 2000

368

December 31

Look to the Tape

Every muscle stands out; the lungs are straining to the bursting-point; the body is one network of painful drive as the runner pushes himself to stay in front of the cluster of athletes. His aching body demands that he fall to the ground and rest, but his athlete's mind tells him he cannot give up even if he does not win this race. So his eyes are not on the grassy borders of the cinder-track, but fixed steadfastly on the finish tape. His goal is not rest, but victory.

It may have been a rough year for you. There are all kinds of reasons why you should give up and fall out of the race. Most people are not driven by the kind of principles that drive you. Why should your high standards give you all the pain, while millions relax and enjoy whatever tickles their fancy? Think of all the fun you denied yourself during the year. Think of what you could have profited if you had "played your cards right." (And if you focus on that stuff, you will head downhill fast!)

369

You know what you have to do. You cannot look back at the pains of the year. You have to look ahead to the goals you want to reach in the next. Your eyes cannot be on the ground, where there is relief; they must be on the tape where there is accomplishment.

Paul spoke of runners and of their focus on the tape. That's the key for the new year—not how your peers do it, or whether they support your value system, but how Jesus would do it. If His priority was not profit or power or pleasure, then yours must not be. If He allowed Himself to be abused in order to remain faithful to His Father's command, then we must (Sigh!) allow ourselves to be misused even when we have the weapons to fight back. If the tape for you is the will of Jesus Christ, then you have the push to keep on running.

Happy New Year!

I press toward the mark for the prize of the high calling of GOD in Christ Jesus. Philippians 3:14

December 27, 1987

INDEX